Negro Soy Yo

Refiguring American Music

Series Editors

Ronald Radano

Josh Kun

Charles McGovern

Negro Soy Yo

Hip Hop and Raced Citizenship
in Neoliberal Cuba

Marc D. Perry

Duke University Press   Durham and London   2016

© 2016 Duke University Press
All rights reserved   Printed in the United
States of America on acid-free paper ∞
Designed by Natalie F. Smith
Typeset in Quadraat Pro by Copperline
Library of Congress Cataloging-in-Publication Data
Perry, Marc D., [date] - author.   Negro soy yo : hip hop
and raced citizenship in neoliberal Cuba / Marc D. Perry.
pages cm—(Refiguring American music)
Includes bibliographical references and index.
ISBN 978-0-8223-5985-2 (hardcover : alk. paper)
ISBN 978-0-8223-5885-5 (pbk. : alk. paper)
ISBN 978-0-8223-7495-4 (e-book)
1. Hip-hop—Political aspects—Cuba.
2. Blacks—Cuba—Social conditions.
3. Cuba—Race relations.
I. Title. II. Series: Refiguring American music.
ML3486.C82P47 2015
782.421649089'9607291—dc23
2015020930
Cover art: Ariel Fernández Diaz.
Photo by Steve Marcus.

For my parents,
Morton and Margie Perry,
and my dear aunt,
Susan Ribner

Contents

Acknowledgments

This book has been a long-awaited endeavor, as many can attest. All said, there are numerous individuals who have lent collaborative time, intellect, guidance, and political investment to bringing this book to fruition, and I am deeply grateful and indebted to them for this. First and foremost are my friends, colleagues, and others in Cuba whose lives, work, and art inspired this project and for whom this book is ultimately dedicated. In Havana these include artists Magia López (and her family, especially her mother, Caridad), Alexey Rodríguez (and his parents, Celso and Maria), Sekou Yosmel Sarrias and Kokino Entenza, Soandres del Río and Alexis Cantero, Randy Acosta and Jessel Saladriga, Odaymara Cuesta, Odalys Cuesta, and Olivia Prendes, Yrak Saenz and Edgar González, Magyori Martínez, Yanelis Valdéz, and Yaribey Collia, Julio Cardenas, Michael Oramas and the EPG&B crew, the Diez y Diecinueve posse, Edrey Riveri and 100% Original, Reyas de la Calle, Roger Martínez, Papo Record, and Telmary Díaz. Other instrumental individuals within this broader community include Pablo Herrera, Ariel Fernández Díaz, Alexis "D'Boys" Rodríguez, Rodolfo Rensoli, Balesy Rivero, Yelandy Blaya, Javier Esteban, and Mateus Da Silva. In Santiago de Cuba I would like to thank Luis Gonzales, Rubén Cuesta Palomo, Omar Planos Cordoví, Aristey Guibert, Café Mezclado, Chucho SHS, Antonio, and Eugenio for their involvements.

Other Havana-based interlocutors with whom I am also humbly indebted are Roberto Zurbano, Tomás Fernández Robaina, Nehanda Abiodun, Assata Shakur, Gisela Arandia, Grizel Hernández Baguer, Norma Guillard Limonta, Rogelio Martínez Furé, Gloria Rolando, Yesenia Sélier, Joseph Mutti, Elvira Rodriguez Puerto, Rita, Mario, Ernesto, Lisnida, Amílcar, Delmaris, Guillermo, and Delbis Gomez. Additional Cuban or Cuba-related individuals who have contributed important form to this book include Tonel (aka Antonio Eligio Fernández), Sue Herrod, Catherine Murphy, Baye Adofo Wilson, Vanessa Diaz, Antonio (Tony) Reyes, Lisandro Perez-Rey, Danny Hoch, Marinieves Alba, Kahlil and Eli Jacobs-Fantauzzi, Dana Kaplan, Javier Machado Leyva, Ariel Arias, Sahily Borrero, Steve Marcus, Sarah Siebold, Ybp Banderas, David Downs, Teresa Konechne, Lou "Piensa" Dufieux, Juliette Barker Dufieux, Vox Sambu, Warda Brédy, Diegal Leger, and the whole Nomadic Massive posse.

The formative stages of this project occurred at the University of Texas, Austin. I would like to thank my advisor Ted Gordon and committee members Charles Hale, Joao Costa Vargas, Craig S. Watkins, and Jafari Allen who was also an important compadre in the field, for their intellectual guidance and support. Here I would also like to thank Aline Helg, Shelia Walker, Stuart Guzman, Bob and BJ Fernea, Deborah Kapchan, Isar Godreau, and Asale Ajani for their early support and engagements. My appreciation goes to my peers who encouraged and intellectually challenged me during this period: Jennifer Goett, Ben Chappell, Keisha-Khan Perry, Kia Lilly Caldwell, Mark Anderson, Peggy Brunache, Lynn Selby, Julio Tavares, Saheed Adejumobi, Denni Blum, Dana Maya, Courtney Johnson, Chantal Tetreault, Elana Zilberg, Vania Cardoso, Scott Head, and David Lynch.

I would also like to thank my colleagues at the University of Illinois, Urbana-Champaign: Arlene Torres, Gilberto Rosas, Ellen Moodie, Matti Bunzl, Alejandro Lugo, Martin Manalansan, Charles Rosemam, Erik McDuffie, Jessica Millward, Tage Biswalo, Fanon Wilkins, Diane Pindergrass, Merle Bowen, David Roediger, Lisa Nakamura, Christian Sandvig, Cristobal Valencia, Anthony Jerry, and Maritza Quiñones. I extend my gratitude to my colleagues while completing this project at Tulane University (2010–15): Laura Rosanne Adderley, Christopher Dunn, Mariana Mora, Felipe Smith, Olanike Orie, João Felipe Gonçalves, Allison Truitt, Michael Cunningham, Beretta Smith-Shomade, TR Johnson, and Justin Wolfe for their intellectual engagement and much appreciated support.

I additionally would like to thank the following individuals for their support and varying involvements during the course of this project: Deborah Thomas, Faye Harrison, Mark Anthony Neil, Ariana Hernandez Reguant, Lisa Maya Knauer, Frank Guridy, Ruth Behar, Henry Taylor, Ivor Miller, Robin Moore, Ron Radano, Tejumola Olaniyan, Frances Aparicio, Steven Gregory, Nitasha Sharma, Arlene Davila, Mark Sawyer, Novian Whitsitt, Emily Maguire, Bakari Kitwana, Laurie Frederik Meer, Nadine Fernandez, Karen Morrison, Katherine Gordy, Ned Sublette, Umi Vaughn, Amrita Chakrabarti Myers, Jed Tucker, Sherwin Bryant, Karine Poulin, Marietta Fernandez Lopez, Antonia Chabebe, Kristin Kalangis, Francoise Grossmann, Joseph Tolton, Jean Cohen, Virginia Miller, and Rosalyn Baxandall. I would like to thank Janet Dixon Keller for her keen editorial eye, and India Cooper and Cyndy Brown for their copyediting. My appreciations to Ken Wissoker at Duke University Press for his patient shepherding of the project as well as to the four anonymous reviewers who provided valuable feedback in bringing this book to final form.

The following institutions provided generous support during the research and writing of this book: the John L. Warfield Center for African and African American Studies and the Teresa Lozano Long Institute of Latin American Studies at the University of Texas, Luther College and the Consortium for a Strong Minority Presence in Liberal Arts Colleges' Minority Scholar-in-Residence Program, The Ford Foundation Diversity Dissertation and Postdoctoral Fellowship Programs, the Illinois Program for Research in the Humanities at the University of Illinois, Urbana-Champaign, and the Roger Thayer Stone Center for Latin American and Caribbean Studies at Tulane. Lastly I would like to thank my partner Maria Hinds for her sharp eye, love, and generous support through the final stages of this project.

Introduction

Siento odio profundo por tu racismo
Ya no me confundo con tu ironía
Y lloro sin que sepas que el llanto mío
tiene lágrimas negras como mi vida

I feel profound hatred for your racism
I am now no longer confused by your irony
And I cry without you knowing that my cry
has black tears like my life

—"Lágrimas negras," Hermanos de Causa

In "Lágrimas negras" (Black tears) by the Havana-based hip hop duo Hermanos de Causa (Brothers of the cause), the artists Soandres and Pelón provide a biting critique of the racialized hardships they, as young black men, encounter in the Cuban everyday. Borrowing the title from the classic *bolero-son* first popularized in the 1930s by the celebrated Cuban composer Miguel Matamoros, Hermanos de Causa poetically refigure the terms of "Lágrimas negras" by placing black life amid Cuba's evolving social malaise at its narrative center. Where the original composition offered a ballad of romantic sorrow, Hermanos de Causa speak of "black tears" of racial marginalization, criminalized gazes, and the simultaneous invisibility and hypervisibility that has come to mark Afro-Cuban life following the island's post-Soviet economic crisis of the early 1990s. The artists in this sense offer a poignant play on blackness that reflects a shifting Cuban complexity of race and nationhood, while foregrounding the salience of black subjectivity itself as a site of political life and contest.

Cut to a humid July evening in 2006 during a party I attended at a rooftop flat in Regla, a residential barrio a quick ferry ride across the harbor from the tourist-laden district of Habana Vieja. Atop the narrow staircase leading to the apartment, one is greeted by a large portrait of Toussaint L'Ouverture, the heroic patriarch of the Haitian Revolution, poised in military garb with his foot pressed triumphantly upon the head of a hissing snake. A photo of Malcolm X sits prominently amid other images garnishing the living room walls, as a large spray-painted figure of an afro-adorned man sits affixed to an outside wall of the flat's rooftop patio. The evening's hosts, Alexey Rodríguez and Magia López of the hip hop duo Obsesión, had invited a collection of local MCs and members of a visiting Canadian hip hop delegation for an informal gathering of food, music, and rum.

As guests assembled, a few clustered casually around an old Soviet television in Alexey's parents' bedroom to view the nightly state-run newscast when it was announced that there would be a notice of national importance within an hour's time. Given the newscaster's tone, word quickly spread through the party. A milling crowd had gathered in front of the television for the impending news when it was announced that President Fidel Castro had undergone intestinal surgery for an unspecified ailment. Governance, we were told, would be temporarily transferred to Fidel's younger brother, Raúl, and a handful of state confidants. The terms of the transfer were read aloud from a statement apparently authenticated by Fidel Castro's dated, frail-looking signature. A pensive mood settled over the gathering as many expressed concern about Fidel's health, as well as the uncertainties regarding the ultimate significance of this news. Despite all, the party continued, albeit with a tangibly more subdued energy.

Meanwhile, throughout the night U.S. news broadcasts were in a frenzy, airing images of euphoric crowds of Cuban Americans in the streets of Miami celebrating the news of Fidel Castro's illness and speculating on his imminent if not presumed death. In the days following, Washington was awash with predictions of chaos, mass hysteria, and explosive retaliation, as "liberated" Cubans were now expected to take their turn in the streets. Statements from the Bush administration vacillated between "support" for a "democratic transition" coupled with veiled threats to those who might hinder the move to "a free Cuba," and urgent calls for calm to counter the potential threat of a mass Cuban exodus fleeing for U.S. shores. The morning following the announcement, however, Havana's two million residents awoke and went about business largely as usual. In short, daily life continued in Cuba, though clearly not without a new set of ambiguities. While Miami's largely white Cuban American establishment overwhelmingly cheered the development, many among the island's Afro-Cuban population—including Magia's and Alexey's families—shared a more ambivalent relationship to the news, given levels of identification with Cuba's revolutionary past.

The announcement of Fidel Castro's retirement and succession to Raúl, while unquestionably historic, did not in the end lead to a popular uprising or a collapse of the Cuban state as prophesized by some. Indeed, the only ensuing hysteria seemed to have occurred among invested parties to the north. The significance and historical complexities of the Cuban Revolution could not in the end be reduced simply to the figure of Fidel Castro. Such would require erasure of over fifty years of mobilization and sacrifice among everyday Cubans in working toward and imagining, in all its lived incongruencies, a socialist future. Negated would be Cubans' own historical presence and agency, not to mention alternative lines of revolutionarily informed subjectivity (M. Perry 2008a). Rather than a singularly disjunctive event, Fidel Castro's passage from central stage should be viewed within a broader ongoing narrative of national transformation as revolutionary Cuba has struggled to navigate its entry into global capitalism following the 1989 collapse of the Soviet bloc. Social flux and its attendant frictions have therefore long been defining facets of Cuban society, ones through which the Cuban state and ordinary Cubans continue to navigate—in varying and frequently competing ways—without abandoning all historical continuity.

I juxtapose the party vignette with Hermanos de Causa's "Lágrimas negras" to underscore a key tension that has shaped and come to define Cuba's movimiento de hip hop (hip hop movement). At one end are rapidly eroding national narratives of revolutionary struggle, lore, and utopic promise within which Cuban raperos (rappers or MCs) live as members of a generation coming of age in a period of prodigious social change. However, on the waning periphery, these young people remain inheritors of the island's revolutionary history and as such both live with and embody those same tensions that mark Cuba's evolving condition and uncertainties. They are at one time a part of and yet critically apart from a previous moment, in essence betwixt and between two Cubas—one of a receding past and one in process of becoming. Such liminality offers this generation of artists a privileged vantage point as chroniclers of revolutionary decline, if not potential custodians of its utopic call.

It is also vital to note that for many core and founding members of Cuba's hip hop movement, race—through its varying confluences with gender, class, and sexuality—has served as a politically meaningful lens through which the incongruencies of a shifting national typography have been most saliently lived and mediated anew. Indeed, Hermanos de Causa's testament to life as young black men speaks to a raced materiality of Cuban citizenship vis-à-vis the island's emerging market economy, one that stands in fraught tension with enduring claims to the contrary rooted in Cuba's nonracial national foundations and elaborated upon during the post-1959 revolutionary period. It is precisely this "irony" to which Soandres and Pelón speak, and whose mystification they proclaim "no longer confuses." Embedded in Hermanos de Causa's read on race and racism then are those disjunctures between the ideological claims and the everyday practice of revolutionary socialism in today's Cuba—a critique suggesting a certain disenfranchisement of Afro-Cubans from the revolutionary national promise in ways that may implicate the Cuban state itself.

This book thus explores questions of social maneuver within the shifting, often frictive fields of global-local interface that mark Cuban life today. At its center is an inquiry into the rise of Cuban hip hop in relation to ongoing elaborations of race and class following the island's post-Soviet-era trauma of the early 1990s. Here I focus on the ways young self-identified black Cubans who comprise a pioneering core of raperos and their followers not only give voice to the lived quotidians of race, but also craft new understandings of black Cuban selfhood and forms of racial citizenship by way of rap music and the broader global imagine of hip hop culture.

Through this twofold sense of articulation—at one time a performative voicing and productive crafting of self—these artists can be seen as moving in strategically flexible, globally attuned ways (Ong 1999) in response to the particular urgencies of Cuba's unfolding economy at the millennium's turn. Amid an era increasingly brokered by market liberalizations, a withering socialist state, deepening social stratification, and—significantly—resurgent

levels of racial inequality, how might such black self-fashionings complicate Cuban legacies of nonracial exceptionalism while advancing alternative
citizenship claims both within and beyond the nation? With these queries
I seek to consider hip hop's rise within Cuba's historical arc and enduring
dilemmas of race and nationhood, while locating it as a social phenomenon
of a particularly fluid moment of neoliberal flux and transformation.

The everyday contours and social complexities of this history are borne
out in the lives and work of a collection of Havana-based rap artists, producers, and DJs who have contributed collective voice and social form to
Cuba's hip hop community. Beyond realms of music, many embrace hip hop
as an alternative mode of identity, in effect a *whole way of life* that transcends
national and temporal boundedness through a quest for global membership
and black cosmopolitan belonging. I explore the ways these evolving social
imaginaries thus operate both within and beyond Cuban fields of vision by
challenging national prescriptions of race and their obfuscating effects,
while embodying multiple claims to citizenship as contemporary Afro-
Cubans. Those involved range generally in age from their early twenties to
midthirties and are largely drawn from working-class barrios with sizable
Afro-Cuban populations.

The book's narrative lines emerge in conversation with these individuals and through engagement with those places where raperos fashion
community by way of music concerts and festivals, recording sessions,
organizational meetings and colloquia, informal classes, and more intimate spaces of home and everyday life. The bulk of ethnographic material
is drawn from research conducted between 1999 and 2006, a period that in
many ways marked the movement's apogee of racial politics. The book's
concluding chapter carries the conversation into the present by addressing
recent developments both in and beyond Cuba. Taken as such, *Negro Soy
Yo* offers a longitudinal and indeed historicized perspective on the evolving story of Cuban hip hop amid ongoing negotiations of a transformative
present.

A critical facet in this mix has been the revolutionary state's varying positions on, and shifting efforts to manage, raperos' emergent voicings and
embedded challenges. Equally instrumental have been raperos' involvements with two important, at times overlapping communities of outside
interlocutors. The first of these entails a range of intergenerational engagements with an older cohort of Afro-Cuban intellectuals and family mem-

bers, along with a select few African American political exiles on the island. Many among this older generation have been drawn to hip hop for what is seen as raperos' vanguardist position vis-à-vis the island's current spectrum of racial politics. An additional set of dialogues has occurred by way of the transnational, enabling Cuban affirmations of black selfhood at the confluence of nation and diasporic geographies of blackness.

Amid the mix, the now hyperglobal field of hip hop continues to be an important cultural space through which cosmopolitan understandings of contemporary black belonging can be marshaled in challenging local conditions of racial subjugation (M. Perry 2008b). Such agencies illuminate the workings of diaspora as a lived social formation, one constituted through certain kinds of identity practice in the making and moving of diaspora in a mobilized sense (Edwards 2003). Here hip hop offers extranational routes (Gilroy 1993) through which some young Afro-Cubans not only envision black alterities but in fact engage in the active "crafting of selves" (Kondo 1990) as globally conscious subjects. Cuban hip hop in this sense evokes what Josh Kun has termed an *audiotopic sensibility* offering, in this instance, not only "new maps for re-imagining the present social world" (Kun 2005: 23), but innovative ways of revisioning both being and moving in the world as well.

What I propose, then, by way of the cultural politics and poetics of Cuban hip hop, is an effort to think through the quotidian play of shifting governmentalities and evolving practices of race as they unfold under the expanding global reach of neoliberal capital. Attending to what Wendy Brown identifies as the political rationalities of neoliberalism (Brown 2003; see also Kingfisher and Maskovsky 2008), the emphasis here is on regulatory effects of neoliberal logics as they impact the social terrain of imagination and practice, if not subjectivity itself. In its broadest sense this approach seeks a historicized understanding of hip hop's ascendance in Cuba as one intimately tied to the island's own ambivalences of neoliberal condition. Here I suggest it is indeed no coincidence that hip hop Cubano has evolved precisely during Cuba's recent period of historic flux. Although the early roots of rap music on the island can be traced back to the mid-1980s, it was not until the national crisis of the early to mid-1990s that hip hop as a self-defined movimiento began to take conscious Cuban form. Cuban hip hop is thus born and acutely reflective of this ongoing moment of national rupture and reformation.

What then are the historical terms that have shaped this particular juncture? Beyond a musing query, it is precisely these terms and their fault lines upon which many raperos and aligned others maneuver in fashioning alternative black Cuban claims to national legitimacy, musically and otherwise. By way of Afro-Atlantic analogy, then, what does it indeed mean in an enduring Du Boisian sense to embody a "two-ness" of being at one time both black and Cuban at the millennial turn (Du Bois [1903] 1989)? Such frictions remain poignant grounds of struggle for many Cuban raperos through both life and art.

Dilemmas of Racial Disenfranchisement

The economic crisis of the early 1990s in the wake of the Eastern bloc's collapse and subsequent suspension of Soviet subsidies unquestionably engendered profound realignments within Cuba's social landscape, revolutionary trajectory, and broader national narrative. Efforts to preserve the salience of state socialism in the face of deepening market realities have exposed, exacerbated, and in many ways elaborated upon a set of historical tensions laid progressively bare in the current everyday. The most immediate of these has been widening social inequality tied to differing levels and means of access within the island's increasingly monetized economy. Amid this flux, a once revolutionary call for la lucha—that collective national "struggle" to build a socialist Cuba—in today's parlance is associated more with the daily hustle for the island's globally pegged currency now so essential to Cuban life.

In addition to urgencies of class, racial difference has emerged as a critical, largely correlative factor in shaping social position and play within Cuba's shifting economic terrain. This reality, in turn, presents a set of fraught complexities for Cuba where the dismantling of racial discrimination is touted as a key triumph of the Cuban Revolution in its professed realization of a racially egalitarian, if not ultimately postracial, socialist society. Indeed, claims to a nonracial exceptionalism have in fact been historically instrumental to Cuba's very formation as a modern nation.

It was of course sugar, that brutal irony of "sweetness and power" (Mintz 1986), that gave rise to the island's inherent entanglements of race and nationhood as colonial Cuba became the Caribbean's largest sugar producer following the collapse of Saint-Domingue's sugar industry at the onset of the Haitian Revolution. Cuba's groundings in modernity were thus born of that very "machine" of plantation-based slavery reiterated throughout the Caribbean region (Benítez-Rojo 1992).

Yet Africans and their descendants were far from simply fodder for a colonial idiom of raced capitalism. Numerous slave revolts occurred during the eighteenth century, with the first large-scale expression unfolding in 1812 in a series of uprisings known collectively as the Aponte Rebellion in which an alliance of enslaved and free people of color, inspired by the recent triumph of the Haitian Revolution, mobilized in shared pursuit of slavery's end (Childs 2006; Fischer 2004). Although violently crushed, the rebellion instilled a deep fear among white elites of a black Haitian-style revolt, setting the stage for the La Escalera massacre of 1844, which resulted in the execution and imprisonment of thousands of enslaved and free people of color in response to an alleged conspiracy to end slavery and colonial rule (Paquette 1988).[1] In both moments state-sanctioned terror as a technology of raced subjugation was leveled at African descendants seeking human freedom, inscribing, in turn, the early parameters of black Cuban subjectivity in the most material of terms.

A foundational confluence of black freedom, citizenship, and national liberation emerged in Cuba's late nineteenth-century wars of independence in which upward of 70 percent of the voluntary rank and file of the independence army were men of color. Many were inspired through manumission along with the independence movement's broader associations with slavery's abolition and a future promise of a racially just Cuba. Instrumental in the mix was General Antonio Maceo—a free *mulato* and leading commander in the independence army who, following the larger movement's refusal to emancipate enslaved blacks en masse, organized plantation raids encouraging liberated blacks to join the anticolonial struggle.

Although killed in battle two years before national independence, Maceo's symbolism as heroic liberator of both black Cubans and the Cuban nation remains complex. Under Maceo and other black commanders' leadership, the centrality of blacks in the nationalist struggle posed a radical challenge to those who sought the exclusion of Afro-descendants from equal participation in a newly liberated Cuba (Helg 1995). Indeed, for many formerly enslaved Cubans, Maceo represented the martyred embodiment of black Cuban citizenship. Among white *criollo* elite, however, regard for Maceo was tempered by fear of a black *caudillo* (leader) ushering a "black" Cuba into being (Duharte Jiménez 1993; Ferrer 1998a). Subsequent efforts to expunge Maceo's raced significance reflect early interests in purging blackness from Cuba's mythic foundations and narratives of national identity (Kapcia 2000: 200–201; cf. Trouillot 1995).[2]

Appeals to a deracialized Cuba were in fact ideologically integral to the independence movement itself. José Martí—the criollo intellectual, prominent independence figure, and celebrated father of Cuban nationalism—recognized racial difference as an obstacle to a unified nationalist front, advancing calls for a nonracial Cuba with lasting resonance into the revolutionary present. Martí's advocacy of a racially transcendent liberation struggle—and by extension an envisioned nation—was also aimed at appeasing white fears of an unleashed black population coming to power on the eve of independence (Ferrer 1998a; Pérez 1999).[3] While blacks may have redeployed Martí's advocacy of nonracialism to justify entitlement to full citizenship (de la Fuente 1999; Ferrer 1998a), the same postracial logic impeded political redress to racially lived inequality. By juxtaposing "race" against "nation" in this way, racial identification (if not subjectivity itself) was ultimately cast as counternational (Martí [1893] 1975). Within this postracial scripting, claiming one's blackness (or whiteness) was akin to antipatriotism, one ultimately treasonous with respect to the nonracial solvency of the Cuban nation itself.

The rise of the Partido Independiente de Color (Independent Party of Color) in 1908 posed an intrinsic challenge to early Cuba's conflictive and otherwise unfulfilled profession of nonracial equality.[4] Drawing the bulk of its membership from former combatants of the independence wars disillusioned with black Cubans' continued confinement to the lower working and peasant classes, the Partido pressed demands for political redress (Helg 1995). While the Partido called for the full enfranchisement of blacks as equal citizens *within* the Cuban nation, its appeal to racial solidarity threatened the early republic's efforts to silence race through a nonracial status quo. In response to legislation prohibiting political parties organized along racial lines that effectively banned the Partido, members staged a 1912 Havana protest in which former independence fighters reportedly carried arms. Beyond symbols of violent threat, Partido members may have alternately displayed arms as testimonials of citizenship rooted in their status as national combatants.

Regardless of terms, the protest was brutally crushed by the Cuban army, decimating the Partido's ranks and agenda as more than three thousand blacks were massacred during an ensuing island-wide reign of terror. The events of 1912 thus stood as a poignant reminder of the disciplining use of state violence in forging and policing national parameters of a regulatory nonracialism.[5] Although its significance was long obscured by official accounts of an infamous "Race War" of 1912, the Partido's challenge and subsequent massacre remain poignant moments of historical memory and recovery within rapero circles.

While 1912 ended overtly political forms of mobilization as Afro-Cubans alternatively sought redress through existing political parties and trade unions (de la Fuente 2001), this did not translate to the demise of all autonomous spheres of black social practice. Black Cubans continued to organize around religious and cultural life forged under enslavement and given institutional form through *cabildos de nación* (ethnic-based social welfare societies) and later *sociedades de color* of the early twentieth century. As mutual-aid and leisure associations drawn from professional urban classes of color, the sociedades laid claims to a black cosmopolitanism nourished in important part through engagement with black communities and political struggle beyond the national (Guridy 2010; see also Fernández Robaina 1998).

With the triumph of the Cuban Revolution in 1959, the soon-to-be-declared socialist state took up the elimination of racial discrimination as a centerpiece of its early revolutionary program. While black intellectuals were reportedly active in pushing for public debate on the issue (de la Fuente 2001), the challenge of promoting interracial fraternity toward a nationalist front, in this case revolutionary socialism, was once again paramount. During one of two notable speeches on race in 1959, a recently victorious Fidel Castro evoked José Martí and his nonracial ideals in declaring: "We have to uproot the last colonial vestiges, conscious of making that phase of Martí's a reality. He said it before, we have to repeat it now: that the Cuban is more than white, more than black, we are Cuban."[6] A ban on racial discrimination in employment and public spheres of education and recreation followed, while a broader approach held that residual forms of racism would eventually disappear with the purging of the class-based foundations of racial inequality. An implicit limitation of this latter facet is that while race, as the late Stuart Hall cogently notes, may operate as a modality through which class is historically lived (1980), the particularity of raced power, practice, and subjectivity cannot, in turn, be reduced simply to an epiphenomenon of class.

This formulation, moreover, tends to posit a false dichotomy between institutional and ideological expressions of racialized power (Essed 2002; Goldberg 1993; Hall 1980; Harrison 1995; Omi and Winant 1994). Such framing finds popular expression in today's Cuban parlance, one that often privileges the individualizing *prejuicio* (prejudice) over more structural *racismo* (racism) when referencing Cuba's enduring racial challenges. The common Cuban refrain "Hay prejuicio pero no hay racismo" (There is prejudice but no racism), for instance, limits the exercise of raced power to that of individual practice, thereby restricting calls that would challenge the broader systemics of racial exclusion and privilege. Rather than recognizing racism as a complexly dynamic and reproductive social process, its workings in this sense are rendered obfuscated through a discursive silencing.

Indeed, within three short years of 1959, racism was officially declared eliminated from Cuban society. From that point on discussions of raced power and/or politics of any form in a now ostensibly postracial Cuba were deemed subversive given demands for a united front to build socialism.[7] Reminiscent of earlier moments, race was again juxtaposed to nation, and racial forms of identification were ultimately rendered counterrevolutionary if not counternational. Black Cubans thus concerned with the persistence of racial inequalities found themselves in a dilemma. If they chose to organize around racially associated grievances, they risked being labeled counterrevolutionary; if they did not, they chanced complacency in their own subjugation.[8] Such silencings were institutionalized by state bannings of black social organizations including sociedades de color (Guridy 2010), along with reported suppression of Afro-Cuban religious communities and organizations (C. Moore 1989). At the very level of the ontological, any enunciation of a black, subjectively lived racial difference was in the end marked suspect, echoing again a raced disenfranchisement of Afro-Cubans from full voice and belonging within purports of a nonracial nation.[9]

Critiques and limitations notwithstanding, it is vital to underscore that black Cubans did in large part benefit from the social gains of the revolution. Although race-responsive efforts were never undertaken, black and darker-skinned Cubans—historically among the poorest and most marginal populations—gained considerably from the revolution's efforts to build a more egalitarian society through state socialism. Expansions of low-income housing, for instance, significantly impacted the black urban poor, many of whom lived in shanty-like conditions prior to 1959 (de la Fuente 2001), while the revolution's socialization of medicine increased health care access and improved outcomes for poorer black and darker-skinned Cubans.

Additional interventions occurred within spheres of education, where the eradication of private schools in 1961 (most of which were racially segregated) and the massive nationwide literacy campaign initiated the same year launched a national educational system radically more inclusive of black Cubans. Accompanying shifts toward professional training in areas like medicine and engineering, moreover, dramatically expanded black professional ranks. Participation in this history engendered levels of Afro-Cuban revolutionary affinity in noted contrast to the waves of wealthier white compatriots who fled the island at the onset of the revolutionary period given threats (both real and perceived) to lines of racial and class privilege. Legacies of these achievements, as we shall see, carry meaningful, if often conflicted, resonance among Havana-area raperos.

The disjoint between the instrumentality of race in the ongoing making of Cuban nationhood and official odes to a nonracial nationalism have been sharply exacerbated by market shifts and a concurrent retreat of state socialism since the early 1990s. Governmental efforts to regulate and police the incongruencies introduced by what amounted to a Cuban neoliberal turn have compounded, at times significantly, the racial marginalization of black and darker-skinned Cubans. Neoliberal reworkings of the social via overlapping lines of racial and class difference have in this sense further complicated the utopic claims of the revolutionary project and Cuba's broader national promise. It is precisely amid these cleavages and their attendant incoherencies that Cuban hip hop emerged and moves.

Yet this neoliberal Cuban condition to which I refer is a deeply ambivalent one. Unlike much of the Global South compelled to accommodate neoliberal reforms by way of international lending agencies and regional free-trade agreements, Cuba's socialist leadership has long renounced participation within such accords. These efforts notwithstanding, it is clear that more informal modes of economic liberalization undertaken by the revolutionary state since the collapse of the Soviet bloc set in motion developments that have increasingly aligned with global workings of market capital. Comparable in this sense with Katherine Verdery's insights into postsocialist change in Romania, this movement has generally been one characterized by a transformative dynamism rather than a linear or teleologic *transition* to neoliberal marketization (Verdery 1996). Reminiscent of a collapsing Romanian socialism, Cuba's evolving condition is a similarly fluid and contingent one, marked by uncertainty and struggle over the future terms of a postsocialist Cuba. Indeed, given evolving gestures toward a Cuban-U.S. thaw, such market elaborations and their unpredictabilities are surely to intensify in the near term.

In light of such ambiguities, Aihwa Ong's notion of neoliberalism "as exception" (Ong 2006) is productive for considering the ways market rationales have permeated to Cuban society as state-induced "exceptions" in the face of ongoing claims to preserve revolutionary socialism, engendering a deeply fraught ambivalence of the neoliberal condition the island presently occupies. Ong's work, moreover, points toward how such neoliberal deviations often produce areas of exclusion as well as inform alternative modes of social practice fashioned at the confluence of national and transnational social geographies. Regarding Cuban hip hop, this framing is particularly helpful when considering the reciprocally raced nature of socioeconomic marginalization on one hand, and raperos' multivalent claims to national/transnational belonging (or, in effect, citizenship) on the other within an unfolding neoliberal moment.

As has been similarly documented in the Caribbean and broader Latin American region (Babb 2004; Desforges 2000; Gregory 2006; Klak and Myers 1998; Scher 2011), Cuba's expansion of foreign tourism emerged as a pivotal postcrisis facet of the island's neoliberal shift. In addition to generating its own logics of class and racially marked exclusion that articulate with other aspects of Cuba's new monetized economy, the tourism industry has enabled a commodification and vending of Afro-Cuban cultural forms for consumption by foreign tourists and the Cuban state alike.

While illuminating interrelated dimensions of racial inequality and neoliberal modes of multicultural packaging, tourism's racial currents have also encouraged an enterprising range of racially coded strategies—often gendered and frequently sexualized—that some black and darker-skinned Cubans have adopted to access an expanding marketplace from which they are otherwise often excluded. In many instances these efforts are mediated through the varying ways "blackness" is performed in light of globally tied, locally articulated economies of consumption and desire. It is thus within the evolving folds of neoliberalization that darker-skinned Cubans find themselves disenfranchised from full participation within Cuba's new economy (if not new market-entitled realms of citizenship), while simultaneously managing creative maneuver through alternative spheres of racial space.

Mobilizing Blackness

Amid such shifting typographies of race, class, capital, and nationhood itself, some black and darker-skinned young people have turned to hip hop to craft new understandings of black selves born of the racial materiality of a particular moment and tension of local-global convergence. Cuban raperos, in this sense, similarly navigate racialized realms of exclusion and possibility, ones in which the active field of maneuver is identity. In exploring these complexities, my approach builds upon recognition of how grammars of racial subject-making are often negotiated through webs of social power that interpellate subalternly raced subjects as such (Du Bois [1903] 1989; Fanon [1952] 1967; see also Althusser 1971; Foucault 1979). And yet it is the space of identity, that outwardly conscious and self-aware expression of subjectivity, that serves as the performative intermediary in the movement from racialized subjects to racially self-aware social actors.

Here, Stuart Hall's emphasis on an analytics of identification (rather than identity per se) is informative in underscoring the operative, self-positioning act of identifying with others as the foundational basis for forging and maintaining group identities (Hall 1996). As historically variable as such collective solidarities of recognition may indeed be, they are the very terra firma upon which social groups act and move in corporately invested ways, be they indigenous social movements or Tea Party activists. The salient question therefore is ultimately one of positioned actors and political ends.

Regarding identity claims among black and darker-skinned raperos, affinities of blackness—at one time nationally moored and globally expansive—are for many instrumental in the crafting of both music and selves. Indeed, as these young men and women navigate Cuba's new monetized landscape, racial status has increasingly come to mark economic location and realms of social mobility. Race in this sense, to borrow again from Stuart Hall, has assumed added importance as a key social idiom through which class is currently lived in Cuba. Hall's framing, moreover, suggests a rethinking of what constitutes a social class per se, particularly in light of Afro-descendant communities whose raciality is grounded in the very class edifice intrinsic to the formation of the modern Western world (James [1963] 1989; E. Williams [1944] 1994). While historically contingent and mediated by way of other axes of social difference, race for these communities has frequently served as one of the more enduring lenses through which inequality is indeed most tangibly "lived."

To evoke Marx's oft-cited distinction between a class-*in*-itself versus a class-*for*-itself, Hall's proposition encourages recognition of the ways racial identity may serve as a socially salient and therefore politically productive mode of collective (i.e., "class") organization and action (cf. Gilroy 1991).[10] This materiality of race—or for the sake of this discussion, "blackness" itself—has thus the capacity to be generative of communal ontologies of being as well as collaborative strategies of practice. For many racially marked raperos, the globally conversant space of hip hop has proved instrumental precisely in this sense by enabling new Cuban grammars of both black being and doing.

By illuminating the narrative lines of such black self-fashionings, I explore a nexus of alliances between raperos and a constellation of interlocutors that have contributed important shape to Cuba's evolving hip hop movement. Key among these have been ongoing histories of exchange with visiting hip hop artists, producers, and cultural activists, primarily from North America, who have provided discursive and material support for raperos. Yet many key figures in Havana's hip hop community also share a cogent set of relationships with two local circles of individuals who have contributed to the movement's trajectory in meaningful ways. The first is an established (as well as an emerging) generation of Afro-Cuban intellectuals who have encouraged formative dialogues around Cuban questions of race, history, and contemporary culture. The second involves two Havana-based African American political exiles who have, through varying and sometimes intimate ways, impacted lives and broader ideological conversations within the community. By way of mentorship and other engagements, these exiles have been influential in expanding transnational understandings among raperos, while facilitating alliances with African American hip hop artists and activists—in effect, elaborating routes of black internationalism within the movimiento.

Arising in part through these varying involvements, many black and darker-skinned raperos tie themselves via their music and everyday lives to reclaimed histories of Afro-Cuban radicality, while simultaneously marking their belonging to Afro-hemispheric traditions of black political life and struggle. In doing so, these artists lay claim as contemporary Afro-Cubans to multiple notions of citizenship both critically within, and decidedly beyond, Cuba's nonracial national imaginary.

Of equal gravitas, I examine the shifting interplay between hip hop Cubano as an ascendant social phenomenon and the Cuban state as it has sought to mediate and contain hip hop's emergent voicings and antiracist challenges. From willful neglect, to institutionalizing efforts, to more recent curtailment of governmental support, the revolutionary state has long been a key interlocutor, albeit ambivalently positioned, with island raperos. Despite (or perhaps precisely through) such labors, hip hop arose as an important site of social analysis and critique by pushing accounts of racial and class dynamics into highly regulated realms of Cuban public discourse.

Cuban hip hop in this sense emerged as a kind of disruptive black spectacle, rendering realties of race both visible and acutely audible. As I have argued, these artists have become significant actors within a nascent counterpublic sphere predicated on black political difference and antiracist advocacy in an ostensibly postracial Cuba (M. Perry 2004, 2008b; see also de la Fuente 2008, 2010; Fernandes and Stanyek 2007; Saunders 2009). While dialogues between Cuban MCs and a current range of black-identified intellectuals and cultural producers have given rise to new spaces and routes of racial self-articulation, they have also evolved in conversation with intermittent state openings to public address and Cuba's expanding market economy.

Raced Ethnography

It has, however, been suggested that scholarly emphasis on an analytics of race vis-à-vis hip hop Cubano has been a largely misplaced enterprise. A diverse field of commentators on contemporary Cuba, including Sujatha Fernandes (2003, 2006; Fernandes and Stanyek 2007), Alan West-Durán (2004), Ronni Armstead (2007), Tanya Saunders (2009, 2010), and Alejandro de la Fuente (2008, 2010), have varyingly foregrounded the role of racial identity within Havana's hip hop community as an integral facet of the movement's politics and social coherence. While my work (M. Perry 2004, 2008a, 2008b) is in dialogue with this scholarship, my intervention is directed at providing an ethnographically grounded and historicized analysis of Cuban hip hop as a multivalent site of racial maneuver in an emerging neoliberal moment.

By contrast, the British ethnomusicologist Geoffrey Baker is highly critical of such approaches, taking particular issue with my work and what he views as its "race agenda" and "overarching race-based narrative" regarding Cuban hip hop (Baker 2011: 268–69). Drawing upon field data conducted just subsequent to my own, Baker suggests raperos' (self-)racialization was a gradual one, peaking in the early 2000s precisely during my primary research period. While broadly accurate, where Baker and I differ concerns the terms, contributing factors, and political nature of such black self-fashionings. In the spirit of intellectual exchange, I offer the following thoughts regarding the core issues and limitations his critiques raise, while providing the opportunity to further situate my analytical approach and ethnographic positionality in the field.

A central contention of Baker involves the suggestion that outside entities, from U.S.-based hip hop artists and activists to North American scholars like myself, introduced "Americanized" conceptions of race to Cuba, thereby imposing a foreign racial construct upon an otherwise autochthonously nonracial social landscape (Baker 2011: 267). Once these foreign influences dissipated, he argues, racial currents of identification waned, reverting back to a more "traditional Cuban style [of hip hop], focused on the presence of people of different skin colors [who] identified hip hop spaces as racially mixed" (285). While levels of black identification among raperos may indeed have lessened in recent years for various factors I will later discuss, to suggest that this shift is reducible to the fading of imposed ideas from "outside" risks not only decoupling the conjunctural circumstances of the moment, but also devaluing these artists'—and, in a wider sense, Afro-Cubans'—historical agency in forging understandings of self and ways of being alternative to dominant national prescriptions.

One familiar with standing scholarship on mestizaje in the Caribbean and broader Latin American region, of which Cuba's nonracial foundations are a variant, is cognizant of the ways national constructions of racial neutrality more often than not obscure the raced workings of marginalization and subordination affecting communities of African descent (see Godreau 2006; Hanchard 1998; Lilly Caldwell 2007; Martínez-Echazábal 1998; Safa 1998; Sagás 2000; Wade 1995; Whitten and Torres 1998). Similar conclusions have been drawn by scholars of Cuba and its history (de la Fuente 2001;

N. Fernandez 2010; Fernández Robaina 1990; Ferrer 1998a, 1999; R. Moore 1994, 1997; Pérez Sarduy and Stubbs 2000; Sawyer 2005).

As has been chronicled of various moments, moreover, Afro-Cubans have long engaged extranationally with other Afro-descended populations in making and mobilizing notions of black Cuban alterity toward antiracist and/or liberatory-directed ends (Brock and Fuertes et al. 1998; Childs 2006; Ellis 1998; García 2006; Guridy 2010; C. Moore 1989; Palmié 2002; Schwartz 1998; Sublette 2007). Such agencies were operative in the 1812 Aponte Rebellion by way of the Haitian Revolution, as they were with the poet Nicolás Guillén's decades-long intellectual rapport with Langston Hughes, with the journalist Gustavo Urrutia's affinities with the NAACP and Booker T. Washington, and, as I argue, with black-identified raperos in crafting political imaginaries beyond the national. All are variations on a theme, yet ones responsive to the complexities of their own historical present. Historicization, therefore, is critical.

Identity claims among raperos can be viewed yet more broadly in conversation with the rise of identity-centered social movements throughout the Latin American region involving indigenous as well as Afro-descended populations, many of them marshaled around a politics of antiracism (Alvarez, Dagnino, and Escobar 1998; Anderson 2009; Hale 1997; Ng'weno 2007; Wade 1995; Warren 2001). Such mobilizations of difference, moreover, have often articulated with the expansion of neoliberal policies and related state turns toward multiculturalist positions, displacing mestizaje as a dominant national paradigm (Hale 2002; Laurie and Bonnett 2002; Postero 2005; Sieder 2002; Wade 1999). As I have similarly suggested here, a comparable mix of identity politics, market transformation, and an ever fluid national landscape are also in dynamic play in Cuba today. Locating Cuban hip hop within such regional shifts may therefore yield analytic perspectives that provide broader contextualization and nuances of understanding regarding its racial undercurrents.

A central focus for Baker's analysis is the U.S.-based Black August collective that participated in a series of annual Cuban hip hop festivals between 1998 and 2003. Among other commitments, the collective organized performances by African American and Nuyorican hip hop artists and related involvements of U.S. cultural activists. Like Baker, I recognize the instrumentality of Black August in animating transnational conversations that have been important in framing notions of blackness within Havana's hip hop community. Yet while I identify the collective as one among various actors and/or factors, Black August figures in Baker's analysis as a primary progenitor of racial thinking among raperos. Dimensions of black identity within this formulation ultimately begin and end with Black August. Along similar lines, Baker critiques my work and that of other North American scholars exploring racial poetics within Cuban hip hop for "describ[ing] and analyz[ing] Cuban culture using terms and theoretical constructs derived from people of color in the United States" (Baker 2011: 286).[11] It is implied that through engagements with island hop hip via scholarship and other involvements, we (largely scholars of color), much like Black August, have imposed foreign modes of racial thinking upon hip hop artists and their followers.

Such critiques are reminiscent of a set of challenges leveled by Pierre Bourdieu and Loïc Wacquant against, among others, the political scientist Michael Hanchard and his work *Orpheus and Power* (1998), which examines Brazil's *movimento negro*. In their article "On the Cunning of Imperialist Reason," Bourdieu and Wacquant take Hanchard to task in arguing:

> By applying North American racial categories to the Brazilian situation, this book makes the particular history of the U.S. Civil Rights Movement into the universal standard for the struggle of all groups oppressed on grounds of colour (or caste). Instead of dissecting the constitution of the Brazilian ethnoracial order according to its own logic, such inquiries are most often content to replace wholesale the national myth of "racial democracy" . . . by the myth according to which all societies are "racist," including those within which "race" relations seem at first sight to be less distant and hostile. From being an analytic tool, the concept of racism becomes a mere instrument of accusation; under the guise of science, it is the logic of the trial which asserts itself. (Bourdieu and Wacquant 1999: 44)

Hanchard in this light is seen as a black U.S. scholar extending a racializing gaze onto Brazil's otherwise alien "ethnoracial order," thereby advancing an imperialist projection of North American power and cultural hegemony into historically differentiated realms of the Global South. In his defense, Hanchard suggests:

> Their critique relies on presumptions and critical analytical methods which privilege the nation-state and "national" culture as the sole object

for comparative analysis, and as a consequence ignore how Afro-Brazilian politics, the U.S. civil rights movements in particular and transnational black politics more generally problematize the facile, even superficial, distinctions between imperialist and anti-imperialist nation-states. . . . Bourdieu and Wacquant ignore the complexity and specificity of black agency in both Brazil and the United States, which leads them to equate black transnationalism with imperialism and U.S. foreign policy. In their version of political ethnocentrism, the politics of nation-states are privileged and the mobilizations of non-state actors are neglected and, when identified, poorly understood. (Hanchard 2003: 6–7)

Numerous scholars have subsequently waded into the debate from U.S. (Lilly Caldwell 2007; French 2003; Stam and Shohat 2012; Telles 2002) and Brazilian (Costa 2002; Pinho and Figueiredo 2002; Santos 2002) vantage points, calling into question the premise of externally imposed racial paradigms of analysis and attendant dismissals of transnational histories of racial thought and practice.

My raced positionality as a black North American scholar is indeed informative—and unapologetically so—of my scholarship and, I would add, embodied position in the Cuban field. This is to suggest that in an immediate sense, my subjectivity as African American is an unquestionable location from which I move and engage intellectually and socially in the world. Notions of a neutral ethnographic objectivity have long been challenged in the field of anthropology (Abu-Lughod 1991; Clifford 1986; Sanjek 1990; Scheper-Hughes 1992) and ultimately undermined by the unveiling of power in the production of all knowledge claims (Foucault [1969] 2002; Haraway 1991; Said 1979). Researchers and scholars all therefore move as situated subjects seeking to understand through interpretive means—positivist claims notwithstanding—the social world. My racial as well as gendered, classed, sexual, and national orientations thus collectively inform the ways I come to approach and engage my research and interlocutors.

Regarding the Cuban field, my experience as a racially marked nonwhite subject navigating the streets of Havana, where I was commonly read as a black or varyingly *mulato* Cuban, unquestionably shaped the ethnographic nature of my query into the ways race is currently lived in Cuba. My at times daily experience of being stopped by Cuban police and asked for my *carnet de identidad*, or national identification card, exposed me, like many of my rapero peers, to a quotidian consequence of being black, male, and (relatively) young within the context of Cuba's new racially charged and policed social landscape. My inability to enter tourist hotels without being challenged by male security personnel was yet another expression of my gendered racialization within the island's expanding market logics. Yet if I presented the questioning officer the tattered photocopy of my U.S. passport I had become conditioned to carry, or spoke my accented Spanish (or better yet English!) to hotel security guards, I would often be permitted to pass without further consequence. In the latter case, I would be free to indulge in the hotel's restricted currency zone otherwise long off-limits to most Cubans. Thus, though I was "black," my positionality as a foreign national clearly remained one of marked privilege.

At the same time, my racial situatedness served as an important site of engagement with my Cuban peers, where the space of blackness, through both its sameness *and* difference, became an initiating ground of dialogue. Again, I speak here of black peers in reference to those individuals within Cuba's hip hop community who politically self-identify as black regardless of how they might be externally labeled within Cuba's graduated racial system.[12] Such political identifications, particularly as they find articulation through the nationally expansive lens of hip hop, became a vital point of entry through which my ethnographic engagement with raperos moves. My project is thus positioned within ongoing conversations around advancing transnational fields of dialogue toward antiracist and broader social justice ends. This book is therefore in part an exploration into the possibilities— and potential limitations—of "blackness" as a methodological framework through which to conduct comparative, cross-national racial analyses among Afro-descendant communities at this current juncture of frenetic geospatial interconnectivity.

I am of course far from the first to travel this path within an ethnographic context. The pioneering work of Katherine Dunham, for one, stands as an example extraordinaire of this kind of transnational intervention. For Dunham, realms of dance provided an embodied medium for diasporic dialogue and translation (Dunham [1969] 1994; see also Aschenbrenner 2002). Zora Neale Hurston's earlier ethnographic forays into the Caribbean (Hurston [1935] 1990, [1937] 1990) are also illustrative of such dialogic pioneering efforts. A later generation of African American anthropologists such as Lynn Bolles (1996), Irma McClaurin (1996), Faye Harrison (1997), Edmund Gordon (1998), and Angela Gilliam (Gilliam and Gilliam 1999), among others, have varyingly approached the question of black transnationality as an ethnographic practice of the field.

In her piece "When Black Is Not Enough," Josephine Beoku-Betts invokes Patricia Hill Collins's notion of the "outsider within" (1990) to think about the locality of Afrodiasporic ethnographers working among differentiated black communities (Beoku-Betts 1994). Rather than present an unproblematized celebration, Beoku-Betts underscores the complexities of raced outsiders doing cross-national research. As a British anthropologist of Nigerian descent working with Gullah women of the South Carolinian Sea Islands, her status as a "black" insider was far from given, but rather an ambiguous one necessitating ongoing negotiation. Analogously, the Haitian American ethnographer Gina Ulysse evokes her position as a "regional native/local outsider" in the context of her work with Jamaican market women in Kingston (Ulysse 2008). Embracing a transnational black feminist methodology, Ulysse underscores the challenges, tensions, and limitations as well as the analytic insights afforded through such transnational race-work. In their respective scholarship on black women's organizing in Brazil, the African American ethnographers Kia Lilly Caldwell (2007) and Keisha-Khan Perry (2012) similarly evoke black feminist epistemologies as a mediated language of Afro-hemispheric encounter and ethnography.

What these overlapping conversations and debates unveil is the centrality of power in shaping the relative positionality of researcher vis-à-vis the "researched"—relationalities in which race among other social vectors can serve as a differentiating, though far from politically transcendent, factor. Indeed, far from claiming that racial semblances elide difference, such approaches elaborate a particular space or standpoint from which to initiate conversation among and between black-identified communities of African descent. Diasporic populations are of course by definition formed in difference, but a difference situated within broader shared understandings of sociohistorical, cultural, and often political forms of affinity. Such recognition in no way elides questions of power and privilege, but instead works to mediate some collective grounding of blackness through dialogic intercambio (exchange), in essence putting blackness reflexively to work toward an affective politics of affinity.

Hip hop today, by its very globalized and dialogically resonant nature, is all about the transnationally affective (M. Perry 2008b; see also Fernandes

2011; Mitchell et al. 2002; Sharma 2010). How and where, then, do I enter this conversation? Raised for the early part of my childhood on Manhattan's Lower East Side, I recall being dragged by my teenage babysitter to local "street jams" in the neighboring Baruch and Jacob Riis public housing projects in the mid-1970s where youth, almost exclusively African American and Puerto Rican, gathered on summer afternoons to indulge in the music of local DJs via makeshift audio equipment powered by way of illicit taps into city streetlamps. Although unaware at the time that what was unfolding around me throughout patchworks of public housing projects would soon give rise to an urban cultural phenomenon, I would come into budding awareness of self amid the formative period of hip hop's early ascendance during the 1980s.

It was during later travels, however, that I became cognizant of how hip hop, once a collaborative expression of postindustrial cultural improvisation among African American, Puerto Rican, and West Indian inner-city youth, was now being refashioned transnationally by other marginalized youth to give critical voice to their own subjective experience and sense of selfhood. In the interim a onetime marginal youth culture encompassing expressive elements of music, verbal lyricism, dance, graffiti art, and fashion had evolved into a multibillion-dollar global industry. I became fascinated with the apparent tension between hip hop as a global site of corporate commodification and simultaneously one of utopic yearnings and their possibilities. My Cuban foray thus springs in important part from this history.

While my work seeks to enter within and build upon currents of Afrodiasporic interchange, scholarly and otherwise, such efforts are certainly not without their challenges. Beyond questions of race, another methodologically related issue pertains to the at times vexed politics of conducting fieldwork in Cuba as a U.S. national. Given the highly charged nature of Cuban-U.S. relations resulting from legacies of Cold War tension and antagonistic posturing by successive U.S. administrations, the most enduring of which is the ongoing U.S. trade embargo, navigating this divide as a U.S. researcher can be a complex undertaking, recent thaws notwithstanding.

An immediate challenge for one sympathetic to many of the egalitarian ideals of the Cuban Revolution, along with its internationalist commitments to anticolonial/anti-imperialist histories of struggle, has been how to develop analyses that address the limitations, contradictions, and very real autocratic tendencies of the revolutionary project without risking misappropriations of such conclusions by interests bent on undermining that same project for deleterious gain. In this sense I find myself in a position somewhat analogous to that of many within Havana's hip hop community regarding how to engage critique without playing into, or at least compounding, injurious designs out of Miami or Washington. The obvious distinction between me and my rapero peers is that my analysis is voiced from a location of a national outsider, a distinction further complicated by the particularities of a U.S. vantage point and ongoing legacies of empire. The realities of these chasms came into rather stark focus during an informal meeting I helped organize in 2001 involving a prominent collection of Havana-area raperos and others in which I was accused by one well-positioned Cuban of being a CIA informant. There was a long-standing and intricate set of dynamics at play that meeting day—some personal, some professional—and while the individual voicing the concern and I later made amends, my location as a U.S. researcher was rendered hypervisible, if potentially suspect.

Yet would such anxieties have been beyond consideration? Some months prior, a close rapero friend expressed concern that Cuban hip hop could offer an opportune site for infiltration and provocateur work by those seeking to debilitate the revolutionary state. Nadine Fernandez suggests Cuba's leadership has indeed long been concerned that the race question in particular could be manipulated by adversaries of the state who would exploit the issue as a nationally divisive tactic (N. Fernandez 2001: 119). Given recent revelations involving covert U.S. efforts through the auspices of USAID to ferment provocateurism within Cuban hip hop (see chapter 6), such concerns were far from folly. During my research Cuban MCs were acutely aware of the political stakes as socially engaged artists in a globally complex era of geopolitics. Raperos in fact repeatedly saw their words and lyrics manipulated by U.S. journalists in order to fit reductive readings of Cuban hip hop as a site of counterrevolutionary dissent rather than one largely committed to critical engagements within conceptions (albeit expansive) of the revolutionary process itself. Such were among the broader implications of the field that necessitated nuanced sensitivity on my part, ones that also carried their own interpellating force and potential costs.

As one invested in black transnationalism as a strategic paradigm in combating globalized forms of racial subjugation, Cuban hip hop was for me a consequential site for both mapping and perusing such Afro-hemispheric commitments. Raperos' own transnationally expansive understandings of black-selfhood in this sense enabled a space of dialogue, one within which I could critically engage as a black "outsider within," complexities and contractions notwithstanding. Such conjoining practices of blackness, I would offer, are potentially generative of alternative political vistas themselves.

Throughout this book's narrative I have chosen to largely forgo the common ethnographic practice of using pseudonyms. The immediate reason is that many of the artists, intellectuals, and other hip-hop-affiliated individuals of whom I mostly write are outspoken public figures. It is thus imperative that I give proper recognition to the art, work, and lives of these individuals as they have contributed to the evolving lines of hip hop's rise in Cuba. Yet by acknowledging the majority of my Cuban interlocutors I assume added levels of responsibility and accountability to them and their histories. Over my years of involvement in Havana, countless Cuban friends and colleagues have lent a tremendous amount of their own time, intellect, and political commitment to this project. I consider many in this sense collaborators who have a long-awaited invested stake in this book and its outcome. I thus feel, in vintage hip hop vernacular, a deep indebted responsibility to represent(!) this history to the best of my ability and positioned understanding.

Narrative Layout

Situating hip hop's Cuban ascent within the immediacies of the island's ongoing transformation, chapter 1 opens with my introduction to Havana in 1998 and the fraught complexities of race and class encountered in the wake of the legalization of the U.S. dollar and the subsequent rise of a dual-currency economy following the economic crises of the early 1990s. Drawing on my initial experience living with an Afro-Cuban family, the chapter folds into an examination of Cuba's new raced economies of commingling exclusion and market assimilation, as well as the entrepreneurial strategies some black and darker-skinned Cubans have creatively fashioned amid its workings.

Interstitial in the mix is a query into the ambivalent nature of Cuba's evolving neoliberal condition, its relation to the island's tourism industry, and their conjoining raced effects vis-à-vis spaces and embodied performances of blackness. Here I explore the ahistoricizing nature of folkloric representations of Afro-Cuban expressive culture and their recent monetizations, as well as the revolutionary state's role in such packaging. The chapter then moves to a discussion of the rise of raced forms of regulation as the Cuban state has sought to police the social incongruencies of the moment, and the questions these developments raise via lived realms of Cuban citizenship. The political urgencies of such developments are brought into focus with the chapter's concluding segue into critiques among Cuban raperos regarding the systemics of raced policing of black youth.

Chapter 2 delves into hip hop's rise in Havana during the rapid social flux of the 1990s. The chapter foregrounds the role of race in the early making of hip hop, while introducing a range of key figures in Havana's nascent hip hop community, as well as the revolutionary state's peripheral engagement with the young cultural movement. Here I discuss the crafting of "black spaces" through the ways raperos and their immediate predecessors arose from local spaces of practice in which self-consciously modern understandings of cosmopolitan blackness were celebrated and enacted in new Cuban ways. The chapter then carries the conversation into an exploration of the Cuban hip hop festival of 1997 as an early and highly spectacular illustration of the ways Cuban blackness found new dynamic play and lyric form through a globally conversant lens of hip hop.

Chapter 3 moves into the ethnographic setting of my own research (1999 onward) with a focus on emerging identity currents within Cuban hip hop. The chapter opens with my early engagements with key actors within Havana's hip hop community, with a particular focus on the pioneering hip hop duo Obsesión. The chapter follows with a descriptive exploration of an evolving range of locales through which raperos constituted themselves as an artistic and cultural community. The chapter continues with an exploration of the 2000 Cuban hip hop festival, which represented a significant turning point in the movement's organizational character vis-à-vis expanding institutional investments by the Cuban state. The festival's frame also offers insight into raperos' involvements with African American and Puerto Rican collaborators from the United States, and the significance of such exchange regarding political discourse and dimensions of identity within Cuban hip hop. I conclude the chapter with a discussion of a stage performance of the Havana-based rap duo Anónimo Consejo, as exemplary of positioned critiques within broader conceptions of revolutionary history and struggle.

Chapter 4 draws upon a descriptive sampling of personal narratives and music-making practices in mapping the performative, often gendered nature of black self-fashioning among members of Havana's hip hop community. The chapter opens with rapero mediations of subjectivity through the coupling of two alternative streams of racial citizenship—one rooted in a recuperative claiming of a critical black subject of Cuban history, the other through national-expansive and often masculinist appeals to Afro-hemispheric histories of black radical struggle. The chapter explores how these creative routes of self-invention were shaped through a confluence of mentoring relationships with Afro-Cuban intellectuals and African American political exiles. This is followed by a discussion of the rise of black feminist-aligned discourse and subjectivity within rapero circles by way of an increasingly vocal presence of women. Through such interventions, I suggest, these women pose challenges to the largely masculinist frames of Cuban hip hop and broader Cuban spheres of racialized patriarchy, while constituting themselves as political subjects through artistic praxis.

Chapter 5 centers on the Cuban state's evolving efforts to incorporate hip hop within institutional frames of revolutionary national culture and raperos' varying negotiations of these moves. While related discussions are initiated in previous chapters, this chapter focuses on later developments culminating in the 2002 establishment of the Agencia Cubana de Rap (ACR, or Cuban Rap Agency) under Cuba's Ministry of Culture, which signified the height of incorporative state strategies. These events are examined in overlapping relation to Cuban cultural policy, intensifying market pressures, and the global commercialization of Cuban popular music. Also examined is the simultaneous rise of Afro-Cuban intellectual involvements with hip hop vis-à-vis a broader interplay of intermittent state openings and an emergent black public sphere. Here it is suggested that black and darker-skinned raperos have been active in shaping a nascent black counterpublic rooted in claims of a black political difference within an otherwise nonracial Cuban national imaginary underscoring, in turn, dilemmas of Cuban race and national citizenship in the neoliberal era.

Chapter 6 focuses on more recent reconfigurations of Cuban hip hop in relation to further economic, social, and ideological erosion on the island accompanied by waning state support. Central to this discussion are efforts by raperos to establish alternative projects and support structures independent of state institutions and influence. This chapter also explores the gradual decentering of hip hop's racial currents in dialogue with two concurrent developments, both of which resonate in one form or another with Cuba's expanding marketplace. The first is the rise of more commercially minded reggaetón music, which has displaced much of the space—official, popular, and talent-wise—that hip hop once occupied. Included here is a discussion of reggaetón's Cuban genesis in eastern Santiago de Cuba and its westward march toward Havana.

A second related development concerns the departure abroad by many key figures within Havana's black-identified rapero community. While informed by a range of overlapping factors varyingly impacting the character of island hip hop, the national exodus has also contributed to an internationalization of Cuban hip hop into diaspora as artists have sought to reconstitute community through social media and international travel. This chapter concludes with the continued challenges faced by black antiracist efforts in Cuba, while acknowledging the role and legacies of Cuban raperos within this unfolding moment of political practice and national transformation.

A short postscript revisits the book's main arguments and contributions, while offering a closing vignette and a related coda.

Chapter 1.
Raced Neoliberalism:
Groundings for Hip Hop

To be a poor man is hard, but to be a poor race in a land of dollars is the
very bottom of hardships.
—W. E. B. Du Bois, *The Souls of Black Folk*

Dicen que Dios no aprieta, pero Cuba estrangula. Pero a pesar de todo,
de mil modos te amo Cuba
[They say God does not squeeze, but Cuba strangles. Regardless of all,
in a thousand ways I love you, Cuba]
—"Mi nación," Los Paisanos

In the summer of 1998 I made my first trip to Havana for a Spanish-language
course I had arranged through online sleuthing and e-mail exchanges. I had
recently completed my MA work on Garifuna youth and performance in
New York City, and having leftover research funds I decided to take the opportunity to visit Cuba while seeking to improve my Spanish skills. Raised in
New York City by leftist parents—my father African American, my mother
Jewish—who met through their early 1960s activism amid the U.S. civil
rights movement, Cuba and its revolution were celebrated in my home as a
defiant counterweight to histories of imperial capitalism.

As was the case within many black left circles of the time, the Cuban
Revolution's early commitments to racial equity and internationalist sup-

1.1. Hip hop producer Ariel Fernández Díaz, as shown on the back cover of *Cuban Hip-Hop All Stars*. Photo courtesy Steve Marcus

port for U.S. black radicals and anticolonial struggles in Africa carried particular resonance in my movement household. Fidel Castro's famed 1960 stay in Harlem and impromptu meeting with Malcolm X at the Hotel Theresa struck an especially intimate chord, occurring around the time of my father's on-air reporting on social justice issues with New York–based WBAI-Pacifica radio, work through which he had interviewed Malcolm X on a number of occasions himself. My mother, moreover, was involved in early solidarity work with the leftist Fair Play for Cuba Committee, while a close aunt visited Havana in the late 1980s as part of a delegation of U.S. health care professionals exploring the island's public health system. Given this familial history, Cuba and its revolution had long occupied a site of intrigue.

Yet while my trip to Havana that summer may have been informed by inherited nostalgias of revolutionary lore, I recognized the necessity of experiencing this mythic Cuba on my own historical terms. Cuba of 1998, of course, was not the Cuba of my parents' era and generation. It had been a decade since the collapse of the Eastern bloc and the end of Cuba's preferential trade with the Soviet Union and its allies. Since the early 1990s the island's ambivalent though ever-deepening engagement with market capitalism had introduced new social incongruencies and heightened levels of contradiction into a once defiant revolutionary socialism. By 1998 the strains were clearly evident even to a foreign visitor such as myself. Of particular note were the ways these developments impacted the island's complexities of race and class, long foci of revolutionary Cuba's efforts to build egalitarianism under state socialism. Such fissures of race and class were also latent sites of historical tension rooted in Cuba's very inception as a modern nation.

I was, as it turns out, fortunate to have arranged an informal homestay with a Cuban family in Havana's western barrio of Playa, a short walking distance from the state-run language school where I was attending daily Spanish classes for payment in U.S. dollars. I met the family through Delmaris, an administrator at the school with whom I had initially been in contact about the program via her workplace e-mail, access to which at the time was highly coveted given Cuba's remarkably (if rather conspicuously) underdeveloped electronic communications infrastructure. Despite recent opens, Cuba has one of the lowest levels of Internet penetration in the hemisphere where private Internet access has long been restricted by the Cuban state as a means of regulating open circulation of information. Delmaris and I were nonetheless able to weave conversation through our exchanges to organize a homestay with her husband's family with whom she lived in a six-story concrete *edificio* (apartment building) dating from the early 1980s. While Delmaris's light skin, long reddish-brown hair, and distant Chinese ancestry would effectively classify her in Cuban terms as "white," her husband, Amílcar, and his family were decidedly Afro-Cuban.

From there began my time in the three-bedroom home of Lisnida. A retired geography professor, Lisnida shared her flat with her son Amílcar, a state-employed architect, his wife Delmaris, and Lisnida's five-year-old grandson Leni, whose mother, Alma, Lisnida's daughter, worked in the eastern city of Matanzas. As Afro-Cuban professionals, Lisnida and Amílcar were multigenerational beneficiaries of revolutionary Cuba's public investments in education and professional training that enabled black Cubans levels of educational access unseen in the prerevolutionary period. In the case of Lisnida, fidelities to the revolution included a dedication to watching Fidel Castro's marathon speeches on state television and her enthusiasm in sharing this living history with me, a visiting outsider.

As my initial introduction to a performing Fidel as revolutionary institution, I sat with Lisnida for the opening hour or so of one such speech. After feeling I had put in a competent beginner's investment, I headed out for a beer with a friend, only to return a couple of hours later to find an aging Fidel still in full pontificating swing. In truth I was never fully out of Fidel's earshot that evening, as I was accompanied throughout my outing by distant echoes of his seemingly omnipresent voice weaving its way through open windows into the otherwise empty night streets. Yet while numerous households like Lisnida's had their TVs tuned to the speech, the ghostly quality of the patriarch's voice resonating across carpetless floors seemed to suggest an ever-receding presence. Though this still may indeed have been Fidel's Cuba; the question, though, seemed to be for how long.

In addition to affinities with the island's revolutionary history, Lisnida and her family also held strong identifications as black Cubans. Aware of my interest in Afro-Atlantic cultural lines, for instance, Lisnida sat me down at her kitchen table on a number of occasions to share nuances of Afro-Cuban religious life. Though not a practitioner herself, Lisnida assumed a familial intimacy as she took time identifying varying characteristics differentiating followers of Santería or Regla de Ocha-Lucumí,[1] for instance, from those of Palo Monte, and the secret fraternal society of the Abakuá.

Lisnida's family's embrace of the *Afro* in Afro-Cuban, however, was not limited to the cultural, nor necessarily bound by the national. I recall Lisnida's son, Amílcar, sharing over dinner one evening the story of his namesake, the late Guinea-Bissauan revolutionary figure Amílcar Cabral, recounting Cabral's leadership in Guinea-Bissau's guerrilla war for independence, along with his 1973 assassination at the hands of the colonial Portuguese. Amílcar's affective ties to this history were far from abstract; Cuba's military involvements in Guinea-Bissau's anticolonial struggle played a critical role in the nation's triumph of independence in 1974. In relaying his narrative, Amílcar expressed a prideful sense of identification with Cabral and Cuba's broader history of anticolonial struggle in Africa, citing key moments from the Congo and Ethiopia to Angola. Having spent significant time in Eastern and Southern Africa myself, our dinner conversations broadened to encompass my own diasporic experiences and solidarity efforts, including media work in Cape Town, South Africa, during the waning years of apartheid.

It was clear from speaking with Amílcar that his understandings of Africa and its recent history—and ultimately his own personal baptism by it—were shaped by legacies of Cuban internationalism and solidarities with African independence movements dating back to the early years of the revolution. Legacies indeed. Guillermo, Amílcar's uncle and Lisnida's brother, who frequently visited the household, served as a mechanic during Cuba's sixteen-year military engagement in Angola.[2] Fighting alongside the ruling MPLA in its war against UNITA rebels backed by the United States, South Africa, and Zaire, upward of ten thousand Cubans were killed during the campaign, significant numbers of whom were Afro-Cuban. While Guillermo spoke little in detail of his time in Angola during his visits—noteworthy given broader official silences around the war's national costs and collective trauma—he did share a sense of pride at having served in Angola's eventual victory. Africa was thus interwoven in the lives of Lisnida's family in complexly imbricated levels of both the personal and national.

Aside from shared ties of diasporic affinity, my relationship with Lisnida's household was clearly also a financial one. While my time with the family enabled entrée to their lives and opportunities to explore relationships, our agreed-upon payment of US$15 per night for food and lodging helped defray, at least temporarily, the family's growing need for U.S dollars. This informal agreement was also clandestine, given recent efforts by the Cuban state to regulate and capitalize on a growing dollar-market for residential room rentals to foreigners. Cubans were now required to pay a hefty monthly dollar-tax for official rental licenses or risk fines upward of $1,500 and the possible threat of property confiscation.[3] For Lisnida and family the risk was apparently worth it; the $15 daily contribution was roughly equivalent to the average monthly peso salary garnered by many public sector employees.

Indeed, despite advanced education and levels of professional achievement, Lisnida's family found themselves dependent on the island's rapidly expanding dollar economy within which it was difficult for most to survive on state-regulated peso salaries. As part of the Cuban state's efforts to capture circulating dollars otherwise destined for the informal black market, basics like soap, clothing, and essential foodstuffs were increasingly restricted to dollar-only purchase in state-run stores. Aptly termed la shopping in Cuban vernacular, these dollar-only stores came to symbolize the early rise of a new dollar-based consumerism in a once definitely nonconsumerist socialist Cuba (see Gordy 2006).

One of the only local dollar stores at the time was, rather ironically, in close proximity to the Russian Embassy with its massive citadel-like office tower peering ominously over the leafy residential barrio of Miramar. With its modest aisles of imported delicacies like pasta, powdered milk, and canned goods alongside cooking oil and detergent, the supermarket was conveniently located to serve Havana's diplomatic corps given the barrio's heavy concentration of foreign embassies. In relatively short order these dollar-only stores became ubiquitous throughout Havana and the broader island. By 2000 some 75–80 percent of dollar remittances by Cubans living abroad—a primary source of circulating dollars—would channel through such state-run stores and into government coffers (Eckstein 2010: 1050).

Within this new reality Lisnida and her family were struggling daily to make ends meet. With no family living abroad to remit potentially life-changing dollars to subsidize their household income, their ability—or was it a sacrificial concession—to rent a room in their cramped apartment to a dollar-paying *yuma* (foreigner) was something of a momentary windfall, one arising from the privileged work-related access Delmaris, the sole ostensibly "white" member of the household, had to foreigners such as myself. Her coveted position within the island's evolving dollar-based tourism economy was far from unique, however. It was already apparent that white Cubans were favored for hire in tourism-related employment, Cuba's fastest-growing generator of foreign currency following its recent post-Soviet-era turn toward liberalized markets. Although Lisnida and her family were clearly better off in comparison to the severe hardships they and most Cubans endured during the depths of the early 1990s economic crisis, they had clearly entered a new moment of challenge in which dimensions of race and class were reemerging as key factors shaping social opportunity and mobility on the island. Was this the utopic Cuba of my parents' revolutionary-tinged era? Did that Cuba indeed ever quite exist?

My time in Lisnida's home and broader experiences in Havana that summer triggered an urgent curiosity regarding the peculiarities and fraught tensions of a rapidly changing Cuba. Most intriguing, I had heard during my stay of an evolving local hip hop scene, one with an apparently significant level of Afro-Cuban involvement. Reared amid hip hop's urban birth and later exposed to the complexities of hip hop communities in Brazil and South Africa (M. Perry 2008b), I was fascinated by the idea of Cuban hip hop and what insights it might offer regarding the island's current condition and future trajectory. Living a thirty-minute *colectivo* (collective taxi) ride from Havana's center and well over an hour from the neighboring municipality of Alamar, areas where much of the local hip hop activity at the time was flowering, I unfortunately had little exposure to the music during that initial trip. I did, however, leave that summer determined to return to Havana to explore Cuban hip hop as a window into what was clearly an island in historic flux.

What, then, is the backstory of hip hop's emergence on the island? In what ways might its rise speak to the particularities of Cuba's shifting economic and social terrain? Given Los Paisanos' conflicted allusion to a Cuba that "squeezes" yet remains beloved in their song "Mi nación" referenced in the chapter's opening epigraph, how might enduring tensions of race, nation, and citizenship in light of the island's unfolding neoliberal uncertainties factor into the mix? As I would come to learn, such questions were of both critical concern and daily consequence for many within Havana's hip hop community, while at the same time instrumental to the broader political nature of Cuban hip hop itself.

Market Transitions

It is unquestionable that the 1990s marked a distinctive juncture in Cuba's history, one largely defined by rupture and dissolution following the collapse of the Eastern bloc and the subsequent suspension of Soviet subsidies upon which the Cuban economy and wider revolutionary project had long been dependent. As a consequence, Cuba fell into a severe economic crisis between 1989 and 1993 resulting in a crippling 40 percent reduction in GDP (Jatar-Hausmann 1999: 46). It was during a now infamous 1991 speech before the Congress of the Federation of Cuban Women that Fidel Castro declared *el período especial en tiempos de paz*, a "special period in peacetime," demanding acute austerity measures aimed at reducing national consumption and expenditure.

While signs of recovery from this special period would begin to emerge after 1996, the resulting and evolving character of Cuban society had unquestionably taken a historic turn. I've heard Cubans painfully recall the early 1990s as *el tiempo de los flacos* (time of the skinny ones), a period in which acute scarcities of produce, shelved goods, and meat of any kind contributed to endemic nationwide levels of undernourishment.[4] Exacerbating if not strategically exploiting the scenario, the United States tightened its trade embargo during this period, resulting in an estimated $67 billion loss to the Cuban economy by decade's close in addition to an accompanying range of social costs (Hidalgo and Martínez 2000).[5]

By 1993 urgent intervention was needed to stem the deepening economic and ensuing social crisis, compelling Cuba's ambivalent dance with global capital and attending openings to neoliberal market forces. I underscore ambivalent here to speak to the complexly fraught nature of Cuba's recent engagements with neoliberalism. Unlike much of the Global South obligated to accommodate neoliberal reforms by way of international lending and regulatory agencies or regional free-trade agreements such as NAFTA, Cuba's socialist leadership adamantly eschewed any participation within such frameworks. Revolutionary Cuba has indeed been a vehement critic of global free trade, assuming, for instance, vocal membership as a founding partner in the anti-neoliberal bloc ALBA (Alianza Bolivariana para los Pueblos de Nuestra América), formally led by Venezuela's late Hugo Chávez.

Such efforts notwithstanding, it is clear that more informal modes of accommodation were undertaken by the Cuban state in ways that clearly resonate with neoliberal monetization. It was the 1993 legalization of the U.S. dollar and the subsequent creation of a dual dollar/Cuban peso economy that most cogently signified a turn toward a market-driven, dollar-intensive economy and implicit erosion of state socialism. While the introduction of *pesos convertibles* (convertible pesos, or CUCs) in 2004 as official tender sought to remedy the incongruencies of dollar-based exchange, foreign currency dependence continues as Cubans remain reliant on foreign exchange in order to purchase the globally pegged CUCs now vital to daily life.

Dollar legalization was quickly followed by a series of deregulatory reforms involving the limited sanctioning of privately owned small businesses and cooperatives, the breakup of state farms and creation of private farmers' markets, and openings to foreign investment and joint ventures.[6] Market-aligned shifts have accelerated under Raúl Castro, who has overseen radical reductions to public sector payrolls and state subsidies, as well as authorizing private home ownership alongside private real estate and car markets. The recent $900 million revamping of the port of Mariel—long infamous for the 1980 boatlift of ten thousand Cubans to the United States during an acute moment of revolutionary crisis—into an expansive internationally financed and operated economic free-trade zone stands as a particularly cogent marker of this neoliberal turn.[7] Given ongoing moves toward normalizing U.S.-Cuban relations, the pace and scope of such marketizations are certain to accelerate and broaden.

On the social front, the once essential state-issued libreta (little book) long guaranteeing families basic monthly levels of subsidized food would eventually provide so little it became a sardonic brunt of Cuban humor.[8] The island's celebrated national health care system has in turn become strained due to the contracting out of tens of thousands of Cuban medical personnel to Latin America, the Caribbean, and Africa for hard currency remuneration and other forms of economic exchange.[9] While Cuba provided urgent medical expertise during international crises like the recent West African Ebola epidemic, the broader leasing of professional personnel like doctors and engineers abroad accounted for almost half of Cuba's hard currency earnings by 2006, more than double the revenue generated by tourism (Sánchez-Egozcue 2007: 7, cited in Eckstein 2010: 1049). The concurrent growth of a "medical tourism" industry catering to foreign-currency-paying elites from Latin America and the Caribbean, moreover, speaks further to a monetization of Cuba's public health care system in the face of a withering socialist state.

Here I turn again to Aihwa Ong's notion of neoliberalism "as exception" regarding the selective introduction of market strategies and intertwined modes of social governance as aberrations to established governing practices in order to more effectively compete in the global economy (Ong 2006). In the case of Cuba, neoliberal rationales and their market-friendly effects have increasingly permeated Cuban society as exceptions to dominant socialist rule, engendering a deep ambivalence of national condition and identity. While the Cuban state continues (ever anemically) to claim state socialism as its guiding principle and mode of governance, its efforts to not only mediate but in the end actively facilitate market reforms suggest a discordant slide toward embrace of a neoliberal state (cf. Hardt and Negri 2004; Wacquant 2012).[10]

In Ong's reading, such incongruencies tend to produce graduated zones of exclusion under which rights associated with citizenship are increasingly afforded along lines of entrepreneurial ability rather than national belonging. In Cuban form, one sees these logics embodied in the rise of cuentapropismo, an evolving state-sponsored self-employment scheme that, while ostensibly regulated, places responsibility for employment on the individual alone, thus resonating with a broader turn toward private sector employment and individuated market competition (cf. Burnett 2011). This shift echoes Alexei Yurchak's discussion of the rise of an entrepreneurial ethic in postsocialist Russia, displacing previous modes of collectivist organization and social practice (Yurchak 2003). Such "creative destruction," to borrow from David Harvey (2007), resonates with the ways neoliberal marketization has similarly encouraged entrepreneurial—and ultimately elite capitalist—class formations in settings like China and India. As in these and other global examples (W. Brown 2003; Comaroff and Comaroff 2009; Vrasti 2011), the rise of the market over the state as abettor of social well-being requires each to refashion oneself as rationally minded *homo oeconomicus* (economic human) (Foucault 1979) in competitive pursuit of individual gain. From doorstep peddling of "street pizzas" to renting rooms to foreign tourists, enterprising strategies to creatively resolve (*resolver*) daily hardships in light of Cuba's diminished capacities for social welfare indeed speak poignantly to the island's neoliberal turn.

Raced Economies

As Lisnida's family's experience suggests, the ways Cubans have come to navigate and compete within the island's new economy have been significantly impacted by dimensions of race. Regarding foreign remittances—long the greatest single source of dollars and other foreign-currency income for most Cubans—smaller numbers of black Cubans living abroad and the tendency for migrants of Afro-Cuban descent to be less financially secure have contributed to marked remittance disparities between white and darker-skinned Cubans.[11] In addition to enabling higher standards of living in an immediate sense, remitted monies may also be invested in small entrepreneurial projects providing additional financial benefits. With limited recourse to remittances and their entrepreneurial effects, black and darker-skinned Cubans are ostensibly left with tourism-related commerce—Cuba's other emergent site of foreign exchange—as a potential source of dollars and CUCs. Yet as Delmaris's case suggests, tourism carries its own raced logics and spheres of exclusion.

While the dismantling of the island's Batista-era tourism industry was a celebrated early achievement of the revolution, in line with similar neoliberal strategies in the region (Desforges 2000; Gregory 2006; Klak and Myers 1998; Scher 2011), tourism was designated as a strategic sector shortly after

1989 and provided more than 40 percent of the island's hard currency income by 2001 (Associated Press 2001).[12] In Cuba's European-oriented hotels and related tour services, however, there is wide acknowledgment of preferential hiring for lighter-skinned Cubans (de la Fuente 2001; Roland 2010; Sawyer 2005). Although these workers receive salaries in Cuban pesos, their incomes are often augmented exponentially by tips and other transactions in foreign currencies and/or CUCs circulating within these contained tourist spaces. For a long time, the only darker-skinned employees visible were male security personnel stationed at hotel entrances vigilantly guarding these privileged currency zones from the public space of la calle (the street).

One rationale offered for these whitened spaces is that many tourist hotels are often jointly owned and/or operated by European hotel conglomerates who exercise foreign racial preferences when making hiring decisions. An alternative explanation offered is that the tourist industry is simply responding to the island's predominantly white European and North American clientele who prefer to be served by people who "look like them."[13] Either scenario presents dilemmas for revolutionary Cuba and its embedded ideals of racial equality. They also suggest a certain abdication of sovereignty and full rights of citizenship in which economic livelihood is no longer ensured or arbitrated by the state, but rather allocated by the market along lines of racial difference.

The experiences of Mario, a dark-brown-skinned Afro-Cuban friend from the working-class barrio of Jesús María in central Havana, testifies to the lived realities of such raced exclusion. While not a particularly invested hip hop "head," Mario was not unlike many I later met in Havana's rapero community: that is, young, largely unemployed—at least formally—black men from working-class backgrounds. With his customary jeans, well-worn athletic shoes, and New York Yankees cap he had acquired by way of a cousin in New Jersey, Mario assumed a stylized flair similar to many local followers of hip hop. When we first met in 1998, Mario, then in his early twenties, frequently complained of his inability to acquire work with a state-run tourism company despite his university education and coveted English fluency. While passing his finger along the inside of his left forearm in the common Cuban gesture indicating color or race (i.e., "the blood"), he explained, "Por supuesto, es el color de piel que me impide este trabajo" (Of course, it's the color of my skin that keeps me from this work). Given legacies of Afro-Cuban support for the revolution stemming from histories of expansion in areas like public education, urban housing, and universal health care, Mario expressed a sense of disillusionment (if not a hint of betrayal) about the current Cuban moment. Frustrations of this kind eventually played into his decision to immigrate to France in 2000 through a foreign fiancé visa acquired by way of his French girlfriend, now his wife, with whom he now shares two children in Nantes.

Mario's departure from Cuba can be seen as a fairly strategic one in this light, fashioned in response to an increasingly monetized everyday in which his racial status constrained his range of opportunity and social mobility. Emigration would indeed become ever more common among young black Cubans, including, as I later explore, many key members of Havana's hip hop community. Yet by immigrating to France in an effort to circumvent such limitations, Mario was compelled in the end to forfeit his legal status as a Cuban citizen. Cubans living or traveling abroad for extended periods are obligated to relinquish citizenship, and upon return must request official permission to visit the island on a temporary basis.[14] Although once abroad Mario eventually became certified as an electrician through a local polytechnic, for a number of years he worked part-time in Nantes as a salsa DJ and dance instructor—tapping in this way into global markets of Cuban cultural trade. Thus while a concession of formal rights with emigration may have been unavoidable, cultural realms of Cuban citizenship remained for Mario not only accessible but relatively viable in a commercial sense.

Interplays of race, citizenship, and economies of exchange have in fact become commonplace in Cuba, where racially marked space and signs of blackness have emerged as sites of tourism-related commerce. Anyone familiar with the island over the last decade or so is aware of a strong tourist trade in Afro-Cuban cultural expression in a wide array of forms, many of which draw upon notions of black "otherness" steeped in exotic and/or erotic kinds of desire. This trade and its packaging has been mediated in important part through an enduring trope of Cuban folklore that, through recent market alignments, has helped facilitate a trafficking of black cultural markers as exploitable assets for tourist revenue (see Ayorinde 2004; Delgado 2009; Hagedorn 2001; R. Moore 2006a).

Rooted, as Robin Moore (1997) has detailed, in nationalist efforts among early twentieth-century artistic movements to imagine a racially syncretic, postcolonial ideal of Cuban nationhood, and intellectually codified by the celebrated ethnologist Fernando Ortiz, the trope of folklore has assumed an implicitly raced meaning in its nearly exclusive application to Afro-Cuban cultural forms. Reminiscent of similar projects in the Caribbean and broader Latin American region (Canclini 1995; Godreau 2006; Guss 2000; Thomas 2004), the labeling of Afro-Cuban expressive realms such as music, dance, and religious community as folkloric has worked to contain these forms (and by extension those who practice them) firmly within the trans-culturated bounds of a Cuban national patrimony (Ortiz [1940] 1963; cf. Yelvington 2001). Such folkloric representations—be they objects of study or appropriated national spectacle—are ultimately resignified and statically assimilated within a race-neutral(izing) discourse of lo popular, obscuring these forms' historical specificity and dynamism as ongoing expressions of Afro-Cuban life and cultural agency.

Building upon this legacy, various cultural institutions formed during the early revolutionary period sought to document and institutionally situate Afro-Cuban folklore within the revolutionary scope of national culture.[15] Although these efforts were in keeping with a broader cultural policy aimed at fostering revolutionary-infused arts and culture by way of state promotion and guidance (Hart Dávalos 1990;[16] cf. R. Moore 2006b), the emphasis has been on institutional representations of afrocubanidad (Afro-Cubanness) as performed national spectacle. Through national stagings of both sacred and secular forms of Afro-Cuban music and dance, Cuba's Conjunto Folklórico Nacional has, since its founding in 1962, been an exemplar of state-sponsored efforts (see Daniel 1995; Hagedorn 2001).

While the Conjunto owes some of its creative impetus to Afro-Cuban demands for inclusion within the revolutionary project and draws heavily upon black artistic leadership, its performative repertoire implicitly builds upon an Ortizian legacy positing Afro-Cuban cultural realms juxtaposed to that of modernity (see Bronfman 2002; R. Moore 1994).[17] Such framings tend to reproduce renderings of Afro-Cuban cultural forms—in particular those associated with African-derived religious systems—as primitive, antediluvian counterpoles to modern socialism (see de la Fuente 2001; Palmié 2002). The language of folklore in this sense engenders a fossilizing stasis of black Cuban cultural forms as bounded sites affixed to, and ultimately contained within, a nonracial Cuban national imaginary. Afro-Cuban cultural spheres are therefore relegated to an unchanging national past, effectively fixing black Cubans within static representations of the "traditional" rather than recognizing the dynamic ever-changing nature of Afro-Cuban cultural practice, subjectivity, and experience.

Within today's cultural marketplace, folkloric framings have also enabled the packaging of black cultural forms as exploitable resources for tourist dollars and other exchange. These moves are tied in a broader sense to what Ruth Behar (1999) once referred to as Cuba's "buena-vistaization" in allusion to *The Buena Vista Social Club*, the 1997 album of classic *son* music produced by Ry Cooder and the subsequent Wim Wenders's documentary of the same title that launched a global frenzy for Cuban music and culture. This commercial wave is embedded in nostalgic yearnings for an old Cuba—a prerevolutionary Cuba of vintage pre-1959 American cars, historic urban architecture, and "traditional" forms of expressive culture and tropical exoticism. Reminiscent of Renato Rosaldo's notion of imperialist nostalgia (1989), buena-vistaization thus speaks to the ways Cuban cultural markers have been reconfigured, packaged, and marketed for Western consumption via appeals to imperialist-laden desires for an untainted prerevolutionary past. As Tanya Hernandez suggests, such ahistoricizing nostalgias are often coupled with quests for an authentically "pure" Afro-Cuban subject and attending musicality rooted in preverbal longings for noble savagery (Hernandez 2002).

There are, for example, numerous locales in Havana where tourists regularly flock to consume and bodily experience Afro-Cuban cultural practices such as rumba music and dance. One such widely attended event is held along Callejón de Hamel. On any given Sunday this small narrow street in the Central Havana neighborhood of Cayo Hueso draws large gatherings of local as well as foreign tourists, numbers of whom may arrive via tour buses that sit just outside the street's ornate entrance.[18] Colorfully awash with Afro-Cuban religious motifs and murals as well as a few ritual altars, the Callejón's aesthetics are largely the creative invention of the Cuban artist Salvador González Escalona, whose gallery sits conveniently adjacent to the space dedicated to the weekly rumba performances. Living only a few blocks from the Callejón, I attended the rumba innumerable times between 1999 and 2006.

I recall one particular Sunday, however, when the artist González Escalona, a mestizo who often performed the role of microphone-wielding host of the rumba's festive play of dance and song—though he participates directly in neither—welcomed the crowd by alluding to the rumba as "nuestro folklore" (our folklore). At that point a dark-skinned black woman who appeared to be in her late thirties shouted definitively from the audience "¡Este no es el folklore, esta es nuestra cultura!" (This is not folklore, this is our culture!), followed by affirmations from some in the crowd. Her remarks laid bare tensions between the performance of rumba as a folkloric spectacle, framed in this instant for tourist consumption, and its lived embodiment as a cultural space of enacted community (cf. Daniel 1995). Such discord draws attention to the market-driven commodification of Afro-Cuban cultural forms and signs of blackness within Cuba's tourist economy, one significantly enabled through the language of folklore.

The Cuban state for its part has played its own role in the commercial marketing and packaging of folklorized blackness. Departing from earlier histories of suppression (Hagedorn 2001; C. Moore 1989), the state has assumed an increasingly active role in the public promotion of Ocha-Lucumí and other Afro-Cuban religious systems as generators of tourist-related income. One notable example is Havana's Museo de los Orishas, housed in the headquarters of the state-sanctioned Asociación Cultural Yoruba de Cuba. For a fee of CUC$10 (equivalent to US$10, roughly half a month's average peso salary), visitors can view upward of thirty religiously adorned, life-size figures of various orishas (deities) of the Ocha-Lucumí pantheon and other religious paraphernalia. Yet farther afield, state-run religio-commerce has evolved to offer not only excursions to designated Ocha houses but, reportedly, government-sponsored tours through which paying customers can participate in rites of initiation into the Lucumí religion itself (Hagedorn 2001). Rogelio Martínez Furé, a prominent Afro-Cuban intellectual and founding member of the Conjunto Folklórico Nacional, refers to such practices as "pseudo-folklore," akin in his view to a prostitution or pimping of traditional religious systems (Martínez Furé 2000: 159).

Folkloric packagings, moreover, often involve gendered and sexualized dimensions as well. In large craft markets in Havana and other tourist areas, one can find a bountiful collection of racialized caricatures of black Cubans for sale. Often venturing into the absurd, many figurines and printed T-shirts adopt racially ascribed stereotypes such as grossly enlarged lips framing big toothy smiles. One variation involves a dark-skinned head with vulgarly exaggerated red lips stretched to form an ashtray to accommodate one's favorite Cuban cigar. Many others play upon gendered specific notions of a black primal hypersexuality. In male form, this can translate into a smiling black figurine with a protruding erect penis complete with pink tip.

More common are tables of brown painted female figurines topped with colorful head-wraps invoking "Mammy" or "Aunt Jemima" figures of the U.S. antebellum South. Yet unlike their sexually neutered correlates to the North, these figurines index a raced economy of erotic desire; their absurdly large breasts (sometimes with protruding nipples) and correspondingly ample backside command a sexualized gaze. Articulating upon enduring representations of the mixed-raced *mulata* as an oversexed temptress (Arrizón 2002; Kutzinski 1993), this motif is often accompanied by a large phallic cigar projecting from a provocative wide grin. As Jill Lane's work on nineteenth-century *bufo* theater has shown, similar gendered forms of black sexualized caricature were formative in the early shaping of Cuba's national imaginary (Lane 2005). These tropes, however, are also clearly in historical dialogue with other North and Latin American variants of racist antiblack caricature (cf. Lott 1993; Rivero 2005). One can, for instance, find strikingly similar figurines circulating in tourist markets in the Dominican Republic.

When I spoke informally with market vendors in Havana (many of whom were not black) about the figures' physical attributes and sexual explicitness, a number told me that these images were simply drawn from Cuban folklore. These responses brought to mind the ways racial fictions continue to operate at a deeply embedded commonsensical level within much of Cuba's popular imaginary. One vendor in fact claimed these figures and their grossly exaggerated body parts actually resemble black Cubans themselves. My suggestion that such depictions might be infused with racist meanings was often meet with adamant denials of any racist content or intent. What is clearly less debatable is that such imagery and attendant discourses align with prerevolutionary black caricatures and broader hemispheric narratives of antiblack racism. These forms, once more, are intentionally reproduced for foreign tourist consumption, a practice that comes into focus when considering that many vendors claimed that these figurines were fabricated foremost to meet foreign tourists' own notions and consumer tastes for iconic representations of Cuba and its "culture." Blackness in a neoliberal Cuba apparently sells.

Racial Entrepreneurialisms and Their Regulation

Amid this raced marketplace some darker-skinned Cubans have in turn found enterprising ways to mobilize markers of blackness within an evolving economy from which they are otherwise largely excluded. While such strategies coincide with broader Cuban trends toward entrepreneurial lifeways, they are in this instance both shaped by and traffic within racialized circuits of desire and its trade. Maneuvers of the kind thus suggest in effect a kind of raced *homo oeconomicus* in their flexible adaption to Cuba's expanding market rationales.

Recall again Callejón de Hamel's weekly rumba. Among its other attributes, the rumba has long been a noted space for the hustling of tourist women by young black men cognizant of the spectacle's racial draw. Here I am reminded of Oscar, a stylish dark-skinned man in his late twenties whom I periodically ran into at the Callejón often in the company of young foreign women. One afternoon over a shared bottle of rum in plastic cups, Oscar explained in essence that he was aware of an economy of racialized desire within which he, as a young black man, operated vis-à-vis Cuba's tourist trade. In speaking of his experiences, Oscar noted unapologetically: "Oye, me gusta cuando las mujeres blancas me persiguen, cuando puedo decirle que tienen que esperar un poco. Imaginalo, en la cara de todo ese rascimo que siempre ha llamado mi piel sucia, sin valor, imagina!" (Listen, I love it when white women chase me, when I can tell them they have to wait some. Imagine it, in the face of all the racism that has always called my skin dirty, worthless, imagine!).

Oscar juxtaposed this experience against the hardships of working in a metal workshop where he claimed some of his white colleagues resented his position of relative seniority. Within the public domain of la calle, he expressed a sense of redemptive gratification in his ability to use his blackness of skin as a mode of social capital, enabling him entrée to privileged spaces and potential opportunities that he might not otherwise have in today's Cuba. I have no idea whether Oscar eventually joined the ranks of young black and darker-skinned men I have known since the late 1990s who, like Mario and ultimately many rapero friends, left the island on foreign fiancé visas with hopes of better lives in Europe, Canada, or the United States.[19] If he did, though, I would not be surprised.

While romantic scenarios of this kind clearly do not preclude mutually loving relationships, it would be difficult to assume they fully operate outside broader spheres of raced desire that permeate Cuba's tourism sector in ways similarly noted in other Caribbean settings (Brennan 2004; de Albuquerque 2000; Gregory 2006; Kempadoo 2004; Sánchez Taylor 2001). Economic inequalities are also frequently salient in these contexts. Given the often prohibitive application costs of Cuban passport and visa fees that ran well into multiple hundreds of U.S. dollars by the late 1990s,[20] foreign women in these scenarios frequently offset such expenditure. Over the years I have known North American women of varying ages involved in such relationships, and it is not uncommon for them to provide additional financial support to their Cuban partners—and often, by extension, their families—during the extended months of bureaucratic processing. While these women clearly exercise agency within these situations, dimensions of race, class, gender, nationhood, and sexuality and their interwoven economies of power are unavoidable within such transnational romances.

An eroticized market for blackness has also been an active component of the island's illicit foreign-based sex trade, which evolve alongside the growth of tourism and the dollar economy.[21] Racial difference in this context emerged as a currency of exchange between largely darker-skinned Cubans and their predominantly white foreign patrons in heterosexual as well as same-gendered spheres of sexual desire and commerce (Allen 2011; Lumsden 1996; cf. Alexander 2006). Offering historical scope, Anne McClintock notes that women of color have long been sites of masculinist conquest through the conjuring of colonial territories as "porno-tropics" in the Euroimperial imagination (McClintock 1995, cf. Stoler 1995). Here, nonwhite women are frequently figured as fetishized objects by male travelers who project imperialist claims as parcel of broader feminizations of non-Western societies.[22]

Building upon these legacies, European magazines and tour operators have long exploited such language and imagery to promote Cuba as a travel destination for sex tourism (Clancy 2002). Along these lines there are annals of Internet sites targeting hetero-male sex travelers that cite Cuba as a top sex tourism destination. As a descriptive example, on one English-language site, cuba-sex.com, I encountered the following anonymous posting: "Cuban prostitutes are called jineteras, or 'jockeys.' Wild, untamed, uninhibited women, they love to get on top and ride a man *hard*. Often displaying Afro-Cuban features, these dusky, scantily-clad native girls with fine asses are very passionate and may cling tightly and fondle you after sex" (italics in original).[23]

This brief passage illustrates in no uncertain terms a racially fetishized objectification of female sex workers circulating globally on sex tourism websites. Indeed, similar sites and language have been documented in relation to the Dominican Republic's foreign-tourist-directed sex trade (Gregory 2006). Not only do such narratives reproduce hypersexualized imagery of black and darker-skinned Cuban women through an electronically disseminated tourist gaze, but they further situate such eroticized representations squarely within fictive bounds of a primal black bestiality. Yet amid such racialized trade there may clearly be more at play.

The expression *jinetera*, derived from *jinete*, the Spanish term for a horse jockey, suggests degrees of social maneuvering regarding the women's "riding"—both literal and figurative—of tourists for economic remuneration or other conferred social privileges. Thus implicit in this allegorical play is the question of who in the end may be pimping whom. Here I do not wish to elide the varying structural inequalities between darker-skinned Cuban sex workers and their foreign johns (or janes); nor do I seek romanticized degrees of social agency. Rather, I seek to underscore that while a sexualized commodification of blackness may operate globally as a site of consumptive desire, it may simultaneously allow some darker-skinned Cubans spaces and gendered modalities of labor within a market economy in which Afro-Cubans are often structurally marginal.

Further to the point, the wider phenomenon of *jineterismo* is not reducible to sexualized markets of exchange, but rather speaks more broadly to the rise of informal, often racially associated street hustling for tourist income via an array of nonsanctioned (that is, illicit) services to foreigners. Consider again Oscar's scenario. Although Oscar is state employed, his ostensible leisure visits to touristed rumba spaces moved him within informal economies of tourist trade and hustle. Jineterismo practices, in their strategic application within spaces of tourist trade, are therefore part and parcel of a wider entrepreneurial range of strategies developed in accordance with Cuba's new neoliberally inclined markets of exchange, markets that are often raced, gendered, and potentially sexualized in particular kinds of ways.

Jineterismo's entrepreneurisms in this sense prefigured the formal advent of state-sanctioned cuentapropismo, which, like its illicit cousin, is also predicated on individuated forms of market hustle.

Within an unfolding economy where racial status is increasingly tied to social inequality by way of global currency flows, illicit strategies for economic gain have in turn become heavily policed by the Cuban state. The escalation of police activity in the streets of Havana since the Special Period offers a poignant expression of the raced nature of such market-inscribed governance. In a speech in January 1999 commemorating the fortieth anniversary of the founding of the National Revolutionary Police, Fidel Castro addressed the rise in illicit activities like street crime, prostitution, and drugs that followed the introduction of the U.S. dollar. In response, he argued, the streets must in effect be taken back. Almost overnight, roughly six thousand additional police were assigned to the streets of Havana (Fernández Tabío 1999, cited in Trumbull 2001: 312). During this period police officers could be found on virtually every odd corner in many central areas of the city. A central focus of this crackdown was petty street crime and underground black market activity upon which large numbers of Afro-Cubans (and many Cubans more generally) had become dependent given limited entrée to sanctioned forms of hard-currency acquisition.

This crackdown disproportionately affected young black men, who are often racially marked and targeted by Cuban police as *delincuentes* (delinquents). Within this scenario preexisting laws under the rubric of *peligrosidad* (dangerousness, or risk of criminal behavior) were expanded into stop and frisk-like practices commonly directed at young black men (see Ayorinde 2004: 142). During a conversation with my friend Rodrigo, a darker-skinned Afro-Cuban intellectual in his early forties, about his repeated experiences with police and similar challenges at hotel entrances, he spoke of a candid exchange he had one evening with a police officer. The officer, he said, confided that Cuban police were instructed to be vigilant of black youth, particularly at night, given a claimed propensity toward crime. Such practices, Rodrigo added, were "sintomático, parte del pensamiento institucional que tiene sus raíces en las instituciones políticas" (symptomatic, part of the institutional thinking that has its roots in political institutions).

While it may be difficult to substantiate Rodrigo's claim, associations of black Cubans with criminalized pathologies via a racially coded language of *marginalidad* (social marginality), to which I will return, have a long history in Cuba, grounded intellectually, once again, in the early work of Fernando Ortiz ([1906] 1973; cf. Arandia 2001; Maguire 2011; R. Moore 1994). An alternative explanation for the targeting I have heard cited by Cubans is that large numbers of Havana's police are drawn from outlying provinces so as to minimize affinities with the local population. The purported provinciality of these officers, it is suggested, lends itself to biases that inform racial profiling. Whether a cultural manifestation, a product of intentional design, or perhaps a combination of both, the historical weight of raced policing is compounded by the fact that darker-skinned Cubans reportedly comprise a disproportionate percentage, if not a majority, of Cuba's incarcerated (Ayorinde 2004; Pérez Sarduy and Stubbs 2000; Sawyer 2005).

In a quotidian sense commonplace in the streets of Havana by 1999, young blacks were routinely stopped by questioning police and asked for their *carnets de identidad* (national ID cards). Officers could then radio in the individual's information to check for previous criminal activity; any discrepancies or prior offenses noted might result in arrest. As I mentioned earlier, my experience as a brown-skinned man of being frequently stopped by police in my central Havana neighborhood conditioned my habitual carrying of a tattered photocopy of my U.S. passport that, upon presentation, usually enabled me passage without further consequence. In one particular experience, however, I found myself inadvertently enabling such policing.

I had joined two friends, Mario's older brother Ernesto and his friend Luis, for a beer one afternoon in the Plaza de la Catedral, one of the touristic and thus highly policed sections of the historic, commercially rehabbed Habana Vieja. As we shared a few cans of Cristal amid tourists weaving busily about restaurants abutting the plaza, we noted a blue-clad police officer within a few paces of us surveying the activity. As we continued in conversation the officer abruptly turned and asked Ernesto and Luis to stand and present their carnets, the information of which he began conferring via radio to some disembodied bureaucracy on the other end. Within short order both men were handcuffed and carted away in a small Russian-made Lada police car despite my protests and unanswered queries as to the reason for their arrest. Once informed of their destination, a regional police station located rather aptly on Avenida Dragones (Dragons Avenue), I followed on foot and sat outside the building awaiting their release. After it eventually became clear that neither Ernesto nor Luis was coming out anytime soon, I returned home discouraged.

The next morning I called Ernesto and found him home; he and Luis were evidently released late the night before. Ernesto explained that the official rationale given for their detainment was the officer's claim that the two men were jineteros who had been harassing me, a foreigner. Given his close proximity the officer was well within earshot of our conversation, one clearly between friends—albeit apparently differentiated by way of accents and levels of Cuban Spanish fluency. When I asked Ernesto about how he made sense of this, he responded almost casually, "Oye, estamos acostumbrados a esta mierda. Para los negros, esto es normal" (Listen, we are used to this shit. For blacks, this is normal).

Raced forms of state policing are of course not limited to men. There are corresponding histories of young black and darker-skinned women in highly touristic areas being racially marked as jineteras, particularly when in the company of foreign men. I recall my friend Yanelsi, a dark-skinned woman in her early thirties, complaining about being repeatedly stopped by police who suspected her of working a *temba*, or foreign john, while with her German husband. African American anthropologist Kaifa Roland has similarly documented personal experiences of being racially interpellated as a sex worker by tourist hotel security staff (Roland 2010), while Amalia Cabezas has analyzed the broader racialized projections of such gendered criminalization endemic to the island's tourist zones (Cabezas 2009).

Some critics have alternatively argued that the Cuban state has tacitly encouraged prostitution as a means of generating tourist revenue, while suggesting that periodic crackdowns have occurred only after drawing negative international attention to the expanding sex trade.[24] Addressing this tension, Mette Louise Berg asserts the revolutionary state has been complicit in marketing Cuba as a locale of black female sensuality, while simultaneously seeking to police darker-skinned women's economic agency as sex workers (Berg 2004). Such complexities underscore the interstitial workings of race, gender, and sexuality vis-à-vis a dialectics of criminalization and governmental regulation (and tacit packagings) within Cuba's new monetized nationscape.

In response to the broader systemics of such raced policing, young men in a couple of poorer, predominantly black barrios in Central Havana began around 2001 wearing their carnets de identidad dangling from their necks as a form of symbolic protest. As markers of citizenship as well as foci of racialized surveillance, these public displays spoke to the mounting tensions around race and the rights of national belonging for young blacks within Cuba's new economy. One noted neighborhood where these protestive performances of nationhood took place was Mario's barrio of Jesús María.

Abutting the heavily touristed Havana Vieja, Jesús María has long been branded as one of the more infamous of Havana's *barrios marginales* (socially marginal neighborhoods), an expression, as mentioned, embedded with racially inscribed notions of black pathological criminality rooted in narratives of Afro-Cubans as primitive, atavistic outliers of a modern Cuban citizenry.[25] Revolutionary efforts to rehabilitate such raced zones of temporal-national deviancy are given poetic form in the opening montage of the 1977 film *De cierta manera* (One way or another) by the late Afro-Cuban filmmaker Sara Gómez.[26] In this sequence, black-and-white images of a wrecking ball demolishing dilapidated urban housing are juxtaposed with those depicting the construction of modern apartment blocks in allusion to Cuba's transformist socialist march toward forging Ernesto "Che" Guevara's mythic "new man" of revolutionary lore ([1965] 2007). In the current moment one might consider Havana Vieja's extensive tourist-related commercial reconstruction and related residential displacement as a neoliberal variant of such rehabilitative renewal.

While recent developments may carry historical resonances, forms of raced regulation and enabling discourses of black criminality have clearly been elaborated upon and emboldened within Cuba's shifting economy. Although the revolutionary project may have expanded realms of national inclusion through a utopic promise of a socially equitable nonracial Cuba, these commitments have been significantly undermined by the growing dominance of market competition and its uneven effects along racial and class lines. With the rise of a new commerce in blackness, however, this terrain has also proved fertile ground for some black and darker-skinned Cubans to fashion creative strategies to tap into traffickings of racial difference.

Such racial entrepreneurialism recalls Robin Kelley's discussion of self-commodification strategies among African American youth seeking to capitalize on today's increasingly global market for black popular culture and creative expression (Kelley 1997). Kelley suggests markers of blackness in this sense are commercially leveraged by young African Americans as cultural assets within a postindustrial economy in which they are otherwise structurally disenfranchised. It is precisely these kinds of globally attuned,

1.2. Rapero performing at Havana Peña. Photo by the author

market-oriented racializations from below, to borrow from Leith Mullings (2004), that can be seen in active Cuban motion today.

Enter Hip Hop

Regarding the rise of island hip hop, it is also worthwhile to consider the productive tensions between racial exclusion and circuits of raced consumption as a space of maneuver for Cuban raperos. As a recent social phenomenon with a pronounced presence of black and darker-skinned Cubans, hip hop found its grounding amid a fluid moment of national uncertainty in which race has emerged as a particularly fraught site of social difference. Arguably the most widely disseminated conduit of "black" popular imagery globally, and one largely conveyed through a masculine persona of urban marginality, to what extent might hip hop afford in Cuban terms a language of political critique and identity by way of expansive vocabularies and extranational notions of black affinity? Pushed yet further, in a landscape where rights and equitable access to resources long mediated by the state are now increasingly arbitrated by the market, might hip hop offer enterprisingly "flexible" forms of alterative belonging and/or notions of citizenship (Ong 1999) for some black and darker-skinned Cuban youth in the neoliberal era?

In dialogue with the protestive display of national identity cards, one central and enduring concern voiced by raperos—many of them also young, darker-skinned, male, and drawn from similar barrios—involved the quotidian realities of raced policing since the late 1990s. From Hermanos de Causa's composition "Lágrimas negras" to Anónimo Consejo's "Las apariencias engañan," Papo Record's "Revolución," and Los Paisanos' "Mi nación," to name but a few, Cuban MCs have long critiqued the targeting of darker-skinned youth by Cuban police alongside an ascendant market economy. Like their carnet-donning peers in Jesús Maria, they too call attention through public spectacle to the raced limits of Cuban citizenship as they are currently embodied and lived.

One of the more infamous challenges along these lines involved a performance of MC Papá Humbertico during Cuba's eighth annual hip hop festival in Havana's outlying municipality of Alamar. That hot August night in 2002, Humbertico walked onstage accompanied by two others carrying a rolled bed sheet. Before an audience of some three thousand mostly darker-skinned youth and an assemblage of international press, the bed sheet was unfurled to expose in large block letters "Denuncia Social" (Social denunciation). Humbertico asked the crowd if they knew the meaning of the expression before lapsing into a series of songs rapped in a fluid Cuban cadence over hard-edged hip hop beats. His lyrics recounted the daily lives and struggles of people in his working-class, predominately black barrio of Guanabacoa, touching on themes of poverty, crime, imprisonment, and prostitution. A sea of hands could be seen waving in the air as the crowd sounded off in spirited agreement whenever the MC hit a particularly salient chord. As energies peaked, however, Humbertico took aim at Cuban police, their blue ranks visible alongside the stage. Citing the frequent harassment of black youth, he riffed:

> Oye tú, contigo mismo, contigo que en paz no me dejas un instante, no te tengo miedo, no me intimida tu vestimenta azul ni el cargo que tengas, para mí no dejas de ser un ignorante, adelante, estoy a tu disposición . . . móntame en tu jodido camión que yo,
> yo no me callaré.

Hey you over there, you don't leave me in peace for a minute, I have no fear of you,
your blue uniform doesn't intimidate me, nor the position you hold, for me you're still
ignorant, go ahead, I'm at your disposal . . .
throw me in your fucking truck because I
will not be silenced.

Rounding out his challenge amid a din of catcalls, Humbertico concluded:

Amo mi bandera, aquí nací y aquí me van a enterrar, seguro puedes
estar de que tengo bien claro el concepto de la revolución cubana.
Estoy con esto, pero no contigo . . .
Esto es contigo, loco, esto es contigo: Policía, policía, tú no eres mi
amigo, para la juventud cubana eres el peor castigo . . . tú eres el
delincuente!

I love my flag, here I was born and here I will be buried, you can be sure
I have a clear understanding of the Cuban Revolution.
I'm with this, but not with you . . .
This is for you, crazy, this is for you: Police, police, you're not my
friend, for Cuba's youth are the worst punishment . . . you are the
delinquent![27]

Standing among the crowd atop one of the endless rows of concrete benches ringing the stage below, I turned to my friends Alexey Rodríguez and Lou "Piensa" Dufleaux—two MCs from Havana and Montreal respectively who were scheduled to perform in the festival's coming nights—in shared surprise. In the numerous annual festivals we had collectively attended, none of us had witnessed so blunt a challenge by a Cuban MC, let alone one launched the opening night of the festival, the premier event of its kind drawing ample national and international attention. My companions and I wondered out loud how this all was going to play out. Although Humbertico was ultimately penalized by Cuban authorities with a temporary ban from public performance, the proverbial cat so to speak was already out of the bag. In testifying, "I love my flag / here I was born and here I will be buried / you can be sure I have a clear understanding of the Cuban Revolution / I'm with this, but not with you," Humbertico marks his inherent claim to Cuban citizenship while underscoring the disjuncture between the ideals of the revolution he affirms and its lived contradictions.

Might such frictions be part and parcel of the "exceptional" nature of neoliberal governance Ong's work points us toward? Amid an evolving marketplace in which blackness itself is imbued with ambivalent kinds of social capital, might some Cuban raperos be engaged in their own forms of racial entrepreneurialism? If so, transnational circuits of consumption in this instance may in the end open up rather than restrict plays of racial alterity and, ultimately, spheres of citizenship. How then might we locate such raced maneuvers amid the narrative lines of hip hop's Cuban emergence?

Chapter 2.
Hip Hop Cubano:
An Emergent Site of Black Life

While the early Cuban roots of rap music and hip hop culture can be traced back to the mid-1980s, it was not until the economic crisis of the early nineties and the island's ensuing market turn that hip hop began to take shape with apparent urgency as a self-defined movimiento. I suggest that Cuban hip hop in this sense has emerged as an organic phenomenon of a particularly acute moment of social disjuncture and transformation, one shaped at a shifting confluence of national and transnational fields of history and power. Popular narratives of hip hop's Cuban birth for their part have become something of urban lore through their telling and retelling by the initiated. Ever-growing numbers of foreign journalists, filmmakers, and academics descending on Havana in recent years have in turn contributed their own renderings to these narratives. Here I do not wish to replicate preexisting accounts, but rather seek to foreground the instrumental role that race has played in hip hop's ascendance in Cuba—a role whose complexities have often been downplayed or obscured by chroniclers. While my work is clearly in dialogue with existing scholarship, my intervention is directed in the end at providing an ethnographically grounded and critically historicized analysis of Cuban hip hop as a multivalent site of racial practice.

Hip hop's Cuban biography inevitably begins in Alamar, a coastal municipality nine miles east of Havana popularly noted as the birthplace of island hip hop. The suburb's sprawling collection of over two thousand multistoried apartment blocks were built in the 1970s and early 1980s with the help of Soviet architects. Though many were constructed through the work of *microbrigadas*—volunteer civilian work crews organized to build housing with state-supplied materials—the cubical form and gridlike orientation of Alamar's semiurban layout reflects a utilitarian functionalism of Soviet-era design. Originally raised to accommodate young couples from Havana's overpopulated center as well as an influx of rural workers from the outlying provinces, the municipality is now home to roughly one hundred thousand residents. While some commentators have noted a black or Afro-Cuban majority in Alamar (Pacini Hernandez and Garofalo 2000; Sokol 2000), my experience suggests that although black and browner-skinned families are a marked component, the municipality's working-class population is generally more multiracial in character.

Racial demographics aside for the moment, a key factor in Alamar's central figuring within Cuban hip hop is simply one of geography. A principal route of rap music's entry into Cuba in the mid-1980s was by way of South Florida radio stations whose FM signal on good days could be accessed by makeshift antennas fashioned from apartment windows or on rooftops in and around Havana. With its high-rise buildings and northern coastal location, Alamar was ideally positioned for such reception. And so it was there, the narrative continues, that a cultural space eventually identified with hip hop first took root. Building on this lore, a number of U.S. accounts have likened Alamar to a massive Cuban "housing project" (Robinson 2002; Sokol 2000), analogous in this sense to the South Bronx's urban topographies of public housing that first gave rise to hip hop in the post-industrial 1970s. Pushing the analogy further, Alamar aligns nicely with Paris's *banlieues* and São Paulo's *periferias* as comparable, often racialized zones of urban marginality and corresponding global hubs of hip hop culture (McCarren 2013; Pardue 2008). While such parallels carry a certain cachet in Cuba and beyond, it is in fact difficult to pinpoint precisely where and when hip hop actually emerged in the Havana area. It is, however, unquestionable that Alamar and the broader region of Habana del Este (Eastern Havana) played a formative role in hip hop's early Cuban ascendance.

Cubans in close proximity to the North American mainland have indeed long accessed U.S. radio broadcasts by informal means for many decades. Now in his fifties, my friend Tonel tells of his early experience in his seaside Havana barrio of Playa listening to North American Top 40 on AM radio in the 1970s from as far away as Arkansas.[1] U.S. rock music, for example, has had a significant following in Cuba since the 1950s despite state antagonisms, including broadcast bans of English-language rock in the early 1960s for its alleged corruptive influence (Pacini Hernandez and Garofalo 2004). Spheres of U.S. popular culture have in fact long been an important, if at times discordant, resource in the making of Cuban popular culture and broader national imaginary. One need only consider Cuba's celebrated national sport of baseball—or *pelota* (ball) as it is lovingly called—which was introduced to the island as early as the 1860s. Underscoring these linkages, historian Louis Pérez (1999) suggests that the omnipresence of North American culture since the mid-nineteenth century has tied Cuban notions of national identity and modernity inextricably to those of the United States.

Emergent Blackness

Hip hop's Cuban entrée, however, not only was inspired by the proximity of the island's neighbor to the north, the genre's extranational dimensions were for many also embedded with racial meaning. Cuban youth drawn to rap music have and continue to be largely darker-skinned, urban, and relatively more marginal—a set of demographics, I suggest, that is neither coincidental nor inconsequential. As I have argued elsewhere, the participation of racially marked subaltern youth in hip hop communities across the globe frequently involves dimensions of racial difference (M. Perry 2008b). In many of these settings a semiotics of black marginality is often reworked in ways that provide cogent expression to local experience and sites of struggle. Such practices assume particular salience within the Afro-Atlantic, where African-descendant youth in an array of locales have used hip hop to fashion notions of black-self in ways that are frequently both contestive and transcendent of nationally bound racial framings (cf. Anderson 2009). In the case of black and brown Cuban youth of the late 1980s and early 1990s, I suggest, engagements with U.S. rap music and broader hip hop aesthetics signified for many a nascent form of racial politics—one involving levels of racial identification and self-meaning making.

Ariel Fernández Díaz's prodigious work as a Havana-based journalist, DJ, hip hop radio host, and music promoter long positioned him as something of an organic intellectual within the island's hip hop movement. His recollections of hip hop's early Cuban rise, in turn, offer insight into the evolving history of the phenomenon. As evidenced by the prolific range of articles he has authored on Cuban hip hop, Ariel has substantial resources to draw upon in his accounting (cf. Fernández Díaz 2000).[2] And yet in a more immediate sense, Ariel's own personal narrative provides a poignant entry into the social complexities of the broader movement as a whole while providing a window into its raced nuances.

Born and raised in the outlying Havana barrio of Lawton, Ariel grew into adolescence and young adulthood as Cuba was undergoing transformative shifts in the early 1990s. With his light brownish skin and short-cropped hair more straight than curly, he would likely be broadly read as mestizo or possibly jabao within Cuba's graduated racial classification system. Politically speaking, however, Ariel evokes his blackness as a primary source of self-identity. As he explained to me during a conversation in 2002: "I consider myself black, sometimes I'm clearly more black, I don't know, it's a bit complicated. Everyone on my mother's side is black, and those on my father's side are white. So my black family came from Africa, and my white family came from the Canary Islands of Spain. So I think I have both cultures, both races. I'm a mix, no? But I feel more black than white. I think it's something positive."[3]

While such black self-understandings may appear to suggest a level of ambivalence, Ariel's evolving and deeply invested sense of black identity has found important mediation through, among other things, his ongoing engagements with hip hop. Similar things can be said of a number of black-identified raperos I have known over the years who would otherwise be classified as mulato, moreno, trigueño, or any additional host of terms commonplace in Cuba for degrees of nonwhiteness. Many cite their involvement in hip hop as influential in shaping black self-affirmations of racial identity.

Elaborating along these lines, Randy Acosta of the Havana-based duo Los Paisanos explained during an exchange: "Me? I'm black. Well, here in Cuba I'm jabao. This is what they tell me here in Cuba, jabao: this light brown hair and eyes more or less all the same color, and with light brown skin."[4] When I asked how long he had identified as negro, Randy replied: "Not very long. It has been a short time, since I began to take the hip hop movement seriously. Hip hop is a thing that frees the mentality, it's freedom. Many people don't understand this, but for us, it's freedom. We have changed our way of thinking and we have completely opened our thinking. I don't know, it's a powerful weapon. Hip hop is a force, it's life, it's a way of life." Randy's comments suggest a shifting sense of racial identity in which hip hop is viewed as instrumental at both political and ontological levels of play. Expanding on this theme, Randy and his artistic partner Jessel "El Huevo" Saladriga would later pen the song "Lo Negro" (The black) addressing racialized stigmas that in their view inhibit black self-affirmation among Cubans of African descent.[5]

In Ariel's case, his impassioned dedication to hip hop as, in Randy's terms, a distinctive "way of life" and focal point of self-identification seemed at times to border on the devotional. Such commitment is exemplified in Ariel's efforts as a self-taught journalist to be the first to publish extensively on Cuban hip hop in the state-run press, his hosting of Havana's first hip hop radio program, La Esquina de Rap, his rise as a DJ, and his eventual position as a coordinator of state-sponsored hip hop projects and directing editor of the government-financed hip hop magazine, Movimiento.

When we first met in 2000 in the lobby of a Havana hotel where a delegation of U.S. hip hop artists and activists affiliated with the New York–based Black August collective were staying, Ariel was dressed in white from head to toe, marking his year-long status as an iyawo, or religious initiate into Ocha-Lucumí. Through our conversations over the years it became clear that Ariel's involvement in the Afro-Cuban religion was as vital a component of his everyday life and sense of self-direction as was hip hop. Rather than competing ontologies, these differentially raced spaces—one sacred, nationally figured yet deeply resonant with lineages of Africanity, the other cosmopolitanly modern and transnationally expansive—have been mutually constitutive parts of how Ariel views and defines himself as an Afro-Cuban man.

Indeed, like a number of other hip-hop-affiliated Cubans I have known, Ariel simultaneously occupies and moves between public and more private, often sacred spheres of black meaning and communal belonging. Such black multivocality finds poetic form in Ariel's professional nom de guerre. Having considered the stage name DJ Afro until he realized the alias had been claimed by a member of the Venezuelan fusion band Los Amigos Invisibles, Ariel eventually settled on what he considered as a more organic and personally meaningful moniker, DJ Asho. The term asho refers to one of the central caminos or sacred paths of the orisha Obatalá, his personal santo.[6] Drawing parallels between Ocha-Lucumí and hip hop as coeval black cultural spheres, Ariel described DJ Asho as a syncretic way of marking his simultaneous belonging—characterized as "en mi sangre" (in my blood)—to both communities.

Further illustrating an overlapping fluidity of sacred and secular, Ariel spoke of receiving spiritual *consejo*, or advice, through the sacred Ifá divination tradition, suggesting his personal path was linked to his need to remain on the island to advance hip hop as a productive force in Cuban society.[7] Such understandings appeared to have emboldened Ariel against a range of obstacles he seemed to often confront in his personal and professional life. He explained at the time that his convictions—at one time both political and spiritual—precluded the idea of immigrating to the United States. This option had become all the more tangible given Ariel's recent participation in a month-long tour of New York City in 2001 as part of a delegation of Cuban raperos, during which time one visiting MC chose clandestinely to remain in the United States. The draw would indeed have been appealing: while there the delegation connected with various facets of New York's hip hop community including foundational figures like DJ Kool Herc, Afrika Bambaataa, and members of the pioneering Nuyorican breakdance troupe the Rock Steady Crew. Recalling these encounters, Ariel spoke of them at the time as fulfilling "a grand dream" of his life. That Ariel lived and breathed hip hop as a "way of life" was unquestionable. This focus, in turn, helped shape his sense of black self while informing his commitments both in Cuba and eventually beyond.

Reflecting upon hip hop's ascendance on the island one afternoon, Ariel spoke to me of a *movimiento de soul* (soul movement) in 1970s and 1980s Havana that preceded rap music's appearance on the island. He recalled the popularity of James Brown's music among its adherents, as well as a group called Los Estivis (the Stevies), who gathered for a period every weekend to celebrate the music of Stevie Wonder. "Los Estivis were completely black," Ariel explained, adding, "I mean it was really a racial space of people who followed Stevie Wonder, James Brown, and the soul music. Los Estivis was essentially a space of blacks." With few circulating LPs coupled with a dearth of functioning turntables, the primary means of accessing this music was through audiocassettes of U.S. radio broadcasts either recorded in Havana or sent by Cuban family in the States. Such informal circulations enabled alternative soundscapes outside official channels of state-run media in ways that recall Peter Manuel's discussion of the impacts of audiocassettes on popular culture and identity in Northern India during a similar period (Manuel 1993).

Along related lines Ariel and others recall glimpses of U.S. *Soul Train* episodes that could be tapped into under ideal weather conditions using improvised TV antennas or viewed on VHS tapes introduced by Cubans living or traveling abroad. As Ariel recounts:

> People recorded the program on these cassettes and would learn how to dance from them. *Soul Train*, you know, is a dance program, and so people learned how to dance from the show as they exchanged cassettes. What helped out this movement a lot were athletes who traveled [abroad]. Almost all athletes—track and field, volleyball, baseball—are blacks, no? They liked this way, the style, the clothing, the large pants. They would buy nice radios to play in the streets, boom boxes, these kinds of things. So these people traveled and would buy records, LPs, which folks then copied onto cassettes.

Ariel's comments raise a number of salient points, including a central one that concerns the role of international travel in exposing Cubans—in this instance athletes—to African American music styles and related forms of black popular fashion from the United States. At the same time he suggests a certain racial dimension at play regarding music reception, circulation, and its redeployment.

Reflecting upon the immediacies of that period, Alexis "D'Boys" Rodríguez, an influential Havana-based Afro-Cuban DJ and producer of hip hop events, also foregrounds questions of travel regarding his early encounters with what he refers to as "la música Afro-americana" (black American music). As he explained to me: "My father was a sailor, a [Cuban] merchant marine. And he traveled a lot spending time in Canada and the United States where he heard a lot of black American music, like funk and all that stuff—he also danced a lot. I'm in this sense like a mirror of my parents. I always liked this music because it was the music I always heard. For all my life, since I was born, I remember listening to funk music, it was simply part of my culture."[8]

Beyond simply questions of exposure, Alexis's account underscores active identification and embodied rearticulation of African American popular music and dance by Afro-Cubans in globally conscious ways. Such practices recall the ways Afro-descendant youth in other contexts have similarly adopted African American music idioms and forms of popular fashion to mark their belonging to a cosmopolitan blackness in ways that often complicate dominant national prescriptions (Anderson 2009; Diawara 1998; Hanchard 1999; Sansone 2003; Thomas 2004; Wade 2002). In this case, participation within a contemporary black globality—this música Afro-americana—offered an alternative lens to imagine and possibly embody Afro-Cuban blackness in ways that ultimately supersede the spatial and temporal bounds of Cuba's official nationscape.

While informal access to and trafficking of U.S. media may have occurred, Ariel suggests such avenues were not necessarily sanctioned by the Cuban state. Regarding U.S. radio broadcasts of rap and R&B music during this period, Ariel recalls: "I don't know if it happened accidentally or intentionally, but there started to be broadcasts of Cuban radio at the same frequency as broadcasts from the United States. I don't know if it was accidental, you know, but it was very funky because they put a radio station on the same frequency as [Miami's] 99 Jamz. They put a Cuban station with such force, you know, it was impossible to get 99 Jamz."

Revolutionary Cuba indeed has a history of disrupting U.S. radio transmissions—the most notable involved blocking the U.S.-funded, Cuban-exile-run Radio Martí out of Miami. These jamming efforts underscore the ways radio has long been a site of ideological struggle in Cuba, including histories of state censorship of local music programming as well (Frederick 1986; Hernández-Reguant 2006). In the case of North American music, these strategies were less about blocking potentially disruptive effects of overly political forms of U.S. propaganda than about guarding against "corruptive" foreign intrusions into the Cuban revolutionary body. As with the banning of U.S. rock music in the early 1960s, the appeal of North American popular music among Cuban youth was one that the state apparently wished to ward off. Considering Ariel's and Alexis's recollections and understandings of the moment, it appears that the circulation of U.S. black popular music among Afro-Cuban youth actively continued despite such state efforts.

Another individual whose memories of this period offer insight along these lines is Pablo Herrera, a pioneering Afro-Cuban hip hop producer whose work within Havana's hip hop community has been equally prodigious. Reflecting on his early experiences with North American music, Pablo explained:

I listened throughout high school to a lot of [U.S.] FM music. I listened to everything they used to play on the Top 40, and I used to write down the Billboard listings. A lot of the mainstream music from the eighties, though, was mostly white music. The minute I found black music I forgot about all the rest of it. I was like, 'I'm not fucking with that shit, this just does not speak to me. This *other* music speaks to me.' This is what I'm saying, I wanted to gain a cultural connection that may have to do with being African, Africans in the diaspora, and our discourses musically and culturally are what draws us to each other. It made it feel like wow, I dig your shit forever, I love this shit![9]

Pablo's comments speak vividly to the ethnomusicologist Steven Feld's notion of music listening as a participatory act, one that Feld suggests "brings out a special kind of 'feelingful' activity and engagement on the part of the listener" in the making of social meaning (Feld 1984: 13). Pablo's involvement with North American music in this sense was both active and deliberate, assuming his own affective structures of feeling (R. Williams 1977) involving levels of racial identification and resignification. Such sensibilities, moreover, evoke Josh Kun's discussion of the African American jazz virtuoso Rahsaan Roland Kirk's iconoclastic celebration of "blacknuss" as a "musical language that exploits and articulates the aurality of race" (Kun 2005: 133). While Roland Kirk's blacknuss may have been imbued with a certain aesthetic depth of black historical life, in Pablo's reading such affects are rendered racially audible in a diasporic sense. Recalling Michael Hanchard's (1998) discussion of Brazil's Black Soul movement of the 1970s that similarly drew on currents of African American popular music in framing cosmopolitan notions of blackness, the interplay between consuming and redeploying racial self-meaning has the potential to shape local identities while laying ground for racially conversant forms of social practice as well.

Indeed, a shift from active listening to artistic crafting occurred as Cuban interest in hip hop spread from the radio waves to *la calle* by the mid-1980s. During this period a cultural space began to take shape as increasing numbers of youth, almost exclusively darker-skinned and largely male, began gathering in both private and public settings. Informal parties called *los bonches* began springing up in homes, parks, and on street corners where young people gathered to listen, dance, and otherwise participate in the collective making of *la moña*—a term coined to refer to U.S. rap and R&B music and the social space that evolved around the following. Musicologists Deborah Pacini Hernandez and Reebee Garofalo (2000) provide insightful documentation of the early contours of la moña as a cultural precursor to the rise of hip hop on the island. Where my account diverges, however, concerns questions of racial identification and their transnational dimensions.

Recalling los bonches, local lore tells of a park in Ariel's home barrio of Lawton, known as Parque de los Policías due to its proximity to the local police station, where in the early to mid-1980s informal la moña parties were held on weekends. In Ariel's recounting, *moñeros* would gather around makeshift DJ tables, "a piece of wood placed over boxes," with rudimentary amplifiers and speakers to party to U.S. rap, R&B, and "funky soul." During our conversation I told Ariel his description sounded remarkably reminiscent of the local street jams of the mid-1970s I had attended as a child on the Lower East Side of Manhattan. Aware of Ariel's sensibility as an astute student of U.S. hip hop, I wondered if his description might have been informed by an awareness of hip hop's lore-laden origins and, if so, whether it might be an effort to position himself and Cuba more broadly within hip hop's now globally disseminated lineage.

Ariel's personal details notwithstanding, I have heard from others of Parque de los Policías' famed reputation for *los bonches de calle*, a central component of which was a local form of breakdancing. Popular accounts of this period describe informal competitions known as *los retos de breakdance* in which dancers challenged one another to the play of la moña music. DJ Alexis D'Boys, one of those early street dancers, explained that, given the scarcity of cassette players, dancers often resorted to the use of improvised chants as background beats upon whose rhythmic tempo moñeros danced. One of the more legendary of these chants etched in collective lore is "la caja, he, he, la caja," referencing a percussive play upon boxes (*cajas*) to mimic the cadence of hip hop beats.

In contrast to suggestions that this participatory space of music and dance had a largely multiracial character (Baker 2011: 268), DJ Alexis recalls Parque de los Policías as a primarily black space:

> El Parque de los Policías was a completely black movement, one that started in a barrio where the population was 90 percent black. This barrio Lawton was one of the marginal barrios. Before the triumph of the revolution it was a barrio of the upper class, and many blacks worked in houses of the rich; this was a wealthy zone. But when the owners of these houses fled to the U.S. after the triumph, the domestic workers moved

into these houses and this became a marginal barrio. This park, Parque de los Policías, where you had b-boys, they were all black. You might find a white [blanquito], but it was fundamentally black.[10]

Pablo Herrera's reflections of the moment echo similar lines: "Communal cultural efforts like la moña and el bonche exist in Cuba sort of like secret societies just to take the music. These were completely black spaces, full-on black. This was nothing but black. So what I'm saying here is that if there existed any previous understanding of, or any prelude to, hip hop in Cuba, it comes from el bonche."

Offering possible nuance to the point, Ariel adds in reference to Parque de los Policías and the broader space of los bonches:

I always say that the prominent color and the strongest presence of people were black and mestizos, you know what I mean, so there may have been some white people, yes, but that wouldn't make it interracial, because the commentary is really coming from the black folks. The leadership is coming from black folks, and the main figures, the major dancers, the people who made a reputation and were most famous at the time were basically blacks. Like the big names, the biggest breakdancers—they were black—so I would say the leadership of those spaces came from blacks and people of color, you understand me?[11]

Beyond simple demographics, realms of racial identification were apparently also active within these emerging spaces. Among early bonche members, Ariel suggests:

There was a language of acceptance that was definitely tied to where we knew we came from—we share a local experience and we share a story. And this was conscious but not exactly spoken about, you know what I mean? But we knew the connection we had between each other locally here in Cuba was also a connection we had with black music in America, because we're black and we feel connected with those black folks. We never felt like we were distant from those black people. And we accepted and embraced this music because we feel we are part of it, and that we can be accepted there. It is something we could assimilate easily, you know what I mean? It's something we can connect with easily, something that we feel beyond words, you know what I mean?[12]

While the crowds and attendant identifications may indeed have engaged vocabularies of blackness, los retos de breakdance were primarily male-centered celebrations of music, body, and movement, the masculine character of which is reflected in DJ Alexis's alias, "D'Boys" (pronounced "da-boyz"). As Alexis elaborates: "When I started, the first element of hip hop culture I became involved in was as a b-boy,[13] which is why I go by 'D'Boys' after the guys who I started dancing with. We became friends and formed a group of b-boys and worked on our choreography, and people wound up naming us 'da-boyz.' I got my name because I was the most active in the group, and I was crazy for those battles."

Evocative of Alexis's personal account, early moñeros fashioned a largely homosocial space of male performativity reminiscent of New York City's early b-boy culture of the 1970s and 1980s. The competitive masculinist posturing central to these b-boy battles grew in part out of urban gang culture from which some young black and Puerto Rican men, who comprised much of the pioneering ranks of New York's breaking crews, drew (Chang 2005; Rivera 2003). While histories of structural violence and racialized class marginalization particular to postindustrial urban America were not inherent to revolutionary Cuba, there nonetheless seemed to be a gendered dimension of cultural translation and embodied identification among moñeros who first took up hip hop music and dance. Indeed, such masculine groundings, as will be explored, continued to be a central (though not necessarily definitive) social contour of Cuba's evolving hip hop phenomenon.

Transnational Complications

Dance and body-centered musicality have of course been enduring facets of Afro-Cuban cultural life in realms of both the secular and sacred. Yvonne Daniel's allusion to rumba as a holistic "complex" of "combined music/dance activity" (Daniel 1995) speaks in this sense more expansively to fields of Afro-Cuban expressive practice writ large. Traditions of Afro-Cuban music making have at the same time long engaged Afro-Atlantic routes of cultural dialogue and interchange in many politically resonant moments and ways. Echoing drumming patterns introduced by relocated Saint-Dominguean slaves following the outbreak of the Haitian Revolution, Eastern Cuba's tumba francesa owes an important part of its history to semi-independent cabildos[14] and the more transgressive palenques (maroon communities) of the former enslaved who formed autonomous communities of black radical freedom. Some more recent histories of the black dialogic kind are recalled through the work of Leonardo Acosta and Ned Sublette regarding cross-fertilizations between Cuban popular music and U.S. jazz via trans-Caribbean currents of exchange between Cuba, Haiti, and New Orleans (Acosta 2003; Sublette 2007). An important chapter here, Acosta suggests, occurred during the first U.S. occupation of Cuba (1898–1902) when African American battalions introduced local Cubans to early jazz, elaborating upon conversations initiated in the late nineteenth century by Cuban migrants to New Orleans—among them musicians who contributed creative form to Jelly Roll Morton's celebrated ode to early jazz's "Spanish tinge."

Closer historically, a long lineage of Afro-Cuban musicians, from Frank "Machito" Grillo, Mario Bauzá, Luciano "Chano" Pozo, and Arsenio Rodríguez to later artists like Mongo Santamaria and Chucho Valdés, were instrumental in the development of Afro-Latin jazz forms through artistic repartee with African American musicians. Here, vocabularies of racial affinity were undoubtedly active in the creative mix (see J. Moreno 2004). Indeed, Dizzy Gillespie's oft-cited reference to Chano Pozo's claim that their collaborations worked from a shared sense that "we both speak African" (Gillespie 1979: 318) suggests a racial transcendence of nation via diasporically envisioned notions of black musicality.[15] The life narratives of bandleaders Mario Bauzá and Arsenio Rodríguez, moreover, speak to the ways jazz cosmopolitanisms enabled artistic mediations of black-self in the space between Cuban and U.S. racial landscapes.[16] Similar translational dimensions can be seen in the work of the mulato poet Nicolás Guillén, whose literary meditations on afrocubanidad arose in conversation with fellow poesía negra writers like Puerto Rico's Luis Palés Matos and the Dominican Republic's Manuel del Cabral, as well as decades of correspondence with the African American poet Langston Hughes (Ellis 1998; Kaup 2000).

What marks more recent lines of diasporic interchange is that their routes of dialogue are more often than not electronically mediated. Recalling Ariel's reference to the ways young people drew upon Soul Train videos in emulating popular styles of African American dance, DJ Alexis speaks with wisps of nostalgia of a video of the classic U.S. breakdancing film Beat Street (1984) acquired by his father as his first exposure to b-boying: "From his travels to Canada he brought me a video of the film Beat Street along with music. From this I first learned how to dance. I lent this video out to many people, who recorded it and copied the music and used it to learn how to dance. And this is how we first learned how to breakdance and about the hip hop culture."[17]

With its colorful portrayal of the South Bronx's early hip hop scene awash with the bravado of breakdance battles, the majority of the b-boys portrayed in *Beat Street* are Nuyorican, reflecting, in turn, the instrumental role of Puerto Ricans in the development of breakdance as an urban art form. As Raquel Rivera has argued, Puerto Rican participation in the early shaping of New York City's hip hop culture involved mediations of blackness and *latinidad* via creative exchange with African Americans grounded in shared Afro-descendancy and local histories of racial subjugation (Rivera 2003). Such diasporic complexities and their raced understandings were not lost on Alexis, an impassioned student of hip hop. Situating breakdance within narratives of Afro-Atlantic cultural synthesis and resistance, Alexis explained to me:

> Look, the research that I have done on hip hop is that its culture comes from Africa, its roots are African. For example, black Africans [*los negros Africanos*] who practiced capoeira used a move, a dance that was at the same time a form of defense against whites coming to exploit them.[18] By coming to Cuba, Brazil, Puerto Rico, and Jamaica they transformed it into a dance, though one used for defense. But at the same time the dance evolved and became breakdance. In terms of its evolution and arrival in the United States, many Africans of course were also brought to the United States, but it was Puerto Rican immigrants there in the States who developed this dance and evolved it into breakdancing.

Alexis then added: "Take DJ'ing, for example, it comes from Jamaica. DJ Kool Herc came to the United States from Jamaica and established DJ culture and MC'ing as well. And graffiti, some of the first graffiti artists were Puerto Rican, you understand. This is why I say hip hop is of Afro-Caribbean (*afrocaribeño*) origin, this is the study I have done. Coming from Africa and the Caribbean and then to the United States it became a big movement, a community of hip hop."

Evoking notions of Afro-Caribbean cultural ownership, Alexis's account imbues hip hop with a certain black authenticity while simultaneously grounding Cuba within its embryonic arc. In the case of breakdance,

2.1. MC Alexis "el Pelón" Cantero of Hermanos de Causa. Photo by the author

Puerto Ricans' Afrodiasporicity offers a creative vehicle through which Afro-Brazilian capoeira—as syncretic bridge between Africa and the diaspora—is transformed into modern breakdancing. In Alexis's formulation, hip hop emerges as a kind of black "changing same," to borrow from Paul Gilroy's elaboration upon Amiri Baraka (Gilroy 1993: cf. Baraka 1966), through which an expression of African historical roots and transnational routes of cultural synthesis mark an evolving black historicity that implicates Cuba's participation and membership along with Puerto Rico, Brazil, and Jamaica.

Alexis's and other moñeros' early involvements with hip hop music and dance thus demonstrated an active embodiment of such diasporic intimacy. Alexis's fluency in hip hop's coming-of-age narrative helps lay further claim to his own membership within this lineage. Like their black and Latino peers in New York City, moñeros similarly appropriated public space in the making of la moña as a racially marked site of cultural (self-)production. And if we consider anecdotal accounts of frequent police breakups of los bonches (Hoch 1999), these emergent spaces were not in turn necessarily well received by the Cuban state.

Frictions of Street and State

Official efforts to regulate public space and the airwaves notwithstanding, it would be inaccurate to portray the Cuban government's position regarding la moña's rise as strictly oppositional. State institutions, in fact, appear to have played a role in introducing Cuban youth to U.S. popular music through various public channels.[19] One such early source was 1980s television programming dedicated to popular music from Cuba and abroad. Both Alexis and Ariel, for instance, recall seeing Herbie Hancock's futurist 1983 "Rockit" video on Cuban television. As Alexis describes it, the video with its hip-hop-inspired scratching techniques and young, track-suit-adorned men b-boying was his first awakening to breakdancing.

Of yet possible greater impact on la moña's early growth was the establishment of state-sponsored parties and spaces in the early 1990s where youth, primarily black and darker-skinned, gathered to listen and dance to African American popular music. Premier among these was La Piragua—an open-air performance space on the seafront Malecón adjacent to the storied Hotel Nacional, where weekend la moña parties were organized during summer school breaks (Pacini Hernandez and Garofalo 2000).[20] Along with other open-air music gatherings in Havana, La Piragua was organized by the Unión de Jóvenes Comunistas (UJC, or Union of Young Communists), which, as the youth wing of the Cuban Communist Party, is charged with promoting socialist ideals and political participation among Cuban youth.

In addition to these larger state-sponsored events, smaller bonches would continue to be organized informally in private homes and public sites like parks. While these developments marked the growth of a cultural movement in the making, they also underscore the beginning of the Cuban government's various efforts to engage, if not institutionally incorporate, this emergent racially implicated space of youth activity. Indeed, this play between street and state remains an enduring and ever defining tension within the evolving narrative of Cuban hip hop.

One likely rationale for these state-sponsored parties was to channel young peoples' energies during the long summer vacation months. Such interests would appear to take on added urgency considering that these spaces were organized in the early 1990s at the onset of the economic crisis of the Special Period, a time when scarcities of food, electricity, and medicine and the collapse of socialist rewards pushed Cuban society toward desperate ends. This is not to suggest a reductive reading of state intentions, but rather to emphasize the multivalence of possible interests that played into institutional actions during this period. It would make sense that the socialist state would want to offer outlets for Havana youth during the hot and extended summer break from state-run schools. Yet such priorities could also dovetail with interests in maintaining effective levels of governmental control amid a time of particular societal stress.

One only needs to recall the summer *huelgas* (riots) of 1994 when hundreds of Central Havana residents—large numbers of whom were young, black, and male—took angrily to the streets, targeting storefront windows displaying dollar merchandise only foreign tourists and a few well-positioned Cubans at the time could afford. In addition to Fidel Castro famously joining the fray to calm the protesters, the state dispatched young members of the Blas Roca worker brigade as a bulwark to help quell the unrest. The brigade's deployment against largely darker-skinned rioters carried a certain irony given that the group was named in honor of Blas Roca Calderío, a venerated black Communist Party committee member. Cuba's leadership in fact was reportedly acutely aware of the racial undercurrents and potential menace of the moment (de la Fuente and Glasco 1997).

Triggered by the hijacking of a Havana ferry in an effort to flee the island,[21] this previously unimaginable expression of post-1959 unrest was a critical link in a chain of events that coalesced in that summer's *balseros* crisis. In response to the huelgas and in an effort to alleviate mounting social pressures of the Special Period, the Cuban leadership allowed some thirty thousand Cubans, many of them poor and darker-complected, to take flight on makeshift rafts (*balsas*) heading north to the U.S. mainland. For roughly a month, a carnivalesque environment ensued in greater Havana as individuals, groups, and families scrambled for materials and resources to construct improvised rafts out of inner tubes and scrap wood.[22] The exodus represented the first time since the 1980 Mariel boatlift that Cubans were granted temporary liberty to leave the island en masse, an episode that also involved significant participation of darker and poor Cubans. Occurring one year following the legalization of the U.S. dollar, the summer of 1994 represented a critical point of crisis and reckoning for the Cuban state, the revolution, and Cubans as a whole.

It was amid the uncertainties of this period that an aspiring DJ, Adalberto Jiménez, acquired a small space in Central Havana at the busy intersection of Avenues Infanta and Carlos Tercero, dubbed *el local*, where he began organizing weekend la moña parties (Fernández Díaz 2000). Similar gatherings centered around the music of Adalberto and other early DJs intermittently proliferated through the mid-1990s in a number of state-run Casas de la Cultura (neighborhood cultural centers) in Central Havana.[23] Falling under the auspices of Cuba's Ministry of Culture, the introduction of la moña parties within local Casas de la Cultura indicated a level of institutional state support. Beyond these sanctioned spaces, other la moña parties are reported to have been frequently broken up by police given their association with foreign cultural influence and alleged antisocial (i.e., deviant) behavior (Olavarria 2002; Sokol 2000)—experiences echoed in DJ Alexis's personal accounts of the period. Taken in tandem, all would seem to suggest an ambivalence on the part of the Cuban state regarding its dealings with an emerging U.S.-inspired youth culture, at one time seeking to regulate through official avenues while policing extra-institutional expressions.

As Pacini Hernandez and Garofalo (2000, 2004) suggest, such state anxieties appear to have hinged on long-standing claims of *diversionismo ideológico* (ideological diversionism) from revolutionary precepts, a charge previously leveled against Cuba's rock movement. Formulated in the early 1970s amid debates concerning the ideological role of culture in forging revolutionary ideals and citizenry (cf. Hart Dávalos 1990), diversionismo ideológico spoke of the need to create a bulwark against counterrevolutionary tendencies (or manipulations) of Western capitalist culture—particularly those emanating from the United States—that could potentially undermine the socialist project (cf. R. Castro 1974). In line with post-'59 conflations of revolution and nationhood, capitalist-infused cultural forms deemed "foreign" to the Cuban Revolution were therefore not only antithetical to socialism but incongruous with an otherwise autochthonous Cuban cultural patrimony. Such forms were therefore "ideologically diversionary" from the socialist path as well as officially sanctioned narratives of *cubanidad*.

While hip hop may have been implicated in such early scriptings, its politically infused associations with blackness—both off and increasingly on the island—posed additional complications to the ideological saliency of a racially transculturated Cuba and subsequent revolutionary investments in a postracial nationalism. The labeling of largely black la moña gatherings as sites of antisocial(ist) potential, moreover, resonates once again with the enduring coupling of black Cubans with pathologized deviance that render

Afro-Cubans ever discordant with the transformist project of revolutionary socialism. Indeed, hip hop's racially disruptive tendencies and state efforts to regulate (if not mitigate and contain) them became a central site of friction between this emerging cultural phenomenon and a wary Cuban state.

Evolving Spaces

State cautions being what they were, the establishment of el local and subsequent gatherings in neighborhood Casas de la Cultura marked a new phase in the development of la moña as an evolving cultural space, one that coincided with an active shift in focus from moñeros to raperos. While small numbers of youth in the Havana area may have started experimenting with rapping by the late eighties, it was not until 1995 that a more formal convergence of what would become Cuban hip hop began to come into focus. That year Rodolfo Rensoli, a late-twenty-something university-educated cultural worker and poet, along with Balesy Rivero founded a small arts collective known as Grupo Uno through which they began organizing local rap competitions in their municipality of Bahia in the Habana del Este zone.

Prior to his involvement in hip hop, Rensoli had been active in Havana's rock scene as a promoter of music-related events. When I first met him and Balesy in 1999 amid preparations for the fifth annual hip hop festival, Rensoli's ebony brown skin and tight-knit Afro made it difficult to imagine him partaking in the frenetic head-banging customary by many long-haired rockeros (rock devotees) at Cuban rock shows. When I mentioned this, Rensoli told me that the common labeling of rock as "white" music in Cuba was a false one, explaining, "If you know the history you know that almost everything that comprises rock music in the first place was invented by black people."[24] Rensoli added that though he considered himself a rockero during his involvement with Cuba's rock scene, he was also influenced by the island's growing reggae movement, with which he eventually came to identify as well. Rensoli's involvements in these music making spaces appear to have been motivated in important part by an intellectual commitment to avant-garde forms of cultural expression through the promotion of what he termed músicas alternativas (alternative music). While his participation in the early shaping of Cuban hip hop may have been inspired along similar lines, questions of race did in fact occupy a meaningful place in Rensoli's understandings of hip hop's significance on the island.

As Rensoli described it, what first drew his attention to this new youth culture in the making was breakdancing, an increasingly visible presence in the streets of his East Havana barrio by 1995. Rensoli recalls his intellectual curiosity deepening after he attended a local folkloric presentation where, reminiscent of DJ Alexis's account, a discussion of the African roots of the dance style occurred. Around this time young men began gathering informally at a local patio to freestyle rap,[25] and while attending a neighborhood "soul party" Rensoli shared a conversation with a group of raperos who were complaining about the lack of available performance spaces. It was at that point, Rensoli explains, that he and Balsey decided to explore the idea of an event to showcase what they recognized as an emergent moment of island hip hop, forming the collective Grupo Uno to undertake the project. In the summer of 1995 Grupo Uno organized three days of local rap competitions in Bahia, drawing MCs from the neighboring East Havana barrios of Alamar, Cojimar, Regla, and Guanabacoa. The following June a similar competition was held across town in a local cultural center in the leafy Havana barrio of Vedado. Organized by the director of the hosting *casa de la cultura plaza*, the event dubbed "Rap Plaza 96" was noted in the state-run *Granma* newspaper as the first festival dedicated exclusively to hip hop.

Although these were all small shoestring events showcasing a handful of local rap groups, they marked the birth and unfolding complexities of what would become Cuba's annual hip hop festival. The events' crosstown locations, moreover, underscored the rise of two potentially competing centers of early rapero activity, one clustered around Havana's eastern suburbs and the other located in its central urban zone. In was in 1997, however, that Rensoli approached the state-run Asociación Hermanos Saíz (AHS) seeking institutional support as a co-organizer for a proposed expanded competition to be held that summer in the eastern municipality of Alamar.[26] With few alternatives outside the all-providing socialist state, the costs of a proposed Havana-wide festival would indeed require greater levels of government support. As the cultural arm of the Union of Young Communists (UJC) charged with promoting (and channeling) music and artistic energies among Cubans under thirty-five, Hermanos Saíz would have been an obvious option.

In the opinion of Pablo Herrera, then manager of the Vedado-based rap group Amenaza, Rensoli may have also been interested in reclaiming and securing Grupo Uno's hold on the festival and Eastern Havana's prominence within the developing trajectory of Cuban hip hop.[27] Regardless of motives, it is clear that by 1997 increased institutional involvement was strategically essential for organizing and securing subsequent festivals, a reality that also marked an escalated governmental stake in the evolving space and future direction of hip hop Cubano.

For those in the Cuban leadership who viewed hip hop with suspicion as a nonindigenous foreign import, there may have been grounds, at least ostensibly, for such concerns. Given early scarcities of production-related resources, the vast majority of island hip hop throughout the mid-1990s involved live performances over prerecorded "background" cassettes from the United States and Europe. This meant Cuban MCs often composed lyrics to foreign instrumental tracks, sometimes rapping over beats from a popular repertoire of commercial hip hop from the States. Accounts of the period also suggest that early raperos tended to mimic performance and fashion styles of African American artists, often donning hooded jackets, skull caps, boots, and imitation gold chains (Fernández Díaz 2000; Smith 1998). While transnationally indebted, such style practice may not have been devoid of political meaning making, however.

Drawing upon his work with young Garifuna men in Honduras, Central America, Mark Anderson suggests that similar displays of African American fashion style often involve the negotiation of contemporary forms of Garifuna identity, offering "a diasporic resource for the performance of a Black cosmopolitanism that sits uneasily alongside images of Garifuna tradition commonly produced by the state, the media, and Garifuna organizations" (Anderson 2009: 175). Rather than passive consumers of U.S. cultural exports, Anderson suggests, these young men tap into stylized dimensions of African American commercial culture in crafting alternative, cosmopolitanly modern notions of black Garifuna-ness in ways that may challenge otherwise dominant, nationally bound representations. Comparable practices have been noted by Steven Gregory (2006) among Haitian immigrants in the Dominican Republic and have been similarly sited by Deborah Thomas (2004) in shaping transnational understandings of black modernity in Jamaica (see also Diawara 1998; Hanchard 1998).

In the case of early raperos, plays upon black-identified U.S. music and style forms may also be seen as efforts to negotiate new grammars of Afro-Cuban-ness as a means of marking racial difference while expanding the terms of Cuban blackness itself. Indeed, for many darker-skinned youth who first took to hip hop, everyday levels and modes of racialized experience as discussed assumed an increasingly charged, transnationally inflected significance amid Cuba's market turn of the 1990s. Governing lines within which blackness had been historically configured and channeled—as folkloric, autochthonously rooted, spatially and temporally bound—were in this sense creatively redrawn via hip hop's globally conversant, racially coded aesthetics. Early raperos can in this light be seen as participating in their own kinds of racial entrepreneurialism, yet ones involving resignifications of style as self-representational practice (cf. Hebdige 1979). If we consider Stuart Hall's suggestion that "it is only through the way in which we represent and imagine ourselves that we come to know how we are constituted and who we are" (Hall 1992: 30), the performative possibilities of black popular style encourages attention to the representational force of style in its capacity to enunciate, rather than simply reflect, identities of blackness and ways of being.

Performing Blackness

In step with the rise of hip hop on the island, Cuba's annual hip hop festival continued to grow in size and artistic sophistication through the early 2000s. Despite limited resources, the festival expanded from an event involving a small collection of East Havana–based raperos in 1995 to a multiday program encompassing an island-wide diversity of groups and an assortment of international artists. Based on my attendance from 2000 to 2003, the event represented not only a culmination of a year's worth of artistic development but also an annual opportunity for many raperos to push their music creatively on multiple levels. Held since 1997 in Alamar's open-air *anfiteatro* before some three thousand predominantly black and brown-skinned youth, the festival was the largest single stage for Cuban hip hop and recognized by many MCs as the pinnacle occasion to showcase their music and talent. The festival's stature was all the more significant given that limited production resources and commercial markets have long grounded island hip hop—like most vernacular traditions of Cuban music making— in the intimacies of live performance.

From the festival's inaugural year the social contours that have come to define Cuban hip hop began to take shape. Key among these were raperos'

2.2. MC Magyori "La Llave" Martínez (foreground) and DJ Yary Collia.
Photo by the author

emphasis on social themes drawn from experiences of a young, largely darker-skinned generation of Cubans as they navigated the daily, often fraught tensions of a Cuba in historical flux—one posed between revolutionary socialism and ever-evolving market realities. Given the centrality of social commentary and critique, raperos referred to their lyric-driven compositions as *temas sociales* or simply *temas* (social themes or themes) rather than the more prosaic *canciones* (songs). The rhetorical significance of *temas*, moreover, marked raperos' textual emphasis on the social message, or *mensaje*, of their lyrics. Although resonances were surely present before, the third annual festival—1997, Alamar's first—marked a move toward more overt incorporations of social motifs, particularly regarding dimensions of race and racial identity.

One related episode etched in the collective memory of raperos and foreign chroniclers alike occurred during the 1997 festival. Primera Base, a pioneering rap trio and the first to record a commercially produced rap album in Cuba,[28] performed their tema "Igual que tú" (The same as you) in tribute to Malcolm X. In prefacing the song's performance, one of the MCs explained to the amassed Alamar crowd, "This is a homage to Malcolm X, because he is our brother and we relate to black people all over the world, even in the United States, and we feel sorry for our black brothers in the United States who have to live the way they do. They have it the worst of the worst" (quoted in Hoch 1999: 194). Evoking themes of resistance and self-determination, the song drew inspiration from the life story and black masculine imagery of Malcolm X. When it came to the chorus refrain, members of Primera Base chanted in Spanish, "Malcolm, we wanna be just like you nigger, a nigger like you."

A handful of North Americans present at the event were reportedly dismayed by the seemingly flippant, decontextualized manner in which the term nigger was affixed to Malcolm X. Among this group was Nehanda Abiodun, a prominent African American political exile living in Cuba who would develop a long-standing relationship with Havana-area raperos. Although clearly fraught, Abiodun speaks of the incident as provoking her interest in the emerging scene, suggesting in turn that the resource-strapped artists were in need of critical engagement.[29] Reflecting on the moment, one of the group's members, Rubén Marín, later recounted: "Everyone here sort of felt the echo of Malcolm mania after Spike Lee's movie, so I read his Autobiography to try to get to the truth of what he was really about. The point I am trying to get across in the song is if a great man like Malcolm X is considered a nigger, then I want to be a nigger too like him" (Verán 1998: 133).

While a sensitivity to the historical violence embedded in the term nigger may have been obscured for members of Primera Base, an identification with Malcolm X as a black liberatory figure apparently was not. Rubén's comments attest once more to the capacity and global reach of U.S. media in conveying images and discursive notions of blackness. Yet rather than being an object of unreflective consumption, Spike Lee's filmic portrait of Malcolm X was drawn upon by these young men, two of them black, in mobilizing alternative narratives of blackness in ways quite similar to those I have discussed in the context of Afro-Brazilian hip hop (M. Perry 2008b). As Rodolfo Rensoli, then the festival's organizer, recalled of the episode:

Never in Cuba has there been a song that expressed anything like "we blacks are equal to you" like Primera Base's tema about Malcolm X. I think that this song marked a new period for Cuban music. After this there was a series of songs in rap where there was a self-affirmation of blackness. I haven't analyzed it thoroughly, but if you were to examine Cuban music the image of blacks is almost always one of drunkards. It is not the image of blacks as social thinkers, or as cultural thinkers. Rap marks in this way an overturning [*vuelco*] in the thinking of the black individual. It is in part a self-reconciliation [*auto-reconciliación*] as black people.[30]

Rensoli's notion of black self-reconciliation does indeed appear to have been a recurring theme during the 1997 festival. A poignant case in point involved Amenaza (Menace) and their performance of "Ochavon cruzao" (roughly, Mixed-up octoroon).[31] In this tema the group's three members of variously mixed-race backgrounds address the lived ambivalences of racial identity in contemporary Cuba. In doing so, the artists both complicate and implicitly contest dominant narratives that present mestizaje as a historically stable and harmonious race-neutral core of the Cuban social body. Awarded first prize for best composition during the 1997 hip hop festival,[32] a lyric excerpt of "Ochavon cruzao" follows:

También soy congo,
también fui esclavo,
también mi esperanza sufre para aquellos
que el racismo no ha acabado
Soy rumba Yoruba Andavo
y no acabo hasta ver lo
mío multiplicado
No ves soy pinto, ochavon cruzao
negro como el danzón y el son cubano
negro como esta mano
negro como mi hermano
negro como Mumia
y negro como muchos blancos, mas quien lo diría, y no me cuentas
Mesafía raza mía.
Dijeron negro pero a mi no me contaron
Dijeron blanco pero en esta clan no me aceptaron
Dijeron tantas cosas
Soy el ser que nadie quiso,
lo negro con lo blanco, el grito de un mestizo

I too am Congo,
I too was a slave,
and so too has my hope suffered for them because racism has not
ended
I am rumba Yoruba Andavo
and I won't be done until I see what's
mine multiplied
Can't you see I am mixed, mixed octoroon
black like the Cuban danzón and the son
black like this hand
black like my brother
black like Mumia
and black like lots of whites, but who could tell, so you don't count me
My race defies.
They said black but they didn't count me
They said white but that clan didn't
accept me
They said so many things
I'm the one that no one wanted,
the black with the white, the cry of a mestizo[33]

While this passage offers poetic voice regarding struggles over racial
self-meaning, it also represents an early foregrounding of the movement's
quest for forms of black identification transcendent of Cuba's prevailing
racial continuum and its lived ambiguities. By exposing the internal dissonance embodied in the celebrated national figure of the mestizo, the
song's first-person narrative undermines a foundational symbol of Cuba's
historical profession as a racially transculturated (i.e., racially neutral[ized])
nation. The tema's mestizo subject seeks to rectify, or in Rensoli's terms
self-reconcile, this dissonance by making its own historical claims to blackness. Such affirmations are voiced at one moment through the invocation
"soy rumba," whose Afro-historicity is further grounded through association with Havana's acclaimed Afro-Cuban rumba troupe Yoruba Andavo.
Amenaza's marking of the *danzon* and *son* as "black" music forms, moreover,
recuperates these historical genres—long-acclaimed national symbols of a
harmonized, racially hybrid Cuban patrimony—as part of an Afro-Cuban
cultural lineage asserting, in turn, a black Cuban presence and historical le-

gitimacy. Amenaza's interventions along these lines thus literally "menace" Cuba's nonracial glorifications.

Significantly, "Ochavon cruzao" also invokes the social memory of Africa (*congo*) as well as the racial terror of slavery, two historical loci central to the shaping of black racial consciousness in the Afro-Atlantic world (Gilroy 1993). And yet it is an enduring racism "that has not ended," which links the living present to that of the past. Thus regardless of one's marked rendering as mestizo, one's nonwhite self in this testimonial ode remains ever subject to raced forms of history and power.

Although struggles over racial self-meaning are framed within the space of Cuban nationhood, recourses to blackness are not necessarily so bound. Here, the tema's brief though pointed reference to the radical figure of imprisoned African American journalist Mumia Abu-Jamal is poignant.[34] Mumia's invocation presents an alternative, outer-national site of black identification—one that transcends conflictive tensions between a racial ideal and the raced realities of being nonwhite amid Cuba's fluidities of the 1990s. Unlike the historical figure of Malcolm X, the immediacy of Mumia's black radicalism lends an urgency to such identifications. While Abu-Jamal became a common lyric refrain alongside an assortment of "Free Mumia" T-shirts by the early 2000s,[35] "Ochavon cruzao" initiated this link within rapero circles. As I discuss in greater detail in the following chapter, engagements with currents of U.S. black radicalism have been critical to the making and moving of black self-understanding within Cuban hip hop. As Amenaza's poetic "cry of a mestizo" suggests, however, despite such self-affirmations, the ontological condition of being racially mixed remained one of marked ambivalence. At least such was the case in 1997.

Lyric-centered analyses of the like might invite concerns regarding the limitations of purely textual readings of social orientation and practice. It is therefore important to foreground the ethnographic context of performance within which raperos' lyrical expression arises. Possibly more than any other contemporary Western music genre's, hip hop's aesthetic form is predicated on the centrality of the spoken word as *performed text*. Among Cuban hip hop artists, such textual prioritizations are reflected in their vernacular use of the phrase *los textos* (the texts) in reference to their lyric compositions.

Yet within Cuban hip hop's live-performance-driven settings, the signifying weight of los textos takes on an additional level of embodied significance. Beyond the initial composition when textual meanings are first shaped, it is through Cuban MCs' public performance of their temas that such textuality assumes self-actualizing force. It is of course the "rap" through which the rapero artistically defines him/herself, marking in the most tangible of terms that movement from textual realms of discourse to those of corporal practice. While it is indeed one thing for a Cuban youth of mixed race to compose the lyric line "[soy] negro como Mumia" (I'm black like Mumia), it is a whole other ritualized undertaking to mount a stage before three thousand peers and verbally proclaim over a microphone "¡[soy] negro como Mumia!" Here it is less about performing a text than the performative embodiment of the text as self-representational practice. Rather than reflecting a preexistent subject a priori, raperos' public performances in this sense seek to enunciate or socially enact that very subject into being.

As public spectacle, then, the performative dimensions of blackness in "Ochavon cruzao" are hence twofold. A blackness of self-meaning is signified in an immediate sense through announcing itself *as such*—a form of performative utterance or speech act (Austin 1976). Yet in the same breath this act is performative in that its enactment is ultimately productive of something subjectively *different and new* (cf. J. Butler 1990). Amenaza's "cry of a mestizo" thus invokes blackness as spectacle by asserting and making conspicuous a black subject otherwise obscured by Cuba's nonracial scripts. Similar to the mimetic adoption of black style previously discussed, raperos' extranational use of racial markers is translated in ways that assume their own locally situated meanings and structures of feeling. And while such black self-reconciliations—to again evoke Rensoli's term—are imbued with autochthonous national claims, they continue to index a modern black globality with which they actively converse.

This discussion runs somewhat counter to previous accounts of the period suggesting early Cuban rap artists tended not to foreground transnational connections with other African descendant populations, thus displaying a conspicuous absence of Afrodiasporic lines of identification (Pacini Hernandez and Garofalo 2000). Here, appeals to an international cosmopolitanism over those of racial diaspora are seen as primary (cf. Baker 2011). While these observations capture salient features of the early hip hop scene, I suggest further exploration might yield additional complexities.

2.3. *Cuban Hip-Hop All Stars* CD. Cover artwork © 2000 by Steve Marcus

Arguments along these lines are drawn in part from an interview with the producer Pablo Herrera, who suggested that contemporary Africa held little attention among raperos as a source of identification and inspiration. As I discuss in greater detail later, Africa would in fact become an important point of reference for many Cuban MCs via the ways they imagine, bodily mark, and performatively enact meanings of blackness. Yet beyond appeals to an African historical rootedness per se, to what extent might contemporary articulations with other Afro-Atlantic sites and histories provide more immediate recourse to an Afro-globality, one self-consciously modern and indeed cosmopolitan in scope?

Black Assemblages

As I myself have come to know Pablo Herrera, there seems little ambivalence regarding his own understandings of and participation within extranational routes of blackness by way of hip hop. Pablo and I first met at the studios of Conjunto Folklórico Nacional in the summer of 1999 while he was doing translation work for a group of North American participants during a dance workshop hosted by the Conjunto.[36] Workshop members had gathered that day for a screening of the Afro-Cuban filmmaker Gloria Rolando's recent work *Eyes of the Rainbow* (1997), a documentary celebrating the life of African American political exile Assata Shakur, who has lived in Cuba since the mid-1980s. Noting Pablo's seemingly flawless U.S. accent and the fluidity of his engagement with visiting students, I mistakenly assumed the brother was from the States. It was not until we spoke after the screening that I realized he was not only Cuban but a key contact suggested to me by a mutual acquaintance in New York City. Our exchanges from that point on were almost exclusively in English, sprinkled with an African American vernacular affecting a sense of a black fraternity, which I came to understand as part of Pablo's facile charisma and charm.

I soon learned that Pablo earned an advanced degree in English and Russian translation at the University of Havana, where he completed a thesis on the poetics of African American culture. This background made Pablo fairly exceptional within Havana's hip hop community where the vast majority of raperos and their largely black working-class followers did not attend university, let alone pursue advanced degrees. Pablo later spent a number of months in the late 1990s living in Brooklyn, N.Y., where he gained a deeper appreciation for African American life and racial history. Pablo's cultural fluency in black American-ness was indeed so well-tuned that I heard of his ability to pass in Havana's streets and tourist hotel lobbies as a yuma (foreigner), a notable feat for a young dark-skinned black man in Cuba. Such skill found comic display in the 2000 film *Jails, Hospitals & Hip-Hop* by the New York–based performance artist Danny Hoch in which Pablo, for ironic effect, plays a monolingual camera-toting African American opposite Hoch's street-hustling (and presumably Afro-Cuban) jinetero character.[37]

This dexterity undoubtedly contributed to Pablo's ability to maneuver fluidly in a space between Cuban and U.S. cultural landscapes, one in which hip hop served as an important medium of translation. Building on an evolving network of North American contacts, Pablo eventually compiled an improvised music studio in his rooftop apartment in Havana's outlying barrio of Santos Suárez. His mother, a reputable Afro-Cuban architect who helped instill within Pablo a grounded sense of black pride and respect for Cuban socialism, designed the apartment-cum-music-studio that sat atop her home. Pablo's rudimentary production equipment, including a digital beat machine, electronic keyboard, and monitor speakers donated by a New York City contact, came by way of Ariel Fernández Díaz, who approached him around 1999 about assembling a compilation disc of local hip hop. The project culminated in the 2001 CD *Cuban Hip-Hop All Stars, Vol. 1*, which represented the first commercial compilation of Cuban hip hop artists.[38] Crafting some of Cuba's earliest background beats, Pablo's home studio became something of a hip hop mecca among established artists seeking music production, including Anónimo Consejo, 100% Original, Obsesión, Grandes Ligas, Las Krudas, Explosión Suprema, and Los Paisanos, to name a few. Until the proliferation of personal computers and music production software enabling a wider range of artists to produce background beats, Pablo held important (though not necessarily uncomplicated) sway within Havana's hip hop community as one of its premier producers.

As Pablo describes it, his sense of black selfhood was first and foremost rooted in his family history and cultural fluency as an Afro-Cuban. Pablo's mother, as mentioned, was a respected architect, while his father, a former director of the radio and electronics section of Cuba's Naval Academy, was the first Afro-Cuban to receive a PhD in his field. Among the first generation of black professionals trained during the revolutionary period, their professional and personal life trajectories were deeply tied and in many ways indebted to the revolutionary project. For Pablo's mother, Daysi Veitia, such fidelity found early expression as a teenage volunteer among the roughly 250,000 Cubans who participated in Cuba's massive National Literacy Campaign of 1961, an experience recounted by Daysi in Catherine Murphy's 2012 documentary film *Maestra*. Daysi's later training and professional development as an architect took shape amid Cuba's rising internationalism, a period that involved her in Cuban-sponsored construction projects as far afield as Vietnam, Cambodia, and Bolivia.

Yet it was his parents' experiences working in Angola during the war period that Pablo claims carried particular salience: "If you talk about the generation of Afro-Cubans who went and fought in Angola in the end of the eighties and in the beginning of the nineties, the ways that they understood Angolan culture and African people, or black people in Africa, the way they talk about them was special. My parents had important experiences and made important relationships with Angolans while there."[39] Though memories of the war's trauma remained present, Pablo recounts, his parents' involvements helped reconcile the human costs of the conflict by foregrounding Cuba's broader "victory" in helping Angola win the war and postcolonial independence. Speaking of his parents' pride in partaking in this history, he added: "The experience of having traveled to Africa and having been part of something so grand as the liberation of a country in Africa was huge in that sense. . . . I wanted to go to Angola when it was my chance, I wanted to go to Angola to be part of that. Angola was seen as victory big time. I mean the war had been won, and the Angolan people were free!"

Thus part of a generational narrative similar to that shared by Lisnida's household,[40] understandings of afrocubanidad were for Pablo and his family intimately entwined with Cuba's revolutionary past, one in which contemporary Africa served as a poignantly lived referent. The singularity of history, Pablo suggests, positions Afro-Cubans uniquely in diaspora vis-à-vis engagements with modern Africa.

As Pablo has made clear in the course of our conversations, familial recourses to a Cuban Africanity were also grounded in spaces of the sacred. Pablo traces such lines back to his paternal grandfather, whom he described as a craftsman of African drums and shekeres used in Afro-Cuban religious ceremony, as well as his mother, a longtime hija or initiated daughter, of the orisha Yemanyá. These lineages extend to Pablo's own spiritual involvement in Ocha-Lucumí as an hijo of Changó and his more recent initiation into the sacred divinization pathways of Ifá.[41] As he describes it, such commitments are rooted in a deep Afrocentric resolve among Afro-Cubans that has endured in his words as "a sacred space of victory that is untouched by anything, and nothing can fuck with that."

Although Pablo's self-understandings drew upon autochthonous readings of Afro-Cuban experience in realms of both the sacred and the profane, hip hop seemed to offer an additionally meaningful site of black belonging. As Pablo recounts, his involvement with hip hop began during a teaching stint at the University of Havana in the mid-1990s when he incorporated Cuban rap lyrics into course material. It was around this period that he came into contact with Amenaza, eventually developing a relationship with the artists that evolved into a managerial role. Pablo recalls initially harboring some concern about what he felt was the trio's lack of political awareness, particularly in relation to dimensions of race. Shortcomings of this kind, he suggests, contributed to a dismissive attitude among local raperos, some of whom viewed Amenaza as superficial "pretty boys" in relation to the more politically charged range of early island hip hop. As manager, Pablo claims he encouraged Joel "Pando" Heredia, the creative head of Amenaza, to engage more explicitly with questions of race and racial identity. This intervention, he contends, helped initiate Amenaza's eventual turn toward "Ochavon Cruzao," a tema that as discussed marked a new moment of racial self-reflexivity within Havana's budding hip hop movement.

When I queried him about the tema's self-referential appeal to Mumia Abu-Jamal, Pablo offered it was he who first introduced Amenaza to Mumia's story. It is indeed worth noting that earlier the same year that "Ochavon Cruzao" was composed, Pablo had connected with a group of African American activists from New York City during an international youth festival in East Havana.[42] A number of these individuals were active members of the Malcolm X Grassroots Movement (MXGM), a youth-oriented collective centered on human rights advocacy and political mobilization among communities of African descent. These contacts eventually led Pablo to Brooklyn the following year.

It was this same period of transnational exchange that gave rise to the launching of Black August, a hip-hop-centered offshoot of MXGM with a strong Cuban focus. Black August in turn became an influential interlocutor with Havana-area raperos through running participation in a number of Cuban hip hop festivals beginning in 1998. A related organizational facet of Black August entailed support for an older generation of imprisoned U.S. black radicals and, by extension, a small circle of African American political exiles residing in Cuba. A key figure among these intergenerational networks was Nehanda Abiodun, mentioned above. A native Harlemite now in her early sixties who has been in asylum in Cuba since the early 1990s, Abiodun shares a tradition of black-left organizing with fellow radical-in-exile Assata Shakur, and has maintained U.S. connections through in part active membership in MXGM.

I will return to a more detailed discussion of Abiodun and Black August's legacy in Cuba; what is worth alluding to here is the instrumental role Black August played in facilitating Afro-dialogic alliances between Cuba and the United States via a transnational vocality of hip hop. Among those key in this conversation was Pablo Herrera, who, along with Abiodun, served as one of Black August's founding Cuban members. Extranational affinities of blackness and their political inflections therefore do appear to have been present from inception in hip hop's Cuban rise.

Chapter 3.
New Revolutionary Horizons

I had the fortunate experience of being introduced to and initially guided through the often frenetic currents of Havana's hip hop scene through my relationship with Magia López and Alexey Rodríguez of the hip hop duo Obsesión. They were then a married couple whose artistic creativity and tireless commitment helped position them among the most productive and respected of pioneering artists in the movement.[1] The couple and their extended families, in turn, offered me a supportive community and an invaluable window into the broader complexities of contemporary Cuban life as a whole. As I explore in more detail, given the varying positions raperos negotiated vis-à-vis state institutions and realms of revolutionary discourse, Magia and Alexey's achievements and chosen involvements placed them at times in somewhat ambivalent terms within some circles of Havana's hip hop community.

Obsesión

When we first met in 1999, the couple, then in their midtwenties, was living at Magia's mother's home in the central Havana barrio of Cayo Hueso. Their second-story flat sat conveniently across the street from a *casa particular* (private apartment) I wound up renting a room in and calling home for the bulk of my time in Havana, all thanks to their initial introduction to the casa's owner, Delbis. Along with Magia's mother, Caridad, and Magia's older sister, Tamara, and her young son, Norberto, the two lived in a small *barbacoa* (improvised loft apartment) in an old five-story walk-up.

In time the couple moved to Alexey's parents' relatively more spacious rooftop apartment in Regla. A fifteen-minute ferry ride across Havana's industrialized harbor from Habana Vieja,[2] the municipality of Regla is known, among other things, for its enduring associations with Ocha-Lucumí and wider communities of Afro-Cuban religious practice. A living embodiment of this history can be found in La Iglesia de Nuestra Señora de Regla. This small eighteenth-century church facing Regla's harborside docks is home to La Virgen de Regla, a black-skinned Madonna who shares a syncretic form with Yemayá, the maternal orisha of the sea. Tradition holds that when traveling to Regla an offering of a Cuban penny is thrown from the *lanchita* (small ferry) into the blue harbor waters for blessings from La Virgen cum Yemayá.

Today, Regla and its neighboring barrio of Guanabacoa remain home to sizable communities of babaláwos and *iyas de ocha* (religious godmothers, or *madrinas*) who live among its narrow streets, while Guanabacoa's small municipal museum is dedicated to local histories of Ocha-Lucumí, and other religious traditions of Palo Monte and the Abakuá. The earliest documented fraternity of Abakuá was in fact founded in Regla in the early nineteenth century (Cabrera 1958, cited in Sublette 2007: 191), and revelers continue to visit the church of Nuestra Señora in homage to Regla's black Virgin, her maternal figure shrouded in Yemayá's oceanic blues.

Alexey was raised in a black working-class family just a few blocks from the waterfront church, and his sense of history and black-selfhood is in turn deeply meshed with that of Regla. Such historicity, however, is largely grounded in the secular rather than the sacred—neither Alexey nor his parents are practitioners of Ocha-Lucumí or other religious traditions, Afro-Cuban or otherwise. As described earlier, a portrait of Toussaint L'Ouverture poised in military garb with his foot upon a hissing snake greets those entering Alexey's home. This heroic icon of the Haitian Revolution stands in this sense in profane analogy to that of Eleggúa, the orisha of the crossroads, whose figure sits in ritual guard at entryways of many *santeros'* homes. Indeed, Haiti has assumed an enduring presence in Alexey's domestic life, one finding artistic form in his composition "¿Viste?" from Obsesión's 2011 album, *El Disco Negro*. An ode of solidarity with Haitians following the devastating earthquake of 2010, the tema is interwoven with a solemn exchange between Alexey and his father, Celso, reflecting upon the traumas of the event and its historical resonances in light of Haiti's struggle for black nationhood.

Currents of Afro-hemispheric affinity within the Rodríguez household are not limited to Haiti, however. Among other visual markers displayed prominently in the Regla flat stands a black-and-white portrait of Malcolm X in iconic pose, while a large spray-painted image of an Afro-adorned man sits against an outside wall of their rooftop patio overlooking Havana's skyline across the harbor. Recalling MC Rubén Marín of Primera Base mentioned earlier, Alexey tells of how his exposure to a Spanish-language Cuban edition of The Autobiography of Malcolm X influenced his thinking about his blackness as well as his broader membership to a black historical world.[3] Yet these varying figures on parade—L'Ouverture, Afro'd figure, and Malcolm X—stand in interesting tension with la Virgen de Regla not only in terms of a scared-secular divide, but also along gendered and temporally divergent lines as well. Such semiotic play, while rooted in the local, were thus more expansive and self-consciously diasporic—if decidedly modern and masculinist—in scope.

Over the years Alexey and Magia's Regla home has hosted countless gatherings of raperos and other hip-hop-affiliated folk, one of which was alluded to in the book's opening vignette. The couple's bedroom eventually doubled as a makeshift studio where Alexey, working with PC-based consumer software, produced many of the duo's background beats and vocal tracks. The room itself is adorned with hip-hop-inspired artwork and images; one of its walls is dedicated to a frenetic collage of photographs and graffitied notes from visitors, both local and foreign. During one of my own early forays to their place on a hot and muggy afternoon in the summer of 1999, I queried the two about what seemed to be a pervasiveness of black-self-affirming lyrics within local hip hop. In response, Alexey explained:

This is a stage of rap. One must first announce "I am black." And when you acknowledge this, we can then move forward from there. I think this is valuable, this is valuable today especially here in Cuba. It seems to me that black people now know more about themselves, and I think our work is contributing to establishing this. And part of what is necessary here is to know your history in a deep kind of way—to know who you are, your roots, and where you come from.[4]

As Alexey's comment suggests, his conception of black identity is an implicitly political one. Rather than passively given, such identity is understood within the Cuban context as a conscious and active assertion of self—"I am black"—which in turn serves as the ground upon which to "move forward," to act. Here, Alexey is not suggesting a notion of blackness as a detached marker to be chosen or rejected at whim. Blackness rather is seen as embodied and lived subjectivity, one that he claims Obsesión and other Cuban MCs have worked to make critically visible.

Years later while speaking to an undergraduate class of mine in New Orleans, Magia spoke similarly of a "process" of coming into racial self-consciousness (auto-consciencia) rooted in a lived experience of race through which, in her words, one "reflects," "learns," and ultimately "acts." She added that in her case such self-actualization grew from an ongoing set of conversations tied to her involvements in hip hop and wider evolving fields of Cuban racial discourse. Magia emphasized that it was through her music that such black self-consciousness and its embedded politics assumed animated form. Such racial practice has been a consistent element of Magia and Alexey's artistic vision over the years, not something eventually discarded and moved beyond (cf. Baker 2011: 277). For Magia and Alexey, whose dark complexion, hair, and facial features unequivocally mark them as negros, such blackness of embodied form and historical weight is largely inescapable.

During that early Regla exchange, Magia explained that in the past she had been hesitant to identify as black despite her family's strong tradition of pro-black affirmation. A striking, dark-brown-skinned woman, Magia recalled her early-school-age tendency to claim any nonwhite identifier other than negra. Prevailing traditions, she explained, taught her that as a young woman of color, blackness was not something to embrace. Those same raced genderings that fixed la mulata as the quintessence of heteromasculine desire and celebrated symbol of a racially transculturated nation compelled darker-skinned women to distance themselves from the term negra and its peripherality from normative centers of racial and gendered privilege.

It is precisely against such historical erasure that the Afro-Cuban poet Nancy Morejón's celebrated poem "Mujer negra" empathically speaks (Morejón 1979). Mapping black women's presence in the making of Cuba from Africa to enslavement to independence struggle and finally to contemporary revolutionary, Morejón's ballad of personal freedom is fused with that

3.1. MCs Magia López (left) and Alexey Rodríguez of Obsesión.
Photo by Sahily Borrero

of national liberation as the first-person *yo* (I) evolves by poetic end into a
collective celebration of *nuestros* (ours) with the arrival of the Cuban Revolution. Here Morejón offers a recuperation of a black female subject of Cuba's
conjoining histories of nationhood and revolution, one analogous in this
sense to Magia's own recuperative efforts of black self-reconciliation.

By 1999 Magia's outlook had indeed shifted. Her identity and performative presentation as a black woman increasingly became a central facet of
her work as one of Cuba's pioneering female MCs, a role that expanded in
scope over the years as one of the movement's most active and accomplished
members. A key current of these labors has been Magia's efforts to challenge
the raced sexualization of black and brown-skinned Cuban women, ener-

gies that arose in conversation with a broader emergence of black womanist voices within Cuban hip hop's otherwise male-centric space. As I explore in more detail in chapter 4, these female artists not only complicated hip hop's highly masculinist orientation, but often also provided critiques of the wider heteronormative workings of racialized patriarchy in the Cuban everyday.

During the many years I have known Magia and Alexey, their sense of blackness has become an ever more celebrated facet of their personal and public lives as artists. When we first met in 1999, Magia wore synthetic extensions braided into her hair, while Alexey kept his in a short-cropped fade. Within a couple of years Magia began wearing her long, reddish-brown hair combed out into a big Afro-like crown, or alternatively bound in colorful African-style wraps reminiscent at the time of the black neobohemian flair of Erykah Badu. For Alexey's part, he began grooming what became a head of mid-shoulder-length dreadlocks, a practice in dialogue with a growing number of young black urban men who, while not necessarily followers of Cuba's nascent Rastafari movement (see Hansing 2001),[5] embraced dreadlocks as a nonconformist, Afrocentric marker of black masculinity.

Such stylized body practice was not free of potential costs, however. There is history of Cuban police harassment of black men with dreadlocks for their perceived associations with Rastafarians and marijuana use, a raced and largely gendered form of social regulation—again tied to racialized framings of criminality—to which I will return (see chapter 6). Despite, or precisely in *spite* of, such racially coded antagonism, Alexey held his locks as performatively integral to his sense of black-self, yet one clearly in dialogue with wider global circuits of black corporal practice and aesthetics of style (cf. Diawara 1998; Kelley 2012). Magia and Alexey would eventually set the politics of black hair to music in their tema "Los pelos" (The hair),[6] in which the duo addresses the restrictions as well as the celebratory possibilities of black hair. As Magia riffs:

Pelo suelto carretera, no hay desriz
y me di cuenta que pa' que si yo no nací así
El hombre que me quiere me acepta como soy,
Africana! Adonde quiera que voy seguro!
Mi naturaleza rompe patrón de belleza no me vengan con que
pa' luciese más fina . . .
Pa'riba los pelos y que crezcan los dreadlocks

Hair loose on the street, there's no relaxer
and I realized that I was not born like that
The man that would accept me as I am,
an African woman! Wherever I go, for sure!
My natural beauty breaks standards of beauty; so don't tell me
to look more refined . . .
To the top with hair and let the dreadlocks grow

A body-centered poetics of black style, however, extends beyond hair. When performing, Magia often appears in West African–inspired gowns and headwraps. While periodically garbing his thin frame in African prints, Alexey is more often draped in classic rapero attire of oversized baggy pants, U.S. footwear, and long, loose-fitting tops—a fashion grammar globally synonymous with hip hop. Regardless of attire, for many years the two never hit the streets without a set of dark wooden amulets about their necks. Fashioned by Alexey as symbols of the couple's bond, these amulets bore carved faces with strong African features and were spoken of as carrying protective spiritual significance.

Such crafting skills drew upon Alexey's former employment in the early 1990s in a state-run workshop of tourist crafts. This early space of tourism commerce is where the artists first met—Magia was then making clay figurines. As Magia recalls, "This was during the Special Period, and people were losing jobs, payrolls were reduced. I was the first to lose my job, and then they closed the entire workshop and Ale lost his job."[7] Magia eventually found employment in a dollar-only tourist shop, while assisting Alexey with the sporadic work he found carving small wood sculptures for the informal tourist trade. Alexey later worked briefly in a printing house, a job that his father, Celso, helped him obtain.

None of this, however, provided much by way of income. Alexey was at one point compelled to take a job collecting street trash and mowing lawns for a monthly state salary of 40 Cuban pesos (roughly equivalent to US$2). While their ability to move between their respective family homes helped manage costs, like nearly all Cubans during this period Magia and Alexey were struggling to make basic ends meet on state-regulated peso salaries. Rather cogently, a common Cuban refrain from the late 1990s mused, "El gobierno pretende pagarnos, y nosotros pretendemos trabajar" (The government pretends to pay us, and we pretend to work).

Forms of public-sector employment that had long provided stable income for the vast majority of Cubans during the revolutionary period were ever increasingly less viable by the mid to late 1990s. As Magia's and Alexey's narratives testify, early state schemes tied to an emerging tourism market did not provide much by way of a living (let alone competitive) peso salary vis-à-vis a rapidly expanding dollar economy. These shifts and their injurious effects were felt acutely by young Cubans like Magia and Alexey entering the workforce, a generational demographic worth noting from which the first wave of raperos was drawn. Indeed, it was amid such fluidity that Magia and Alexey got married in 1996 and, significantly, formed Obsesión as a trio initially with comrade-in-arms DJ Roger Martínez.[8] From that point they began performing informally in small venues as their music became increasingly central to their personal, artistic, and ultimately political lives.

Along similar lines mentioned earlier, Alexey explains that his early exposure to hip hop came from FM radio broadcasts from southern Florida in the 1980s. With the help of an improvised wire antenna fashioned outside his bedroom window, his parents' rooftop apartment in Regla afforded ideal access to these otherwise elusive radio waves. Alexey soon took to Havana's emerging b-boy scene. With the coming of the economic crisis in the early 1990s, however, Alexey had to curtail his street dancing to preserve his lone pair of shoes or risk, as he put it, "corriendo descalzo por la calle" (running barefoot in the streets). Thus, in tune with broader trends within Cuba's evolving hip hop scene, Alexey's pivot from dance to music making marked a shift in artistic direction amid a backdrop of economic and related social flux.

Transnational dimensions being what they were, Magia and Alexey nevertheless understood their blackness as deeply rooted in Cuban narratives of history, nationhood, and revolution—renderings that find poetic form in their music. One of Obsesión's early signature temas, "Mambí," offers a vivid illustration of such interwoven autochthony. Released in 2000 on the artists' debut album and awash in historical references, "Mambí" draws its name from los mambises, the machete-wielding largely black and formerly enslaved regiments of soldiers who fought among others under the famed mulato general Antonio Maceo during Cuba's late nineteenth-century wars of independence. Rather than a historical recounting, the composition's first-person narrative likens Obsesión's members to modern-day mambí.

When asked about the song's thematic significance, Magia put it simply: "Somos mambises, luchando lo mismo" (We are mambises, we are fighting the same struggle). Below is the opening salvo of "Mambí."

Pa' el pueblo aquí estoy yo
[coro]: Yo estoy aquí diciendo
Obsesión Mambí pinchando
Que nadie espere ningún tipo de chance
Si Quintín Bandera nunca dio masaje,
¿por que yo entonces?
¡A fajarse!
Que la manigua está gritando: Yo soy yo
Y es por mí por quien doblan las campanas,
no metan forros
El morro sabe que al combate corro y corro junto a los Bayameses
¡Cuba, orgullosa de mí!
No le temo a una muerte gloriosa
Estense quietos que insurrecto y prieto es un lío ¡Rebambarambara! . . .

For the people, here I am
[chorus]: I am here speaking
Obsesión Mambí in the battle
Nobody should wait for chance
If Quintín Bandera never gave up,[9]
then why should I?
Let's fight!
The manigua is screaming: I am me
and it's for me for whom the bells toll,
don't tell lies[10]
The Cuban fortress knows that in combat I run and run together with the Bayameses
Cuba, proud of me!
I don't fear a heroic death
To be a rebel and black is still trouble. Making hell! . . . [11]

The tema's allusions operate on various overlapping levels. In an immediate sense, foregrounding the racial significance of los mambises underscores the historical instrumentality of blacks in Cuba's national liberation struggle. The intimacies of such history are marked through figures like the mambí leader Quintín Bandera,[12] a celebrated black general of the independence wars who served directly under Antonio Maceo, and the legendary Manigua Brigade of mambí fighters from Cuba's eastern Oriente region. These references stand in tension with enduring, largely race-neutral(ized) renderings of Cuba's early national beginnings (Ferrer 1998b; Helg 1995). In line with postracial framings previously discussed, los mambises are framed in official revolutionary discourse as liberators of the Cuban nation in ways that often supersede if not mask their historical agency as Afro-Cubans.

Historical recuperations of this kind are further evoked by Obsesión through their self-fashioning as present-day mambí, situating themselves and their work within counternarratives of black struggle elemental to the modern forging of Cuba itself. Indeed, in running "with the Bayameses," the artists index Cuba's national anthem, "La Bayamesa," and its opening call "¡Al combate, corred, Bayameses!" (Run to battle, men of Bayamo!) as a marker of national legitimacy—one through which antiracist struggle is held intrinsic to Cuba's own national liberation and birth. Sacrifice in the nation's wars of independence—Cuba's "first" revolution in the discursive teleology of the post-1959 revolutionary period—therefore warrants a historical national indebtedness to black Cubans, tying Afro-Cubans inseparably to national-revolutionary citizenship. Temporal imbrications of black citizenship and revolutionary virtue in this sense provide a rhetorical bridge between revolutionary past and present. "Yo estoy aquí diciendo . . . pinchando . . . corro y corro junto a los bayamese . . . ¡Cuba orgullosa de mí! . . . insurrecto y prieto es un lío ¡Rebambarambara!" declares in essence: "I am black, and Cuban, and revolutionary, recognize me, hear me speak!"

It is, however, noteworthy that "Mambí" opens with a dedication to the African American imprisoned radical Mumia Abu-Jamal, expanding political claims and forms of citizenship into realms of the contemporary outernational. Revolutionary articulations do nonetheless appear to grow first and foremost from an organics of Cuba's own history. As the two explained to me early on:

> **Alexey:** We are rapping from the perspective of a socialist society, from a point of view of socialism, and we engage it from a positive position.
> **Magia:** Our role [as raperos] within the society is well defined within socialism, and this is independent of whether we communicate, cri-

tique, or denounce certain things in society. Our position is well defined in this sense.

MP: Well, do you then consider your music somehow connected to the revolution?

Alexey: Yes, we cannot separate one from the other. I cannot make music by putting aside what is significant about the revolution for me. I can make a song that is critical of something, but never against the revolution. Never against the revolution, because it is not like this, not for Obsesión.

Magia: Since I was little my mother always told me, "Gracias por la revolución" (thanks to the revolution), because black folks have had more possibilities under the revolution. I get annoyed, though, when a black person makes a lot of noise criticizing the revolution. Before the triumph of the revolution my mother told me that even light-skinned [black] women could only get work as maids. The revolution allowed black folks to study, to work, to be who we are today. From here on it's us who have to work double, triple, whatever it takes to arrive at who we are to become. It depends on us.[13]

In comparison to many of their peers, Magia and Alexey were among some of the more adamantly self-identified and vocal supporters of the Cuban Revolution and, by relative extension, the Cuban state. I recall numerous discussions with the two regarding current tensions in Cuban society in which my critical readings as an "outsider" were often met with fervent defenses of "the revolution." Here I mark the (Cuban) Revolution with quotations not only to reiterate the artists' use of the term but also to underscore the tendency within post-1959 discourse to conflate *la revolución* with *el estado*, and ultimately *el pueblo* (the revolution, the state, and the people/nation). Within this secularized trinity where one-is-all, as all-are-one, perceived challenges to one are deemed antagonistic affronts to all. While such framing might serve the ends of curbing public critique, it can take on additional charged significance when critique is leveled from *afuera*, or the outside. Such dynamics informed the tone of some of our more animated exchanges around Cuba's shifting landscape, with Magia in particular frequently impassioned in her positions.

Yet as Magia implies, the artists' strong identifications with the revolution were shaped in important part by their close relationships with their parents, who, like many of their generational peers, share deep-felt attachments to the island's revolutionary history. Such familial affinity is reflected with comic flair in Alexey's 2011 tema "Esta es mi mamá" (This is my mother), dedicated to his mother, Maria. Shot against the domestic backdrop of their Regla home, the song's YouTube video centers on a playful back-and-forth exchange between son and mother, with Maria spiritedly contributing her own rapping to camera.[14] Recalling numerous conversations with Alexey's father, Celso, and Magia's mother, Caridad, I was often moved by their fervent faith in both the principles and the achievements of Cuban socialism. Yes, there may have been *errores*, mistakes, but the revolution had worked and was continually working to correct them.

While widespread disillusionment and cynicism regarding hardships of Cuban life were commonplace among *habaneros* (Havana residents), with the phrase "no es fácil" (it's not easy) assuming mantra status since the onset of the Special Period, I often found Celso's and Caridad's perspectives refreshing given the conflicted assessments one commonly hears and lives in Havana. Celso and Caridad are in this sense among that generation of Afro-Cubans who share a lived memory of what Cuba was for poor and working-class blacks *before* the revolution, as well as the hard-won transformations achieved *through* it.

In Celso's case, as a retired engineer he owes much of his education and professional training to revolutionary openings of Cuba's long racially exclusionary educational system—a similar generational narrative of black professionalism shared with Lisnida and with Pablo Herrera's parents. Celso's fidelity to socialism as it turns out dates back to early adulthood when he won a poetry contest dedicated to the Russian Revolution, an award that afforded him a trip to the Soviet Union in 1970. He later traveled to Czechoslovakia for a course in cartographic design, during which he also briefly visited Bulgaria. Circuits of Cuban internationalism also brought Celso to Ethiopia, where he spent two years during Cuba's military involvement in the Ogaden War of the late 1970s. For Magia, recollections of her mother's account of social mobility under the revolution—Caridad having been a domestic worker herself—are illustrative of the affective power of this narrative in Magia's own life.

Legacies of mobility notwithstanding, like many of their hip hop peers neither Magia nor Alexey attended university, and as described they spent most of their young adulthoods scrambling to make ends meet until eventually devoting themselves full-time to their music. As one of the more accomplished of Cuban rapero groups, the duo have been fortunate to have garnered income, as inconsistent as it may have been, through local performances and national tours, informal sales of their two recorded albums, and eventually artistic tours aboard. They are relatively exceptional in this sense—most raperos have not been as consistently productive in translating talent into income. While the majority are generally unemployed in a formal sense, like large numbers of young Cubans many have found resourceful ways of getting by, or in Cuban terms *inventar y resolver* (to creatively invent and/or resolve) by one means or another.

Magia's recollection of her mother's account of the prerevolutionary limits of black women's opportunities for employment also underscores gendered dimensions of racial regulation, a theme with which she is intimately familiar in her own life. Revisiting Obsesión's "Mambí," Magia gives voice to her own raced gendering in her opening volley:

¿Como e'? Yo soy niche
Mi intención no es salir como negrita linda
en los afiches
Y si me ven así es porque
sé que todavía hay
quien quisiera ser mayoral
Pa' verme trabajando sin descanso
en los trapiches
Eso lo he sufrido, lo he visto . . .

What's that? I'm black
My intention is not to be a pretty black girl in the posters
And if they see me this way it's because
I know that there are still those
who would like to be an overseer
So they can see me working without rest
in the sugar mills
I have suffered that, I have seen it . . .

Here Magia evokes her blackness through the expression *niche*, a vernacular Cuban term for blacks long inscribed with a racially derisive, if not overtly racist, meaning. The phrase has, however, worked its way into the parlance of Afro-Cuban youth and, reminiscent of African American inversions of "nigger" (i.e., nigga), is frequently employed as a marker of pro-black unity and self-affirmation. Indeed, the Santos Suárez–based trio of 100% Original give flamboyant expression to such verbiage in their tema "Pa' mis niches" (For ma' niggaz), which proclaims: "Nígga, niche abre tus ojos / Si hoy hemos sobrevivimos porque en el ayer luchamos para juntos hoy estar unidos" (Nigga, niche open your eyes / If today we have survived it's because we fought for our unity in the past).

For both Magia and 100% Original, the term *niche* evokes legacies of racial subjugation as well as liberatory possibilities. Yet in contrast to 100%'s masculine rendering centering "hombre negro" (black brother) as cardinal protagonist, Magia's niche is decidedly female, one unwilling to conform to normative prescriptions that would fix her body—"a pretty black girl"—as an object of heteropatriarchal gaze and consumption. Magia alternatively historicizes such raced genderings by invoking the memory of enslavement: "I know that there are still those who would like to be an overseer / So they can see me working without rest in the sugar mills." By proclaiming "I have suffered that, I have seen it," Magia marks a historical link with racial slavery, while testifying to its everyday vestiges in the life of black women. Though Magia too declares "somos Mambíses, luchando lo mismo," her gendered positionality would in fact become an increasingly vocal part of her artistic voice and identity as a performer.

Obsesión nonetheless represents something of an enduring older-guard within Havana's hip hop community, most of whom have tended to range between their late teens and early twenties during their music-making years in comparison to the duo's thirties (and eventually beyond)—an age difference that often translated into having relatively younger parents. This contrast may in part account for Obsesión's relatively less conflicted identifications with the Cuban state and its institutions in comparison to many of their peers. As I discuss shortly, forms of revolutionary affinity are often a central and defining component among many Cuban MCs. A key distinction, however, lies in raperos' varying mediations in that space between the Revolution with a capital R and alternative revolutionary conceptions vis-à-vis dimensions of identity and political positioning. Magia and Alexey's comments do nonetheless underscore the tendency among many Cuban raperos during this period of viewing their work as critically engaged from *within*—rather than *against*—the Cuban Revolution.

It is also clear that in addition to a range of autonomous, self-financed projects, Magia and Alexey share a long history of working collaboratively with state institutions—a history at times generating ambivalence among more institutionally wary members of Havana's hip hop community. In 2000, for instance, Obsesión was among four hip hop groups to join the state-run *empresa* (venture/project) Benny Moré established to promote performance opportunities nationally for Cuban musicians—the first such institutional inclusion of raperos. Magia explained that their involvement came about through months of struggle that, in the end, bore little fruit given limited resources and an organizational inexperience regarding the needs of hip hop artists. Obsesión's debut album, *Obsesión*, produced that same year, nevertheless remains the one commercial hip hop album released on Cuba's state-run music label EGREM.[15] Further along, Obsesión was one of the first of the coveted few hip hop groups to join the newly formed Agencia Cubana de Rap (ACR, or Cuban Rap Agency) in 2002—a state organ set up specifically for the commercial development and promotion of Cuban hip hop with an eye toward both domestic and international markets. Magia would in fact eventually assume leadership of the ACR, a complicated tenure to which I will later return.

While such involvements may not necessarily imply compromise, they did mark both a dexterity and an ideological (if at some level strategic) willingness to engage institutionally with the revolutionary state. Magia and Alexey were indeed often adamant in conversation that institutional collaborations in no way menaced their artistic vision or craft, and if this were to arise, they argued, they would cease to participate. Though Obsesión's temas were often critically attuned to thorny questions of race and moved from antiracist positions, unlike some of Havana's more outspoken hip hop artists, they generally avoided launching direct critiques at the Cuban state and its institutions. While degrees of *autocensura*, or self-censorship, were frequently part of the negotiated politics of artistic production in Cuba (cf. Fernandes 2006), given the duo's strong inherited identification with the Cuban Revolution—and possibly by extension the Cuban state—they seemed in my experience less concerned with these tensions than others.

Elaborating Spaces

During my early foray into Havana's hip hop community I developed relationships with a set of individuals who either were or soon became key players within the local hip hop scene. In addition to the likes of Magia and Alexey, and later Pablo Herrera, Rodolfo Rensoli, and Ariel Fernández Díaz, I befriended a dynamic crew of hip-hop-affiliated folks in el Vedado, where DJ Alexis D'Boys among others was active. This seaside barrio with its tree-lined streets was one of the more affluent (and whiter) of Havana's neighborhoods prior to 1959. With the onset of the Cuban Revolution, however, many residents joined the exodus of wealthy and middle-class Cubans, given the threat—both real and perceived—the revolution posed to established lines of racial-class privilege. Vedado today nonetheless remains home to some of Havana's relatively more well-off residents, many residual family of those who emigrated during the "white flight" of the early 1960s.

In addition to benefiting from racially skewed patterns of foreign remittance that privilege such lighter-skinned Cubans, Vedado residents live in some of Havana's most coveted real estate, which in today's foreign-currency-driven tourist economy translates into marketable capital. As one of the barrios with the highest concentration of casas particulares that rent rooms (both legally and illicitly) to tourists, Vedado benefits disproportionably from this niche of Cuba's new economy. The barrio does, however, have pockets of black and darker-skinned Cubans, some of whom acquired housing vacated by fleeing employers in ways similar to those mentioned previously by DJ Alexis D'Boys in the context of barrio Lawton. Analogous in this sense to the multi-unit solares of Central Havana, many of the onetime palatial single-family homes in Vedado accommodate multiple households among now-partitioned units.

One such site and surrounding black pocket centers around the intersection of Tenth and Nineteenth Streets, known locally as Diez y Diecinueve, where Deno, a dark-skinned early-twenty-something dreadlocked black man, lived with his extended family. Deno's home and adjoining patio, part of a formerly grand two-story house now in need of significant restorative work, became a communal center for the EPG&B crew (the Executive Plan Ghetto and Barbito).[16] Founded in the union of Grandes Ligas, a local hip hop duo out of Vedado; Junior Clan, a duo from the adjoining Central Havana barrio of Cerro; and a spoken-word circle known as Jóvenes Rebeldes, EPG&B

3.2. Producer Pablo Herrera (*left*) and DJ Alexis "D'Boys" Rodríguez.
Photo by Sahily Borrero

celebrated themselves as among the more subversively "underground" MCs in the Havana area.[17] Increasingly graffiti-adorned, the patio beside Deno's house became something of a local hip hop institution where, beginning in 2001, a series of EPG&B street concerts were held, involving guest appearances by many of Havana's established raperos.

Taking on the flavor of a festival block party, these informal concerts regularly drew hundreds of overwhelmingly darker-skinned youth into the adjacent cobblestone streets in an otherwise sedate, predominantly white Vedado. Claiming space at levels of both the material and the sonic, these public spectacles often drew the attention of the police, who on numerous occasions shut the events down. This eventually changed, however, as the revolutionary state, through the conduit of the Asociación Hermanos Saíz, began lending support to these events in the early 2000s by supplying audio equipment and arranging greater police tolerance. Such moves illustrated a gradual shift in the state's approach from one of cautious suspicion to institutional incorporation—a strategy I return to in detail in chapter 5.

While Grandes Ligas and Junior Clan members had close associations in 1999, EPG&B as a collective had yet to be formed. It was during this early period, however, that I developed many of my connections with these artists and their extended Diez y Diecinueve posse. Many contacts grew out of regular visits to La Pampa, a small cabaret-style club down the street from my flat in Cayo Hueso. Sitting rather apropos in the shadow of General Antonio Maceo's statue at the corner of Parque Maceo and the seaside thoroughfare of El Malecón, La Pampa was the latest local incarnation of la moña where Adalberto Jiménez held court as resident DJ. Here on any given Thursday through Saturday night, well into the morning, an animated crowd of black youth could be found extending into the street. While many lacked the 20 peso entrance fee (the equivalent of US$1), others preferred the cooler night air to the stifling heat within. Given that the club's beats often resonated well beyond its doors, the adjoining street was indeed integral to La Pampa's social space and party.

Regarding attire, many young women attending wore tight-fitting tops and some fluorescent spandex tights that were au courant across a notably wide generational range of Havana women at that fashion juncture. Young men donned baggy pants, loose jerseys (including a small number of NBA and NFL jerseys), U.S. baseball caps, and for a privileged few FUBU and Eckô designer gear—among the latest in hip-hop-aligned youth style. These style practices were often informed by dog-eared U.S. rap magazines and videocassettes of hip hop videos that found their way to Cuba via visiting family members, friends, and tourists from the United States. They also spoke broadly to expanding circuits of transnational exchange and a growing culture of consumerism in a once definitely anti-consumerist Cuba.

Inside La Pampa's small, sweltering, barely lit space, DJ Adalberto Jiménez played U.S. hip hop and R&B with intermittent microphone shout-outs before a moving mass of sweat-soaked bodies. Rather than LPs or the later proliferation of CDs, Adalberto's music was "spun" from second-generation audiocassettes over a dilapidated speaker system at deafening levels. The sound quality though never seemed much of a concern to those gathered in celebratory communion with and through the music. To my half-attuned ear at the time, many beats often seemed slightly dated given the lag time it took most North American music to make its way to the island.

Over subsequent years, however, such lag was less the case as consumption habits evolved, fed in large part by the increased trafficking of North Americans with linkages to Havana's hip hop community. It was in fact not long before many were as abreast with the most recent beats as any professed hip hop head in the United States. Indeed, upon my repeated returns to Havana I frequently found myself schooled on the latest U.S. tracks by my rapero friends, many of whom had a particularly strong command of music out of New York City and the Oakland, California, area due to established bicoastal ties with local hip hop communities. The eventual access to computer-based CD-burning technology dramatically increased the pace and range of new-music dissemination within Havana's tight-knit networks of hip hop devotees.

Regardless of how relatively current a track may have been on any given La Pampa night, scores of dancing revelers, hands aloft, could be found singing along with the lyrics though most spoke little if any English. Hip hop for these young people was more than simply music; it was an active and deeply lived facet of social life and identity. As DJ Alexis D'Boys, whom I first met at La Pampa, once put it: "My life is hip hop, hip hop is my culture, I am hip hop. Hip hop is my life wherever I am until I die."[18] Though it was one of the only Havana-area locations at the time where the hip hop devout could commune, La Pampa's dance-only format precluded live performances. Local MCs had to rely on Thursday or Friday night open-mic events held a half-hour bus ride away in Alamar's amphitheater as the only semi-reliable performance venue. This, however, was 1999.

By 2000 another local hip hop peña (event party) emerged at a small venue, Club Las Vegas, located just a few blocks from La Pampa on Infanta Avenue at the border of barrios Cayo Hueso and Vedado. Prior to its hip hop christening, I had visited the club to catch a small revue-style cabaret that turned out to be a nostalgic retro-pastiche of a classic teatro bufo performance complete with the archetypical trio of el negrito, la mulata, and el gallego caricatures. I recall the largely Cuban audience at the club being highly amused with the buffoonish exploits of el negrito—the "little black man" played in blackface opposite the gallantly masculine "Spanish" gallego figure—as he ran around farcically trying to win the affection of the alluring mulata adorned with her prerequisite long flowing hair and complementary fishnet stockings. As Jill Lane's work (2005) illustrates, Cuba's comedic teatro bufo tradition offered a popular blackface casting of dominant racial, gendered, and class scriptings in the early framing of Cuba's racially triangulated national imaginary—one apparently alive or revived in the contemporary moment.

A decidedly different shade of Cuban blackness emerged Wednesday afternoons, however, when Las Vegas transformed into a weekly performance space for local raperos and their fans. Descending into a sunken windowless space on a given afternoon, one refreshingly cool thanks to its privileged air-conditioning, groups like Anónimo Consejo, 100% Original, Junior Clan, Raperos Crazy de Alamar, Grandes Ligas, and Obsesión performed original material over prerecorded background tapes. The overwhelmingly black, early to midtwenties crowd collected around cocktail tables beside the floor-level stage came out religiously to indulge in music and drink while rooting on local MCs.

Reflecting the expanding growth and sophistication of local hip hop, a subsequent and in many ways intuitionally significant site for Havana-area MCs emerged in 2001, Café Cantante. A comparatively glitzy nightclub at the crossroads of Vedado and Cerro barrios famed for salsa performances, Café Cantante was located in the basement of the Teatro Nacional (National Theater) overlooking Havana's storied Plaza de la Revolución. With its towering monument to Jose Martí and iconic building-side portrait of Che Guevara, the normally empty square is home to Havana's mass rallies, including Fidel Castro's legendary May Day speeches. It was thus notable that hip hop established a niche at the foot of such a sanctified space (and in the institutional bowels of the National Theater), access to which was afforded by the state-run Asociación Hermanos Saíz (AHS) in conjunction with the Instituto Cubano de la Música (Cuban Institute of Music).

While Pablo Herrera recalls encountering the pioneering hip hop crew Amenaza during a show in Café Cantante in the mid-1990s,[19] my first experience of the locale was in 2001 during recently instituted Saturday afternoon matinees devoted to local hip hop performances. By this time Pablo and Ariel Fernández Díaz (aka DJ Asho) were cohosting the afternoon hip hop event under the auspices of AHS involving a mix of U.S. hip hop music and live performances. From this moment on the café emerged as the preeminent weekly showcase for Havana-area raperos. By 2002 the venue was incorporated into an expanded multiday Cuban hip hop festival, reflecting again the Cuban state's growing institutional investment in hip hop during this period.

One final site instrumental to hip hop's ascendance in Havana at this formative juncture was La Madriguera. A small compound located on the dilapidated grounds of Parque Quinta de los Molinos in Central Havana,[20] La Madriguera had long served as a central administrative point for AHS's involvements with Havana raperos. Here Rodolfo Rensoli's Grupo Uno, through the institutional sponsorship of AHS, organized a number of Havana's early hip hop festivals, including annual MC auditions for festival entry. By 2003 La Madriguera began organizing regular nighttime peñas hosted by DJ Ariel Fernández Díaz, now institutionally positioned within AHS as the principal liaison between the revolutionary state and the island's hip hop movement.[21] Far from the earlier days of Adelberto's pirated audiocassettes, Ariel held court with state-of-the-art CD-based electronic mixingtables broadcast over high-end mobile speakers.[22] Some of the latest East Coast beats were spun before an energized local crowd of young, demonstratively black and darker-skinned hip hop heads. While La Madriguera's peñas made occasional space for impromptu free-style sessions among local MCs, the spot was primarily one dedicated to body-centered celebrations of U.S. hip hop. To gain broader perspective on the evolving dimensions of rapero performance, however, one needs to revisit Cuba's annual hip hop festival as a cumulative marker and apogee of creative innovation among Havana-area artists.

Performing Blackness at the 2000 Festival

In the summer of 2000 I returned to Havana after a few months' absence just a week or so prior to the sixth annual Cuban hip hop festival, customarily held during the sweltering month of August. Part of the logic behind the August scheduling was to hold the festival during the summer recess when school-age youth, who comprised a sizable component of Alamar's hip hop fan base, would be free to attend evening performances that often ran late into the night. Another key consideration was that Black August, a New York–based hip hop collective that participated in the two previous festivals, was set to partake again in 2000. The collective traditionally organized events in August in remembrance of the August 1971 murder of Black Panther George Jackson[23] and preceding August histories of black resistance dating back to Nat Turner's 1831 slave rebellion. Through modest donations to Havana's rapero community and, most significantly, the shepherding of U.S. hip hop artists to the island for annual performances, Black August had become an integral facet of the festival since 1998. Unlike the previous year, when I had failed to attend, I recognized in 2000 that I could ill afford to miss another year's festival.

Once back in Havana I immediately headed out to reconnect with people, finding everyone feverishly in preparation for the upcoming festival. A common complaint in rapero circles at the time concerned the disorganization on the part of the festival's lead coordinator, Grupo Uno. In attending subsequent festivals it was indeed my experience that there was often confusion over the details of the event's preparation, necessary resources were rarely in place, and schedules were habitually in flux. It is also worth noting in retrospect that this 2000 edition of the festival would be the last year that Rensoli and Grupo Uno would be coordinating the event. Since 1999, the Cuban state had become increasingly active in the festival's organizational structure, a development reflecting increased efforts to incorporate hip hop within institutional folds of the state. For the immediate moment Rensoli and company were still the lead organizing force behind the festival's four nights of performances.

The afternoon of the festival's opening night, I headed out to Alamar's amphitheater to attend the evening's sound check and to retrieve a promised credential tag that would allow me backstage access during the festival. On that muggy August afternoon in front of Havana's stately Capitolio building, I boarded a 20-peso máquina—one of the old, often ramshackle pre-1959 American cars that operate as privately run collective taxis—for a twenty-minute ride east to the coastal municipality of Alamar. Between the colossal Capitolio, the prerevolutionary seat of Cuba's legislature styled after the U.S. Capitol that looms over Havana's skyline, and the antiquated fume-engulfed máquina, I was reminded of the everyday intimacies of U.S. imperial legacies and the improvisational nature of their transformation on the island. Might Cuban hip hop, I mused, be yet another variation on this proverbial theme? Or, now in hindsight, in what ways might the unfolding hip hop festival reveal neoliberal countercurrents of empire and revolution at the millennial turn?

Following the ride and an additional fifteen-minute walk down from the main road past countless rows of high-rise apartment buildings, I arrived at Alamar's amphitheater. Atop descending concrete tiers of empty seats leading to a large stage below, the festival's organizer, Rodolfo Rensoli, was in the control area scrambling to pull together final details for the opening night's performances. While waiting to speak to him about my credential tag, I joined in on a cajita lunch provided to all working the festival prep. Named for the small brown paper boxes stuffed with fried pork, congri (rice with a sprinkling of red beans), and raw cabbage—long a Havana street staple— these lunches represented a limited, though at the time much appreciated, gesture of governmental support for an otherwise resource-strapped festival.

While absorbed in my cajita, I listened in as the MC trio of Alexei, Amaury, Ransel of Reyes de las Calles rehearsed their tema "El mundo va a acabarse" (The world is coming to an end). The track's instrumental built upon a sample riff from the classic 1974 hit "La Habana Joven" (Young Havana) by the immortal Los Van Van, Cuba's premier dance band since the early 1970s. I later found out the track was produced by Pablo Herrera, who often spoke of the need to create an "authentic" Cuban sound behind Cuban MCs rather than relying on U.S.-produced background beats.[24] In marked contrast to the buoyant Van Van original, however, Reyes de las Calles offered a markedly different rendering of a "young Havana."

Though deceptively playful in delivery, the song painted a grim portrait of the social hypocrisy of the Cuban everyday. Thick with liturgical allusion, "La Habana Joven" evoked the wrathful coming of a black God to a society riddled with racism and duplicity, taking retribution against racists under whose weight blacks have been perpetually "squeezed." Like many raperos, Reyes employed metaphor and *doble sentido* (double meaning) to veil more overt forms of critique, while further masking the bite through a stylized use of humor and satirical play. For further effect, the artists went on to perform the track during the festival equipped with a small blow-up raft and plastic oars in a thinly disguised reference to los balseros, the thousands of disillusioned Cubans who fled in rafts to the United States following the onset of the economic crisis (see chapter 2). It was as if the trio were abandoning a torn and sinking Cuba while testifying to its demise. "El mundo va a acabarse," as it turns out, was the opening performance that first night of the festival.

I returned to Alamar later that evening with Magia and Alexey of Obsesión, who were scheduled to perform later in the festival's multiday run. Within a few blocks of the amphitheater we could feel the reverberations of bass-heavy beats echoing off buildings, ever intensifying as we drew closer. The music was of U.S. rather than Cuban origin, suggesting that the evening's performances had yet to start despite our late arrival. The organizers were evidently priming the crowd with recent tracks by Common and the Roots, two favorites of local hip hop followers who had or would soon perform in Cuba. As we made our way toward the entrance flooded with attendees purchasing tickets at five Cuban pesos apiece (roughly US$0.25), we encountered a few police officers at the doorway who allowed us passage after viewing our credential tags.

Once inside we were met by a descending sea of roughly three thousand young people milling about in energized anticipation of the festival's first night of music. Surveying the scene, it was a significantly darker-skinned audience in comparison to the multiracial range of Cuba's broader population. Also notable was the apparent youth of those attending; the median age could not have been much beyond seventeen. This was clearly a younger following in comparison to those I had encountered at smaller hip hop events throughout Havana, where, in line with most artists, the audience generally ranged between their early twenties and early thirties.

A key difference was that the majority of these young people were drawn locally from Alamar, as the distance and scarcity of reliable night transport for return to Havana made it difficult for many outsiders to attend. This, however, did not deter the most devoted who managed by one form or another to make it out to each of the festival's four nights of performances. Much like La Pampa's patrons but thirty times its multitude, many of the young men donned baggy pants and tops, baseball caps and skullies (skull caps), and athletic team jerseys, while a few flaunted hip-hop-associated U.S. attire like FUBU. Among the young women, spandex tights and shorts along with form-fitting tops were again standard fare. Yet draped squarely behind the stage below sat a towering Cuban flag basking in the multicolored stage lighting as if to remind all: "This is Cuba, be there no confusion!"

Once the evening's performances began, all attention was directed to the onstage spectacle below. In addition to Reyes de las Calles, groups performing that opening night included Raperos Crazy de Alamar (RCA), Pasión Oscura, and the female trio of Instinto. Waves of call-and-response moved through the crowd, while in classic hip hop fashion a sea of arms bobbed in rhythmic call with the music as energies rose. With performances wrapping up around 1:30 AM, the crowd filed out into Alamar's darkened, now quiet streets, heading home in anticipation of the following night's performances. For some of us the night was far from over. The public buses and máquinas that brought many to Alamar from Havana earlier were now nowhere to be found. Sweat-soaked, dehydrated, and exhausted, we dragged ourselves up to the main road to wait for a passing bus carrying early morning commuters, eventually arriving back to Havana by 4 AM, only to do it all again the next night.

The following evening Alamar had a notably different energy, however. On approaching the amphitheater one could immediately sense a heightened buzz and nervous tension among the milling crowd as scores of blue-clad police stood in front of the entrance overseeing crowd control. Inside, additional stern-faced columns of police were positioned in front of and beside the stage below. These numbers were in marked contrast to the relatively sparse police presence on the festival's previous night. A key distinction was that in addition to a list of Cuban groups slated to perform, the hip hop duo of Dead Prez and the DJ-cum-MC Tony Touch—all from New York City—were topping the bill that night. This was Black August's (aka Augusto Negro's) night at this year's festival.

Upon entering the amphitheater, members of Black August's New York contingent handed out flyers in Spanish introducing the collective. The flyer was adorned with a graphic composite of Afro-adorned images of George Jackson beside Assata Shakur, the onetime Black Panther member and Cuba's most renowned African American political exile. The two profiles were framed by a large five-point Cuban-style star. Inscribed below in large block letters read:

BLACK AUGUST 3RD ANNUAL BENEFIT CONCERT 2000
DEDICATED TO ASSATA SHAKUR AND VIEQUES, PUERTO RICO

The eight-page handout in Spanish opened with the question "¿Por que el agosto negro?" (Why Black August?), followed by a brief history of events that began:

The Tradition of Black August was established during the 70s in the Californian penal system by men and women of the Black/New Afrikan liberation movement as a way to remember and investigate a heritage of resistance in the Americas.

This preface was followed by an outline of the collective's central principles, which included:

- The global development of hip hop culture as a means of facilitating international interchange between communities of youth with the intention of promoting greater consciousness around social and political issues.

- Collective opposition to the criminalization of youth and youth culture.
- Organizing against the international prison industrial complex and the escalated incarceration of political prisoners in the U.S.
- Fighting the persistence of white-supremacist propaganda and violations of human rights.

The text closed with the following statement:

> Through a powerful union of hip hop culture and political information, Black August promotes our own hip hop aesthetic which emphasizes sincere self-expression, creativity, and the sense of responsibility to the community.

The remaining six pages were devoted to Spanish translations of song lyrics by Dead Prez and Tony Touch.

As is evident from this material, Black August organized around a set of political commitments in dialogue with recent histories of U.S. black radical thought and practice. Drawing upon an earlier prison movement of the same name aimed at political education among African American inmates, Black August formed in the late 1990s in New York City as a project-offshoot of the Malcolm X Grassroots Movement (MXGM), a youth-centered activist collective grounded in a black nationalist orientation and human rights advocacy. While in conversation with an earlier moment of radical organizing, Black August's program reflected cultural priorities of a younger generation of activists who invoked hip hop as a global medium of political mobilization and youth outreach. Beyond Cuba, such transnational bearings led to Black August projects involving U.S.-based hip hop artists' and activists' tours to South Africa, Brazil, Tanzania, and Venezuela. In the case of South Africa, the 2001 tour was coordinated to coincide with the UN's World Conference against Racism in Durban, with artists performing at the adjoining NGO antiracism forum.[25]

Internationalist orientations being what they were, Black August's ideological groundings—along with its mother organization, MXGM—remained significantly shaped by nationalist traditions of U.S. black radicalism.[26] Black August's use of the term New Afrikan in its literature to refer to Afro-descendant populations marked an alignment with a particular post-1960s vein of black-left nationalism along those of the Black Liberation Army (BLA) and the New Afrikan People's Organization (NAPO), members of which have been imprisoned or, as in the case of a few including Assata Shakur and Nehanda Abiodun, forced into exile. Black August's support for an older cohort of imprisoned radicals and broader anti-prison focus grew in important part out of intergenerational networks of solidarity with this history. Hip hop in this light is viewed as a temporal bridge through which political sensibilities sought translation into a new era of social activism.

Amid these converging currents of black radicalism, revolutionary internationalism, and hip hop itself, post-1959 Cuba has played its own historical part. Building upon legacies of support for African American radicals dating back to Fidel Castro's impromptu 1960 meeting with Malcolm X in Harlem, the U.S. black left has shared a long, if at times ambivalent, history of solidarity with revolutionary Cuba (Joseph 2002; Reitan 1999). Concurrent with Cuba's anticolonial involvements in Africa, a stream of prominent figures including Black Panthers Eldridge Cleaver and Huey Newton, and others like Stokely Carmichael and Angela Davis, visited or spent time in exile in Cuba during the 1960s and 1970s. As one of the first African Americans to receive asylum, the radical iconoclast Robert Williams hosted a Havana-based AM radio program, *Radio Free Dixie*, whose 1961–65 broadcast mingling music, news, and political commentary targeted black communities along the southeastern United States. Yet Williams, like a number of subsequent African Americans, left Cuba disillusioned about the perceived shortcomings of the Revolution's antiracist commitments (cf. Clytus and Rieker 1970). There have been related suggestions that Cuban support for U.S. black radicals not only served as a proxy challenge to U.S. imperialism, but also offered a popular means of deflecting domestic attention from Cuba's own incongruences of race (C. Moore 1988).

Tensions notwithstanding, such histories have engendered their own structures of feeling and forms of social memory in Cuba. Tapping into a moment of this history, I recall my friend Rita reminiscing about her school-age experience singing the popular solidarity song "¡Por Angela!" calling for the freeing of Angela Davis from imprisonment in the United States during the early 1970s.[27] As Rita shared the song, clenched fist raised high, she began to cry as emotionally laden memories of the period returned to her. Although she was not Afro-Cuban herself, Rita's nostalgias were rooted in an affective sense of political solidarity that she, as a child of the Cuban Revolution, shared with African Americans in their labors for social justice.

A more immediate set of conversations began with the arrival of Assata Shakur, who, following a prison escape and period of underground activity in the United States, was granted political asylum in Cuba in the mid-1980s. A former Panther long active in black radical circles in the New York area, Shakur was also the godmother of the late hip hop artist turned global icon Tupac Shakur, an association not lost on many hip hop devotees in both the United States and Cuba. Indeed, given narrative form in her 2001 autobiography, *Assata*, Shakur's life of radicalism has attracted popular support among a younger generation of politically minded U.S. hip hop artists and affiliated activists, their ranks comprising much of the energy behind a 2005 "Hands Off Assata" campaign organized in response to a U.S. Justice Department's $1 million bounty for her capture.[28] Black August's co-dedication of the 2000 festival to Shakur reflects these solidarities.

Black August's conjoining of Cuban hip hop and the lives of African American political exiles was held as part and parcel of the same project. To these ends Black August hosted a series of annual benefit concerts in New York City with the dual purpose of raising funds in support of imprisoned African American radicals and their families, while providing modest material assistance to Cuba's hip hop community. With 1998 marking the project's inaugural year and initial Cuban foray, artists Mos Def (aka Yasiin Bey) and Talib Kweli, then of the duo Black Star, alongside MCs Sticman and M1 of Dead Prez, performed under Black August's umbrella at the festival. Mergings of music and politics endured the following year as the Chicago-born artist Common interrupted his festival performance to read a letter of solidarity addressed to the audience from Dr. Mutulu Shakur—a former NAPO member and stepfather of Tupac Shakur currently imprisoned in the United States. Provoking a stir among Cuban higher-ups, the impromptu presentation was prompted by Nehanda Abiodun, who I am told provided the letter and encouraged its reading.[29] Common later released the track "A Song for Assata," likely evolving out of his time in Cuba, on his album *Like Water for Chocolate* (2000), which recounted Shakur's experience of imprisonment in the United States.[30]

Black August's political affinities were not limited to nationalist claims of blackness, however. The collective's 2000 co-dedication to Vieques, Puerto Rico, underscored a transnational frame of social justice that, reminiscent of internationalist orientations of earlier moments, recognized the often imbricated linkages between antiracist and anti-imperialist struggle. Black

August's attention to Vieques also reflected the New York–based collective's sensitivity to histories of Puerto Rican radicalism and labors for national independence, legacies of which found current expression in the campaign to free the island of Vieques from over sixty years of U.S. military occupation, an effort in which mainland Puerto Ricans played a vocal role.

A number of Nuyorican cultural activists were in fact integral to Black August's formation and inaugural Cuban launching. Key among these was Clyde Valentine, cofounder and editor of the now defunct hip hop magazine *Stress* and a founding member of Black August. Another who shares enduring connections with Havana raperos is Marinieves Alba, a Nuyorican activist, writer, and events producer who helped organize a 2003 U.S. tour of Havana-based artists culminating in a concert in Harlem's historic Apollo Theater alongside the Roots. The Oakland, California, area brothers Kahlil and Eli Jacobs-Fantauzzi are two other enduring Puerto Rican supporters of Havana's hip hop community, with Eli's 2003 film *Inventos: Hip Hop Cubano* marking one of the earliest documentary treatments of Cuban hip hop. The New York–based journalist Cristina Verán, moreover, was one of the first in the United States to document Cuba's emerging hip hop scene (Verán 1998), while the Bronx-born performance artist Caridad De La Luz, aka La Bruja, accompanied the bill during the 2001 hip hop festival.

These collaborative involvements, once more, elaborated upon legacies of Spanish colonial and U.S. imperial antagonism shared between the island nations of Cuba and Puerto Rico. Such communion finds poetic form in the celebrated verse "Cuba y Puerto Rico son de un pájaro las dos alas, reciben flores y balas, sobre el mismo corazón" (Cuba and Puerto Rico are a bird's two wings, receiving flowers and bullets in the same heart), penned in 1863 by the Puerto Rican abolitionist and *independista* poet Lola Rodríguez de Tió and later memorialized in Cuba by Pablo Milanés in his 1978 ballad "Son de Cuba a Puerto Rico." Yet his moment also built upon a rich history of Nuyorican participation in hip hop dating back to its artistic birth in the mid-1970s. Hip hop's early development is indebted to the cultural interchange and political affinity-making between African American, West Indian, and Puerto Rican youth in New York City (see Chang 2005). Such intimacies, Raquel Rivera argues, were grounded in Nuyoricans' shared experiences of racial marginalization and histories of Afrodiasporic belonging forged, as mentioned, through overlapping lines of blackness and latinidad (Rivera 2003). Black August's Cuban project can therefore be seen as elaborating on such interwoven affinities of race, diaspora, and hip hop via circulatory solidarities of U.S.-Cuban exchange.

Black August's involvements with Cuban hip hop ran in close conversation with efforts of another noted New Yorker, Danny Hoch. As a Jewish hip-hop-identified performance artist, playwright, and cultural activist raised in Queens, Hoch has long been an active interlocutor with Havana's hip hop community. Building upon a network of relationships developed with local MCs and others involved in Havana's scene since the mid-1990s, Hoch organized a number of collaborative projects including the previously mentioned 2001 tour of Havana-based raperos to New York City. Hoch has also incorporated lines of his Cuban experience into a number of his performance pieces, including the previously mentioned *Jails, Hospitals & Hip-Hop* and later *Till the Break of Dawn* (2007). As Nehanda Abiodun recalls, Hoch, along with the venerable early hip hop notable Fab 5 Freddy (aka Fred Brathwaite), hosted the first installment of Black August's Havana concerts during the 1998 festival.[31]

Returning to that August festival night, a heightened energy of excitement was ever tangible as the audience milled about in anticipation of the evening's performance. Though both Dead Prez and the Nuyorican DJ turned music producer Tony Touch were headlining the bill, it was Dead Prez's Afrocentric duo of M1 and Sticman who set the night's tone. In a build-up to the artists' entrance, their support crew projected images of Nelson Mandela, armed African soldiers, and black shackled fists raised aloft on two giant screens that framed the Cuban flag at stage rear. When Dead Prez finally arrived, the crowd roared with excitement, many of them possibly recalling their initial festival foray two years earlier. The duo opened with their nationalist ode "I'm a African" from their 2000 debut album, *Let's Get Free*. The scene was spectacular. The two dreadlocked artists, surrounded by a stoic cordon of Cuban police below, rallied close to three thousand darker-skinned youth in unison: "I'm a African, I'm a African / And I know what's happenin'! / You a African, You a African / Do you know what's happenin'?" English proficiency was apparently not necessary for shared intelligibility, one that seemed to be conveyed at least in part along lines of racial identification. Directly following Dead Prez's lead, Tony Touch received a notably cooler response from the crowd, this despite his efforts at Nuyorican Spanish and self-billing as Tony Toca (Tony "Touch").

Dead Prez spoke not a word of Spanish, yet they appeared to turn the house out.

I recall Obsesión's Alexey Rodríguez, with whom I had traveled to the festival that evening, commenting on how impressed he was with Dead Prez's performance, noting, "Su mensaje tenía tremenda fuerza" (Their message had tremendous force). Although Alexey had little fluency in English, he was quite familiar with Dead Prez and the politically charged nature of their music, relying like others on translation assistance from English-speaking friends like myself. He expressed concern, however, about one of the duo's songs that evening, "They Schools," which offered a blistering rebuke of the U.S. public education system. Alexey felt Dead Prez's indignation was way over the top, taking particular issue with the line "All my high school teachers can suck my dick, telling me white-ass lies and bullshit," which he felt was excessively disrespectful. I shared with him my reading of the song as a critique of a corrupt and racist education system, rather than a personal attack on teachers per se—one systemic rather than individual in nature. Alexey was not particularly swayed by my interpretation. I wondered at the time if our disconnect might relate to long-standing tendencies in revolutionary Cuba to privilege understandings of individual over structural expressions of racism, often obfuscating broader systemic workings of racialized power and privilege. In a more immediate sense it was likely that Alexey, as an Afro-Cuban, simply had difficulty identifying with Dead Prez's level of black anger and societal alienation.

This discord reminded me of a distinction raperos often made between their music and much of the more commercially oriented hip hop in the United States. Gangsta thuggery, hyper-materialized bling, and virulent misogyny, so ubiquitous in corporately promoted U.S. hip hop, were conspicuously (and often self-consciously) absent from Cuban hip hop. While hyperbolic in their seemingly endless commercial reproduction, such masculinist tropes nonetheless emerge in conversation with histories of structural violence painfully endemic to postindustrial U.S. black urban life. Thus while lines of racial affinity may have been in play that festival evening, Cuba and by extension Cuban hip hop were in this sense indeed different.

This cultural divide resonated with an experience I later had following a screening of the documentary film *One Dollar: El precio de la vida* during the Havana Film Festival in 2002. Directed by the Panamanian American filmmaker Héctor Herrera, *One Dollar* chronicles the aftereffects of the 1989 U.S. invasion of Panama on poor working-class Afro-Panamanians in Panama City, depicting in brutal fashion the subsequent intensification of violence, guns, and drug trafficking within these communities. Having attended the screening with a handful of friends, I asked MC Michael Oramas of the hip hop crew Junior Clan about his thoughts on the film. Michael responded incredulously, "Todo lo que presentó no puede ser real—algunos son falsos, fabricados. Era demasiado" (Everything they presented cannot be real—some are false, made up. It was too much). As critically minded and self-declared "underground" as Michael considered himself, he found it difficult to imagine such a violently desperate set of circumstances plaguing black folks. While the dollar was also rapidly transforming the lived everyday in Cuba, there were still few if any Caribbean, Latin American, or for that matter U.S. cities as relatively free of drugs, guns, and violent crime as Havana. Cuba and its revolutionary history remained (if for the current moment) notably different in this sense, a distinction that defied simple intraracial translation while underscoring divergent historical positions vis-à-vis the destructive tendencies of global capital and legacies of U.S. hegemony.

That said, there did appear to be salient connections that festival evening between Dead Prez's racially charged message and their young Cuban audience. A shared sense of social belonging and/or common vocabulary seemed to resonate. Reflecting on the internationalist dimensions of the moment, the festival's coordinator Rodolfo Rensoli cited Black August's participation and hip hop as enabling dialogue between Cuban and U.S. MCs by way of diasporic currents of black identification. Regarding such workings, Rensoli explained:

> I used this idea of diaspora to help understand how blacks in the United States, or blacks in the Caribbean, or blacks in other parts of the Americas are all brothers. Part of our family went here, another part went there, and for a long time we've hardly looked into each other's faces. All these reflections came to me after my own experience with the festival, after the level of communication between North American and Cuban raperos helped me realize that there was a lot more in common between us.[32]

Reflecting further on the moment's dialogic possibilities, Ariel Fernández Díaz recalls:

The racial identity in the hip hop movement was there, the connection with Black August just helped frame it, you know what I mean, to give it better form and a better way to articulate itself. Because we definitely needed and we definitely didn't have the intellectual and conceptual understanding of what we were trying to express. So we're not saying that they taught us what we need to be addressing or talking about—we knew that we needed to talk about—we were doing it way before. I mean, look at "Ochavon cruzao" from '96 way before Black August.[33] We were talking about race before Black August.

So when Black August came we felt like someone had our backs. We had support and another platform to validate the points that we were already making. Black people have helped create the history of this country, and black people who have fought in the independence war and the revolution have not been fully recognized by the state, which is mostly dominated by white people. And with the denial of any kind of black racial identity with this thing "we are all Cuban" and "there is no thing as black or white Cubans," you don't have anything to grab onto or gravitate to. So suddenly you had people who helped us understand better what we were trying to talk about and give it better intellectual form.[34]

Echoing similar lines, Pablo Herrera adds:

When Black August started coming to Cuba we found that we could identify with them, the same way they could identify with us. It wasn't that they brought the politics to us, that they made us understand what race meant, this is false. . . . That was a beautiful moment to be part of a major moment of Pan-Africanism and solidarity between the people of the United States and Cuba, African Americans and Afro-Cubans. Becoming aware of the resources and the political activism that they were doing in New York and San Francisco gave us tools to try and understand how to deal with the shit here. We need to deal with the shit here in a radical way. So I think something that is really important to talk about here is how cosmopolitan Cuba became through Black August.[35]

While diasporic affinities and appeals to a black cosmopolitanism may indeed have been instrumental during that and subsequent festivals, there did appear to be limitations in their practice. I recall frustrations arising during the 2000 festival over the limited degree of contact between local raperos and Black August's New York entourage. In the case of Dead Prez, the only opportunity most Cuban MCs had to engage the duo was a few fleeting minutes backstage just prior to their festival performance. Given their connectedness, Pablo and Ariel were considerably more adroit in accessing the visiting artists. Pablo in particular, with his English fluency and local position as a Black August liaison, appeared to spend significant time during the festival in the company of artists and other Black August members. For others, handshakes, embraces, and autographs were plentiful, but often not much else. For many in the Black August delegation, the priority of the Cuban trip appeared more centered on connecting with African American political exiles on the island rather than intentional structured time for *intercambio* (exchange) with Havana's hip hop community.

The afternoon following Black August's festival program I attended a meeting in an Alamar cultural center as part of the festival's *coloquio* (colloquium) series. In a dimly lit room with a handful of metal chairs and small desks, roughly a dozen raperos and a few supporting cast members engaged in a freewheeling discussion around issues, concerns, and grievances affecting the hip hop community. One complaint concerned a lack of access to visiting U.S. artists. Some members of the Diez y Diecinueve crew, for instance, complained of their efforts to visit the Black August delegation in their Vedado hotel only to be denied entrance beyond the lobby by hotel security. I had myself spent time with the Black August entourage during the festival, and in most cases these spaces largely conformed to the logics of Cuba's new apartheid economy that tended to segregate Cubans from dollar-paying foreign tourists and their restricted zones of consumption. Revolutionary appeals to solidarity notwithstanding, global hierarchies of social difference did not in the end appear to dissolve.

Another key issue raised at that afternoon's exchange concerned the festival's large police presence. Veteran MC Yrak Saenz of Doble Filo, for one, was incensed by what he felt was the disrespectful treatment from police the night before. Yrak recounted how he was harassed and questioned as he tried to move about the stage—behavior that in his mind amounted to "¡una falta de respeto en mi propia casa!" (a lack of respect in my own house!). While sharing his account he rubbed his finger along the underside of his forearm, invoking the everyday Cuban gesture for blackness (i.e., "it's in the blood") to underscore the raced significance of his encounter. During the ensuing discussion there were complaints that hip hop shows seemed to always draw more attention from the police than salsa concerts, which they claimed were notorious for drunken spats of violence. Others chimed in about rock shows, whose gatherings of mostly "white" youth rarely, if ever, garnered the police attention with which hip hop had to contend.

The difference, they claimed, was hip hop's association with black youth, whom Cuban police often indexed, again in a historically resonant sense, with antisocial behavior aligned with violence and criminality. Many pointed out that in fact fights rarely if ever occurred at hip hop events in Cuba. In my experience this was indeed largely the case, remarkably refreshing given the history of hip hop concerts in the United States where one often had to be on guard against the looming specter of violent confrontation. By contrast, my forays into Havana's hip hop spaces often exhibited a camaraderie and absence of animosity among audience members. Havana's hip hop community was not free of internal tensions and interpersonal grievances—far from it. Yet violence, criminality, and other so-called antisocial(ist) tendencies in my experience were largely absent from hip hop followings in Havana. Nonetheless, the large police presence (and by extension the Cuban state) appeared to think and act otherwise, perpetuating a long-standing Cuban practice of policing black bodies and spaces.

Anónimo Consejo

The energy set in motion by Dead Prez and company that second festival evening continued to build throughout the night as local Cuban groups passed the torch. Closing out the show was the duo Yosmel Sarrías (aka Sekou Messiah Umoja) and Maigel "Kokino" Entenza of Anónimo Consejo (Anonymous Advice). Donned in a collage of Vietnamese-style straw hats, oversized Che Guevara T-shirts, and amply baggy jeans with a single pant leg hoisted aloft in au courant hip hop fashion, the duo hit the stage to a ruckus reception. Although I had been aware of Anónimo Consejo and their reputation as two of the most dynamic and lyrically provocative MCs in Cuba, I had yet to see them perform.

Natives of the neighboring seaside municipality of Cojimar, Anónimo Consejo were among the local favorites, and it showed. Working the crowd through a series of call-and-response riffs, the duo had the riled-up audience singing in animated harmony with many of their songs. The most exuberant response seemed to arrive with their performance of "Las apa-

3.3. MCs Sekou Umoja (*left*) and Kokino Entenza of Anónimo Consejo.
Photo by Sahily Borrero

riencias engañan" (Appearances can deceive). Couched in tones of indignation, the tema offered entry into the hardships of black youth navigating
the island's new dollarized geographies, and the Cuban state's often raced
efforts to police and regulate these marked spaces of exclusionary privilege.
An extended excerpt of the tema follows:

"Las apariencias engañan"

¡Anónimo Consejo Revolución!
¡Yosmel y Kokino Revolución!
No me la aprietes más
que yo sigo aquí
No me la aprietes más, déjame vivir
Por mí Cuba lo doy todo soy feliz
Y tú sigues reprendía en mí,
suéltame a mí
No te confundas con la arena que pisas
Dos pasos más y se te recuerda
que estas en área divisa, Varadero

Todo no es como lo pintan
y yo sigo aquí de frente a los problemas
Aguantando con mi mano el hierro caliente
Sin pasarme por la mente coger una balsa
Y probar suerte en
otra orilla—a 90 millas
Todo no es como lo pintan
y yo sigo aquí
Cada paso en la calle es una preocupación
Extranjero en busca de comunicación
Con la población,
5 minutos de conversación
Policía en acción sin explicación
Andando pa' la estación
Trabajes o no trabajes,
ellos no pueden creer
Que estés hablando de cualquier otra cosa
. . .
Entonces te vas a reprender en mí
Yo que vivo y muero aquí
Yo que nací con el concepto y el ideal de
José Martí
Déjate de abuso
Coge mi coro cubano que dice
Yo sigo aquí, jamando el mismo cable que tú
Yo sigo aquí, preparando el mismo vaso de agua con azúcar que
bebes tú
Yo sigo aquí, cogiendo el mismo camello insoportable que coges tú
Yo sigo aquí, con el mismo pan de la
libreta que te comes tú
Con el apagón que molesta
Piénsalo antes de arrestarme
Justifica tu pregunta, yo tengo mi respuesta
. . .
Entonces porque ¡coño! Te reprendes en mí
Yo que sigo aquí junto a ti
Sal de mí no me la aprietes más

¡Déjame vivir!
Esto no es pa' que te erices
Esto no es pa' que me caces la pelea
Esto es para que entiendas de una vez y por todas
Que todos los jóvenes no somos basura
Porque la divisa ha cambiado la forma de pensar de mucha gente
Y mucha de esa gente no somos nosotros,
los jóvenes cubanos, quienes apoyamos
la idea de lo que es revolución en todos los momentos

Anónimo Consejo Revolution!
Yosmel and Kokino Revolution!
Don't squeeze me anymore
because I'm still here
Don't squeeze me anymore, let me live
For my Cuba I give all, I am happy
And you continue to hassle me
let me go
Don't confuse yourself with the sand you step on
Two more steps and you'll be reminded
that you are in a dollar zone, Varadero[36]
Everything is not how it is painted
and I am still here confronting problems
Holding with my hand the hot iron
Without considering taking a raft
And trying my luck on
another shore—90 miles away
Everything is not how it is painted
and I am still here
Every step in the street is a preoccupation
Foreigner looking for communication
With the population,
5 minutes of conversation
Police in action without explanation
Going to the station
Whether you work or don't work,
they can't believe

That you're talking of other things
. . .
So then you're going to hassle me
I that live and die here
I was born with the concept and the ideal of
José Martí
Drop this abuse
Take my Cuban chorus that says
I'm still here, in the same situation as you
I'm still here, preparing the same glass of water with sugar that you
drink
I'm still here, taking the same horrible bus
that you take
I am still here, with the same bread from the
libreta [ration book] that you eat
With the same annoying [electrical] blackouts
Think about it before arresting me
Justify your questions, I have my answer
. . .
Then why the fuck do you hassle me
I who am still here together with you
Leave me alone, don't squeeze me anymore
Let me live!
This is not to make your skin crawl
This is not to make you fight with me
This is so you can understand once and for all
That not all the young people are garbage
Because the dollar has changed many peoples'
way of thinking
And many of those people aren't us,
the young Cubans who support
the idea of what revolution is at all moments

This selection is an exemplar of Anónimo Consejo's contestive brand
of music making that long positioned them as two of the most respected
MCs in the movement. It also vividly illustrates the political character and
highly poetic use of social critique in rapero lyricism. Most immediately,

"Las apariencias" voices in bold undiluted fashion the frustration and social anger experienced by black youth, while introducing a key set of problematics around questions of citizenship recurrent in Cuban hip hop. A central concern addressed here is the systemics of police harassment within Cuba's new monetized economy. Although not explicitly sited, race and racialized profiling are integral in the tema's critique. Allusions to being "squeezed," "reprimanded," and arrested by police for simply speaking with foreigners evokes the experience of darker-skinned youth as discussed of being racially marked as jineteros/as when in the company of foreigners.

Citing the sands of Cuba's famed tourist district Varadero—"en área divisa" (a dollar zone) and one largely off-limits at the time to Cubans—underscores the limitations of Cuban citizenship within the island's new market-driven landscape. Rather than "coger una balsa" and flee to the United States like so many from their seaside barrio, including one of Yosmel's older brothers during the 1994 balsero crisis, Anónimo Consejo proclaim their determination to remain faithful to Cuba through the struggles of everyday life—the same struggles, they point out, faced by their compatriots, the police. While "the dollar has changed the way of thinking of many," they have stood fast in their support and belief in "the idea" of revolution. Here, the duo's claim "I was born with the concept and the ideal of José Martí" is ripe with significance. The statement moors their demands for fair and equal treatment by the police (and state) as *black* Cubans squarely within the island's grounding narrative of nationhood. Such assertions of citizenship—to be both black *and* Cuban—are in this sense implicit in the very historical inception of *cubanidad* (Cubanness). Yet the emphasis here is one centered on the "ideal" (rather than the "appearance") of Martí's vision and the ensuing "idea" of revolution "at all [its various] moments" to which Anónimo Consejo remain committed.

Overlapping frames of race and revolution, as discussed, have occupied an important place among many black-identified members of Cuba's hip hop community. Such framings, however, are often predicated on implicit (or not so implicit) critiques of contemporary Cuban society and, by extension to varying degrees, the Cuban state itself. The emphasis here is on the nationally imbricated *ideals* of racial equality and revolutionary struggle— ideals understood as unrealized, if not significantly compromised, within the current Cuban moment. The key tension lies then between the principled claims of a postracial revolutionary society and the quotidian realities of race as presently lived. Cuban hip hop thus emerges precisely amid these incongruencies of race, nation, and revolution, while engaging those same incongruencies from a vantage point of a racially positioned critique. Within this context, discourses of revolution take on a marked racial signif- icance; there is no "revolution" without racial equality and justice, the two intrinsically joined at the hip (hop), so to speak.

Yosmel and Kokino's signature chant "¡Anónimo Consejo Revolución!," which both opens and closes "Las apariencias," is emblematic of their flam- boyant use of revolutionary discourse and imagery in their music. This same phrase, encircling an iconic image of Che Guevera's star-capped portrait, is inscribed in the form of matching tattoos on the duo's right shoulders as markers of their fidelity to, and embodied membership within, the revolu- tionary nation. This discursive play on revolution finds further expression in Anónimo Consejo's celebrated mantra "Hip Hop Revolution," a motto that assumed collective resonance among many local raperos.

When asked about this call to revolution, Yosmel and Kokino explained that their invocations of "revolution" were not in fact reducible to the Cuban Revolution, at least not directly so. Rather, they directed me to the term's dictionary definition referring to radical, progressively directed social change. Such positions appear to differ from more explicit forms of Cuban revolutionary identification voiced, for instance, by Magia and Alexey of Obsesión. This is not to suggest that Obsesión did not share in the move- ment's articulations with broader notions of revolutionary struggle. In the case of Yosmel and Kokino, however, the emphasis seemed placed on al- ternative revolutionary horizons, ones not necessarily beholden to national proscriptive frames.

Internal Revolutions?

One potentially productive way to consider how raperos and their follow- ers view their relationship to overlapping discourses of revolution is via the oft-touted analogy of Cuban hip hop as a "revolution within a revolution." The implication here is that hip hop is organic to, and ultimately operates within, the broader terrain of revolutionary society—the struggle and ef- forts of change therefore emanating from "inside" rather than "outside." Such posturing is in line with refrains long voiced by many raperos that their work is by no means positioned *against* the revolutionary project. Claims of this kind undoubtedly carry a certain tactical currency given the Cuban state's general intolerance for public forms of dissent that might undermine the holy trinity of la Revolución, el estado, and el pueblo—one given embodied authority in Fidel Castro's famed declaration "Dentro de la Revolución, todo; contra la Revolución, nada" (Within the Revolution, everything; against the Revolution, nothing) (see Castro 1961).

Yet on another level, as I have suggested, many raperos held genuine degrees of identification with the ideals and principles of the Cuban Revolution, many of which they were devoted to fight for and defend. Indeed, these youth represent a generation of socially engaged artists shaped by socialist-derived notions of egalitarianism embedded in revolutionary Cuban society. Many saw their public role in this light as internal, socially productive agents of change. Their stance resonates in this sense with strategies mediated by critically positioned intellectuals during the revolutionary period. The Cuban cultural critic Desiderio Navarro argues, for instance, that such intellectual currents are vital to the revolutionary process itself, suggesting that their intervention,

> far from being a threat to socialism, is its "oxygen," its "motor": a necessity for the survival and well-being of the revolutionary process. The critical intellectuals believe that social criticism can constitute a threat only when it is silenced or even met with reprisals, when it is confined to a closed guild or institutional enclave, when it is placed in a communicational vacuum under a bell jar, or—and this above all else—when it goes unanswered or when, recognized as correct, it is not taken into account in political practice. (Navarro 2002: 201)

One finds a similar analysis echoed in the words of Kokino, who qualified: "Our critique or our protest is constructive. The idea of Anónimo Consejo is not to throw the revolution to the floor. It is rather to make a revolution within the revolution. It is to criticize the things, or to protest the things, that are not well within the Cuban Revolution. But our objective is not to harass or be destructive, but it is to make a new Cuba for young people."[37]

For many raperos like Kokino, demands for a socially and racially just Cuba and broader world stem first and foremost from the principles embodied within the promise of Cuban socialism. Their task, as expressed by many, is to reveal and critique the limitations, contradictions, and at times hypocrisy rooted in the chasm between the enduring claims and lived realities of Cuba's neoliberalized landscape, all toward the end of strengthening Cuban society. The commonly expressed sentiment "somos constructivos, no destructivos" (we are constructive, not *destructive*) resonant in Kokino's response above speaks directly to this sense of social responsibility. Ariel Fernández Díaz similarly elaborated along these lines:

> I think that hip hop takes on the necessary critique in our country to edu-cate. I always say that the best way to be a revolutionary is to be critical, you understand? The best form of art is the one that says what is good, what is bad, what is harmful, or what is missing, this is valued, this is critical, you understand? The position *most* revolutionary is to speak the truth. Art has to say what is good and what is bad. If you hide your prob-lems, or if you escape from them, nothing will be resolved. . . . Rap is a music of resistance—it is fighting for rights that the revolution *notes* but that society has not delivered.[38]

Among raperos and their followers, however, Cuba was not the sole source of revolutionary inspiration. Over the years Yosmel and Kokino have, for example, invoked the lives and struggles of African American radicals such as Malcolm X, Mumia Abu-Jamal, and Shaka Sankofa (Gary Graham), as well as Nelson Mandela in their music. When I asked what sources im-pacted their awareness of such black radicalism, the two cited Black Au-gust's participation in previous festivals as a significant influence. As I will discuss shortly, Black August was for the artists but one transnational route of engagement with U.S. black radical traditions of discourse. As I came to know Yosmel and Kokino, their music and evolving political sense of self were also significantly informed by a more immediate locus of black radical inspiration, Nehanda Abiodun. This was especially the case with Yosmel, who, under Nehanda's tutelage, eventually took on the African-signified name Sekou as an expression of his continued, ever-evolving efforts toward critical black self-fashioning.

Chapter 4.
Critical Self-Fashionings
and Their Gendering

What must whites think of the black who prides himself on his color?
—José Martí, *La cuestión racial*

El cimarrón ya no tendrás que huir en busca de nuevos horizontes.
[The cimarrón now no longer has to flee in search of new horizons.]
—Anónimo Consejo, "Cimarrón"

Although voiced a century apart, the citations above speak rather poetically to Cuba's enduring tensions of race and national citizenship. José Martí, the celebrated late nineteenth-century criollo intellectual who gave visionary form to the island's nonracial national foundations, poses a cautionary query to black Cubans who might foreground racial identity over the national. The consequences of such moves were soon laid bare in the infamous "Race War" of 1912 involving the island-wide massacre of thousands of Afro-Cubans in the wake of state efforts to eradicate the perceived threat of an emergent Partido Independiente de Color (Independent Party of Color) and its calls for full citizenship rights for blacks within a new Cuban republic. Echoes of this trauma abound; the Havana-based hip hop duo Anónimo Consejo offer a present-day rejoinder to this history in the redemptive figure of the African *cimarrón* (maroon), whose radical pursuit of black freedom and sovereign community is deemed no longer hollow.

As previously discussed, expressive realms such as music and the literary arts have long served as creative mediums through which Afro-Cubans imagine alternative understandings of blackness in ways that varyingly articulate with and diverge from a racially hybridized, if ultimately postracial, cubanidad. Afro-Cuban efforts to navigate the historical constraints of a nonracial Cuban nationhood have in turn had to grapple with a key dilemma of citizenship: how to be mutually yet non-self-negatingly both Cuban and black. Such discord evokes a certain contradictory "twoness" of Afrodiasporic condition that W. E. B. Du Bois addressed so eloquently roughly a century ago (Du Bois [1903] 1989). Although Du Bois was concerned in an immediate sense with the struggle of post-emancipatory African Americans, his reflections on black subjectivity and racialized marginality speak to the wider hemispheric ambivalences of national belonging and citizenship lived by African-descendant communities throughout the Americas.

For Afro-Cubans, mediating the enduring friction between blackness and Cubanness as discussed has included efforts to reach beyond the island's territorial and ideological bounds in the fashioning of coherent understandings of black Cuban selfhood. As with previous moments, Cuban raperos have sought their own performative routes to such black alterity through polyphonic claims to black citizenship via both the national and the transnational. Indeed, it is precisely to these nuevos horizontes (new horizons) that Anónimo Consejo's cimarrón currently turns.

Pedagogies of Black Radicality

Between 2000 and 2002, a pair of rapero-affiliated spaces emerged in differing yet complementary ways as sites of racial politicization for a number of key individuals in Havana's hip hop community. The spaces in question were two informally organized "classes" geared toward redressing, in their respective nationalist frameworks, themes of black radical struggle and history. These venues also provided meaningful dialogue between local raperos and members of an older generation of black intellectuals, in this case one Afro-Cuban and one African American in political exile. One individual who embodied a vibrant confluence of these two spheres of black radical (re)articulation was Yosmel Sarrías (aka Sekou Messiah Umoja) of Anónimo Consejo. His involvements in both classes were very much a critical outgrowth of, as well as a significant contributing factor to, his ongoing political, artistic, and personal maturation as a prominent and highly respected "old-school" Cuban MC.

In 2000 the African American political exile Nehanda Abiodun began holding occasional gatherings in her home in one of Habana del Este's high-rise apartment blocks. Stemming from an initial conversation with a visiting U.S. college student friend, the gatherings grew out of a desire among some Havana-area raperos for dialogue about legacies of African American struggle and forms of radical organizing. As Nehanda described it:

> That open space started out with rappers coming to me and asking me about Malcolm X, asking me about the movement in the United States, not only the Civil Rights Movement but also the Black Power Movement. "What is the Black Liberation Movement? What was the participation of white people? What was the relationship between various movements in the United States?" they asked. And they were not only interested in finding out about the history, my history, or *their* history in the United States because we are all in this together as people of African descent, but how that history pertains to them here in Cuba. And what it is that they could use to create something here on this island without being opposed to the status quo.[1]

When I asked about raperos' particular interest in the narrative of Malcolm X, Nehanda explained: "Malcolm X represents a certain militancy for the freedom of black people; it's not only here in Cuba but it is all over the world. He talked about unity as Marcus Garvey did, but in a language that everybody could understand. He was defiant against the powers that be, and he's a hero among many. My opinion based on my observations is that for too long Cuba has been devoid of talking about their own heroes of African descent. So youth therefore are looking for answers to certain questions."

When I encountered these gatherings in 2001 they had become fairly regular weekly events, drawing an informal collection of two dozen or so young people composed of Cubans as well as an assortment of North American college students from various educational programs in Havana. Although these gatherings had an informal and often festive atmosphere, the meetings were used for serious discussion of issues ranging from the imprisonment of African American political activists, to the workings of patriarchy, to interracial dating and homophobia. These classes, as Nehanda referred to them, regularly drew a core group of local raperos, and were unique in providing a regular forum for cross-cultural dialogue around questions of race, gender, and sexuality within comparative contexts of Cuba and the United States. This kind of exchange had yet to occur in any significant way elsewhere within Havana's hip hop community, and in my experience the discussions were highly engaged and often impassioned as diverse perspectives vied and were negotiated among group members.

The impetus and conceptual framing of these exchanges were shaped in an important sense by Nehanda's commitments to a nationalist tradition of radical organizing. These efforts, she explained, were simply an extension of her ongoing work as a black revolutionary. Just because she was now in Cuba, Nehanda asserted, did not mean that her dedication to transformative change ceased to be an active part of her life. When I asked if she viewed her classes as a space of politicization, she responded: "Oh, without a doubt! I mean, why would I even have bothered? [Laughs] I am very proud of those classes, not because I was involved in them but because of what the students, what those individuals within themselves created. I mean, I was just a facilitator, but they created that space and made it what it was. And not only did they take what they learned, but so many of them both here and in Cuba pursued further investigations, further studies following their involvements in the classes."

In the several gatherings I attended, MC Yosmel Sarrías of Anónimo Consejo was consistently among the most outspoken of participants, Cuban or otherwise. His engagements always struck me as especially thoughtful and self-reflective. It was through these meetings that I first got a sense of Yosmel's rather impassioned quest for personal growth and critical self-education. Nehanda was no doubt an inspirational facet of this process. Over the years she developed close relationships with both Yosmel and his artistic partner Kokino, given in part the shared proximity of their neighboring barrios in Habana del Este. Her involvement as a mentor figure was clearly significant for the artists, in meaningful conversation with their thinking, sense of black selves, and ultimately their music.

As an illustration of the mentor-like intimacy that Nehanda shared with the two young men, sometime around 2002 she presided over a neo-African ceremony in which the artists were anointed with new Afrikan-signified names; Yosmel assumed the name Sekou Messiah Umoja and Kokino adopted Adeyeme Umoja. While Kokino would continue to be known primarily by his original name, Sekou, by contrast, came to fully embrace his new identity as testament to his evolving sense of black selfhood. Marking this ontological shift on his physicality, Sekou soon added a large tattooed image of Africa to his left shoulder encircled by the prose "Mi mente mi espíritu y mi corazón vive aquí" (My mind, my spirit, and my heart live here). This professed fidelity to Africa now sat opposite the previously discussed tattoo of Che Guevara and accompanying slogan "Anónimo Consejo Revolución" that he and Kokino jointly displayed on their right shoulders.

Poetically revealing, these juxtaposing images reflected competing narratives of citizenship—one revolutionary Cuban and decidedly masculinist, the other grounded in Afrocentric claims to a racial diaspora mediated in part through a female mentor figure, Nehanda Abiodun. As such, these discursive intersections evoked a duality of nationalist lenses through which Sekou mediated his evolving self-understandings as a black Cuban man. Indeed, similar couplings of citizenship and their overlapping revolutionary belongings serve as key self-referential paradigms of black self-making for many raperos. In Sekou's case, such alignment found performative and varyingly gendered expression through their material inscription onto the body itself.

While Nehanda's gatherings contributed to one nationalist current of black self-fashioning within Havana's hip hop community, another pedagogic space emerged during the same period intended to redress the "other side," so to speak, of Sekou's revolutionary shoulder. In 2002 Tomás Fernández Robaina, a bibliographic archivist and pioneering scholar of Afro-Cuban history at Havana's Biblioteca Nacional de José Martí, initiated an informal weekly class at the Biblioteca on themes of Afro-Cuban history. Although he had offered similar courses in the past, this most recent class evolved in dialogue with raperos themselves. Tomás's first introduction to Cuban hip hop occurred in New York City when, during an academic stint as a visiting scholar in 2001, he connected with the previously mentioned group of touring raperos composed of Pablo Herrera, Ariel Fernández Díaz, Magia López and Alexey Rodríguez of Obsesión, RCA's Julio Cardenas, and (the then) Yosmel Sarrías and Kokino Entenza of Anónimo Consejo. As Tomás explains:

In New York City I had an invitation to meet with these raperos and got a sense of their music. I realized that something good was going on—I didn't know exactly what, but I knew something was happening. When I came back to Cuba, I began to attend hip hop concerts and pay attention to the lyrics of the songs and I realized that they were doing something that none of us who have been trying to expand the idea of the black identity were able to do, or do it in the *way* they were doing it. They were showing that blackness is something important, and that we can organize and defend blackness and our black ancestors.[2]

Among an older generation of Afro-Cuban intellectuals who had fought for critical recognition of black culture and histories of struggle in Cuba, Tomás eventually embraced hip hop as part of an ongoing continuum of black political expression on the island. Rather, apropos, it was during a 2001 Havana roundtable held at the Unión Nacional de Escritores y Artistas de Cuba (UNEAC) on the Partido Independiente de Color that drew a collection of raperos and local Rastafari that Tomás decided to revive his course on Afro-Cuban history at the Biblioteca.

While Tomás's work El negro en Cuba, 1902–1958 (1990) represented a pioneering scholarly treatment of the Partido during the revolutionary period, renewed discussion of its significance among black intellectual circles at the time was sparked by a 2000 Cuban publication of a Spanish translation of historian Aline Helg's Our Rightful Share (1995) chronicling the party's rise and the ensuing 1912 massacre. Helg later collaborated with the Afro-Cuban filmmaker Gloria Rolando on Rolando's independent film Raíces de mi corazón (Roots of my heart) (2001), which represented the first major filmic treatment of the Partido in Cuba. All told, these efforts sought to restore the Partido from an obscured national memory while gesturing toward the party's long-silenced call for an inclusive citizenship both *for* and *as* black Cubans. Such reclaimation would in turn find creative resonance among many a rapero.

Among those present that day at the Partido roundtable was Ariel Fernández Díaz, who, Tomás recalls, promised to encourage a number of friends to attend the class. Regarding the subsequent involvement of raperos, Tomás explained:

They were doing certain things already, but they hadn't realized that there were many others who had done these kinds of things before. Many black intellectuals and organizations in the past had done similar social critiques about racism and social inequality. But raperos and Rastafarians in Cuba didn't know about this. So I identify with the movement through my involvement in teaching them about other black intellectuals who've done what they're doing now. And by working with these people I was trying little by little to encourage those who could teach other people.

The class, open to all, was held in an open-air corner of the Biblioteca Nacional's second-floor reading room. As small and informal as it was, the fact that a class of this kind was held in a public institution like the Biblioteca— a towering edifice abutting Havana's celebrated Plaza de la Revolución— reflected the Cuban state's recent opening to more public discussions of racial themes within institutional spheres. Similar conversations were occurring in places like UNEAC, where a well-attended symposium organized around Nicolás Guillén's poetic theme "Color Cubano" occurred that same year. On an average day Tomás's class drew roughly a dozen or so participants, the vast majority of whom were young men and women, almost exclusively black or darker skinned. The core among those classes I attended were graduate students, politically oriented artists, and a number of Rasta and hip-hop-affiliated individuals, among whom Ariel, Sekou, and Magia López and Alexey Rodríguez of Obsesión were among the most consistent. Predicated on Tomás's similarly titled work, the class "El negro en Cuba" centered on black antiracist and antidiscriminatory activism during the twentieth century prior to 1959,[3] and sought to expand on his text's central thesis: Afro-Cuban mediations of the island's historic tensions of race and nationhood. Here the fundamental struggle framed by Tomás was one tied to Afro-Cuban efforts to attain full citizenship rights within a Martí-envisioned nonracial Cuba.

Foregrounding raced agencies in the making of Cuban national history in this manner represented something of a revisionist undertaking aimed at redressing historical omissions of Afro-Cubans as critical subjects from Cuba's official past (Ferrer 1998a; Kapcia 2000; cf. Trouillot 1995). I underscore critical here to foreground a distinction between Afro-Cubans as positioned actors rather than consumable objects of historical processes as they have all too often been cast within prevailing national scripts, be they incorporative grammars of transculturation or folklore. Tomás's class offered a space for precisely this kind of recuperative intervention, albeit a notably male-centered one. Antonio Maceo, the Partido Independiente de Color, the Afro-Cuban journalist Gustavo Urrutia, and more recent figures such as the author-activists Juan René Betancourt and Walterio Carbonell figured centrally within discussion, while narratives of black women's contributions remained largely absent.

Gendering notwithstanding, Magia of Obsesión reflected on her experience of attending Tomás's class:

> Back in technical school I got into arguments with my teachers and the principal because they used racist expressions, but I only started to develop race consciousness through hip hop culture, especially after a workshop given by Tomás Robaina sometime between late 2001 and early 2002. He talked about the 1912 Race War in Cuba, the black leader Evaristo Estenoz [founding member of the Partido Independiente de Color], the black massacre—it was a shock. I remember Alexey and I going away feeling angry. (Rodríguez 2011)

Echoing similar understandings, Randy Acosta of the hip hop duo Los Paisanos recalled the following about his participation in Tomás's class: "As I started to attend the class I soon realized I was learning things I didn't know about myself. I found a bit I didn't know, and I kept going. I came to know things I wouldn't even remotely have known, things my family did not know. One day we were asked if we knew anything about Evaristo Estenoz, and no one knew who he was." When I asked why this was important, Randy responded:

> This is our history! It's the history here in Cuba that has to do with me, one that I identify with. It's part of the [national] struggle and it's that black part of me that fought and gave its part to the Cuban Revolution. They always talk about [General] Máximo Gómez[4]—all the things he did in developing war strategies and combat. But where is Antonio Maceo? Where is the Partido Independiente de Color? Why not talk about these people? They were people in Cuba's history and you know nothing of their story. That's what we were talking about in class.[5]

As a partial outgrowth of such conversations, Randy and his artistic partner Jessel Saladriga Fernández aka El Huevo composed "Lo Negro" (The Black). The song aimed at addressing stigmas attached to blackness viewed as inhibiting affirmations of black identity among many Cubans of African descent. As Randy explained, "Lo Negro" was intended as "a warning to blacks who don't want to be black due to long histories of disinformation." Such concerns held personal resonance for Randy, who, as discussed earlier, moved through hip hop to embrace a political sense of black identity despite his light-brown color of skin. Indeed, as if to add exclamation to the point, the duo riff in the chorus to "Lo Negro": "Negro, es mi pensamiento / Negro, son mis movimientos / Negro, es como me siento / Negro, por fuera y por dentro" (Black, is my thought / Black, are my movements / Black, is how I feel / Black, outside and inside).

While reclaiming histories of black radicality may have been of mutual interest to those in Tomás's class, interpretations of these narratives were not necessarily always aligned. One dynamic that emerged involved subtle differences in positionality between Tomás and some of the younger participants in the course. For example, one afternoon Tomás turned to Antonio Maceo's celebrated quote "Nunca pedir como negro, sólo como cubano" (Never ask as a black, only as a Cuban) to underscore the ways Afro-Cuban struggle has long been predicated on citizenship claims *within* a nonracial national logic as opposed to calls for racial autonomy (cf. de la Fuente 1999; Ferrer 1999). While speaking with Sekou after class, he told me he took issue with Tomás's suggestion, drawn from Maceo's statement, that Afro-Cubans were implicitly Cubans before they were black. In contrast, Sekou responded definitely, "Soy africano antes de todo" (I'm African [first] before all). In later conversation along similar lines, Alexey Rodríguez of Obsesión suggested he too considered himself a *negro* before his Cubanness—something I found a bit surprising at the time, given Alexey's strong identification with and fidelity to the nationalist ideals of the Cuban Revolution. In both cases these statements suggested evolving forms of self-identification, if not multiple citizenship claims, rooted in notions of racial diaspora that transcended both the territorial and discursive bounds of Cuban nationhood.

An important nuance of difference between Tomás and his younger class participants was generational. Now in his sixties, Tomás is from an earlier generation of Afro-Cuban intellectuals socialized and trained during the height of the Cuban Revolution. As such, his identity as an intellectual and as a black man is deeply intertwined with the rise of the revolutionary project in complexly lived ways. As a gay-identified, light-brown-skinned man who would commonly be read as mestizo, Tomás often spoke of his long fight for recognition as a gay black man within exclusionary circles that might otherwise deny him entry on both grounds. Full inclusion and acceptance of his multiply queer subjectivity—that is, black *and* gay—within the prevailing frames that have long rendered these markers of difference ideologically incoherent with the revolutionary project (Allen 2011; Arenas 1993; Bejel 2001; de la Fuente 2001; González Pagés 2004; Lumsden 1996; Saunders 2009; Sawyer 2005) was thus a committed facet of Tomás's intellectual politics and scholarship (cf. Fernández Robaina 1996).

Among Sekou, Alexey, and others, however, such nationally moored commitments to inclusion did not necessarily articulate in the same kinds of ways as those of an older generation. In the immediate sense, these young people are coming of age at a moment in which the grammars of racial materiality have assumed new levels, if not pernicious forms of lived exclusion and disenfranchisement vis-à-vis an evolving neoliberal landscape. Within an increasingly market-oriented Cuba where ambivalences of race and nationhood are arguably at their highest level in revolutionary memory, there may indeed be a greater urgency for racially grounded languages of identity that contest and ultimately supersede national parameters of nonracialism that tend to obfuscate and/or deny antiracist forms of redress. These young people therefore can be seen as seeking new, transnationally expansive social imaginaries—whether through hip hop or Rastafarianism—in ways that clearly translate into alternatively structured kinds of affective feeling. Generational differences being what they were, it was also clear that class participants were accessing historical material to which they otherwise had little other recourse. Such archival reclamations in this sense helped shape present-day black claims to citizenship within a now-expanded historical frame of Cuban nationhood.

In an effort to address such recuperations, Sekou soon composed a new tema titled "Afrocubano," which quickly assumed a privileged position in Anónimo Consejo's performance repertoire. The song builds on an innovative background track composed by Nicolas Nocchi (aka Miko Niko), a Paris-based producer with a working history with Cuban raperos[6] that fused Afro-Cuban percussive elements with somber harmonies and choral lines. Lyrically, the tema sweeps through a largely male-centered homage to black resistance figures and narratives of Cuba's history and beyond. Opening with the cause and following demise of the Partido Independiente de Color,

"Afrocubano" locates the duo as spiritual inheritors of an ancestral legacy of black struggle.

"Afrocubano"

Benny Moré, ibaé
Zoila Gálvez, ibaé
Evaristo Estenoz, ibaé
Gustavo Urrutia, ibaé
Aponte, ibaé
Antonio Maceo, ibaé
A nuestro mártires del Partido Independiente de Color, ibaé
Pedro Ivonnet, ibaé, yo con usted
Por la justa causa moriré . . .

Benny Moré, ibaé
Zoila Gálvez, ibaé
Evaristo Estenoz, ibaé
Gustavo Urrutia, ibaé
Aponte, ibaé
Antonio Maceo, ibaé
To our martyrs of the Independent
Party of Color, ibaé
Pedro Ivonnet, ibaé, I'm with you,
I will die for a just cause . . .

The tema launches with a ritualized evocation of black historical figures starting with the immortal Benny Moré, Cuba's famed vocalist of popular song. Moré is followed by Zoila Gálvez, a soprano vocalist of classic training from the early twentieth century who, daughter of a mambí colonel under Antonio Maceo, was denied full recognition and professional success in Cuba due to her brownness of skin. With this segue, Anónimo Consejo turn to a string of resistant figures including José Antonio Aponte, alleged conspirator of the early nineteenth-century slave rebellion, Antonio Maceo and the leaders of the Partido Independiente de Color, Pedro Ivonnet, and Evaristo Estenoz—all key historical focal points of Tomás's class. Each name is followed in turn by the ritualized refrain *ibaé*, a truncation of the Yoruba-derived phrase *ibaé bayé tonú* uttered at the start of Ocha-Lucumí ceremonies to invoke the presence and participation of ancestral spirits. A connection with the present is then marked through the duo's professed fraternity with Ivonnet's commitments and heroic martyrdom in dying "for a just cause." Within this narrative, moreover, Antonio Maceo's racial subjectivity is recuperated from dominant Cuban frames that have sought its historical erasure or hybridized assimilation into a multiracial and ultimately nonracial national body.

While Ivonnet and his compadres are referenced in nationalist terms as "our martyrs," this same history—and by extension that of Sekou and Kokino—is grounded within broader diasporic narratives of black liberatory struggle through these figures' evocation as "guerreros de África" (warriors of Africa). References to Zumbi and Ganga Zumba, leaders of Brazil's famed seventeenth-century maroon community Quilombo dos Palmares, in turn provide subsequent linkages to Afro-hemispheric histories of resistance beyond Cuba's territorial bounds. Repeated allusion to Rastafari imagery have a similar diasporic impact. Although, as mentioned, some raperos began during this period to wear dreadlocks as body-centered markers of black cosmopolitanism, Sekou's growth of locks and attention to a more vegetarian-centered "ire" lifestyle stemmed from direct involvement with the island's Rasta community (cf. Hansing 2001) and reflected a growing influence of Rastafarianism in his life and sense of black selfhood.[7] The refrain "Erguidos ante la policía / Dreadlocks p'arriba / Orgullo fortalece nuestra fila" (Standing [tall] before the police / Dreadlocks raised up / Pride fortifies our position) is emblematic of such extranational symbolism as defensive posture.

Yet as the song's title implies and as is reiterated throughout the chorus line "Afrocubano soy yo, soy yo" (Afro-Cuban I am, I am), Anónimo Consejo's central claim to identity and historical rootedness is as *Afro*-Cubans. Indeed, to bring closure, the tema concludes with "shout-out" tributes to a number of contemporary black Cuban figures such as the eminent cultural historian Rogelio Martínez Furé, the filmmaker Gloria Rolando, and Tomás Fernández Robaina himself. In a cadence similar to the song's opening salvo, each name is followed by chants of *"aché!"*—a Yoruba phase tied to divine productive force of the orishas—with declarations of "Sekou and Adeyeme!" and "Anónimo Consejo!" bringing the tema to conclusion. In choral chants proclaiming, "La lucha continúa / Hoy, micrófono cultura / Anónimo defiende, los ancestros acentúan!" (The fight continues / Today, microphone culture / Anónimo defends and the ancestors reinforce us!), Anónimo Consejo assert their claim to this continuum of Afro-Cuban radicality within broader Afro-hemispheric fields of emancipatory struggle.

Thus while Tomás's class may have been an informative experience in Sekou's penning of "Afrocubano," the transnational dimensions that undergird the tema's revisionist renderings of Afro-Cuban subjectivity and historical experience clearly also draw inspiration from other diasporic sites of black life and meaning. As previously discussed in the case of Obsesión, who claim a mantle as modern-day mambises and heirs of the fighting force's liberatory tradition, critical recuperations of Afro-Cuban historicity vis-à-vis legacies of racial disenfranchisement find thematic recurrence within lyrical realms of Cuban hip hop.

When considering the artistic scope of innovation along such lines, the work of Hermanos de Causa demands rightful attention. Drawn from the adjoining barrios of Cojimar and Alamar, respectively, the duo of Soandres del Río and Alexis "el Pelón" Cantero were long recognized among the most poetically sophisticated and politically uncompromising of old-school raperos. A key trope employed by Hermanos de Causa as alluded to in the introductory opening involves the satirical resignification of blackness as social commentary on Cuba's current incongruities of race and national belonging. Although garnering scholarly attention elsewhere (Fernandes 2006; M. Perry 2004; West-Durán 2004), one of Hermanos de Causa's lauded temas that warrants brief mention here is "Tengo" (I have).

First performed around 2000,[8] "Tengo" plays upon venerated Afro-Cuban poet Nicolás Guillén's famed 1964 poem of the same title celebrating black social gains under the revolution's early efforts to address Cuba's legacies of racial inequality. Guillén's "Tengo" offers a rhythmic refrain of gratitude for all "I (now) have" (tengo) as an Afro-Cuban thanks to the revolution, a parable collectively etched in Cubans' imagination through the poem's canonic teaching in state-run primary schools. Working transgressively with these parameters, Hermanos de Causa offer a subversive inversion of Guillén's "Tengo" by foregrounding the limitations of rights and access that Afro-Cubans currently hold within the island's new monetized realms of racial exclusion. In the duo's rendering, Guillén's "I have" is figuratively transposed to "I lack" as testament to the lived constraints of black Cuban citizenship at the millennium's turn.

As another poignant illustration of Hermanos de Causa's satirical play

4.1. MC Soandres del Río of Hermanos de Causa. Photo by Sahily Borrero

on blackness, I return to their "Lágrimas negras" (Black tears), cited in the
introduction. Signifying on a classic bolero-son of the same title popularized
in the 1930s by the *trova* bandleader Miguel Matamoros of Trío Matamoros,
Hermanos de Causa's translation of "Lágrimas negras" turns from the original
composition's ode of romantic sorrow to offer a stinging commentary on the
quotidian contours of racism in present-day Cuba. The tema opens with an
upbeat sample clip of a popular mid-1980 version of "Lágrimas negras" by
the venerated salsa band Conjunto Rumbavana. The tone abruptly shifts as
a brassy salsa tempo gives way to a relaxed hip hop beat accompanied by a
sparse melody accented with percussive conga riffs. Unhurried, Soandres's
voice eventually chimes in to reframe the terms of "Lágrimas negras" by
placing black life amid Cuba's current social malaise at the narrative center.

Opening with "¡Yo! Yo de frente, todo el tiempo realista / No digas que
no hay racismo donde hay un racista" (Yo! I'm in front, all the time a realist
/ Don't say there isn't racism when there is a racist), Hermanos de Causa
claim a position as truth tellers deconstructing the lived "ironies" of race in

Cuba. Testifying "No me niegues que hay oculto un prejuicio racial que nos condena y nos valora a todos por igual / No te dejes engañar los ojos de par en par, no te dejes engañar" (Don't deny that there's a hidden racial prejudice that condemns us and values us all as equal / Don't be fooled, eyes wide open, don't be deceived), the duo take aim at the intrinsic contradictions of racial life versus nonracial fictions.

Thus juxtaposed to the romantic melancholy expressed in the original "Lágrimas" composition, Hermanos de Causa speak of the "black tears" of racial marginalization, criminalizing gazes, and a dichotomous invisibility and hypervisibility of Afro-Cubans within an increasingly monetized Cuba. Here the narrative pivots from blackness as the site of racialized fear— "Black delinquent, legendary concept / Seen as the adversary in whatever hour"—to blackness as an active field of subjectivity, one "heavy armed, thick caliber, high precision / Strongly impacting white targets with my vocation."[9] In doing so the artists offer an unapologetic resignification of blackness in ways that unmask the current incongruency of race and Cuban citizenship while foregrounding blackness itself as a consequent site of social agency and contest, one in this sense "demostrando como siempre lo que hay" (demonstrating as usual, what's going on).

Fraternal Elaborations

Yet as Hermanos de Causa's gender-marked name and masculinist posture reminds us, the prism through which race is lived, imagined, and performatively expressed through hip hop is often a highly gendered one. In the case of Anónimo Consejo and others, reclaiming a black radical past is frequently predicated on appeals to masculinist narratives of heroic valor as groundings for reimagining the terms of afrocubanidad in male form. Such recuperations are thus intimately tied to performing a black masculine present. Although conversant with the outer-national, these masculinist framings are deeply meshed with those of Cuba's broader male-centric traditions of national identity and citizenship.

As alluded to earlier, from their very inception ideals of Cuban nationhood and citizenship have been heavily rooted in masculine tropes of armed struggle for national redemption (Ferrer 1999; González Pagés 2004), a tradition fervently elaborated during the post-'59 period. Under revolutionary formulations from José Martí to Fidel Castro, the citizen-as-soldier is cast as the quintessential Cuban subject vis-à-vis a continuum of anti-imperialist struggle aimed at remasculinizing an otherwise emasculated prerevolutionary Cuba (cf. Schwartz 1999). For his part Martí was compelled in the end to affirm the very valor of his citizenship by taking up arms during the independence struggle, only to be killed (and posthumously elevated to martyrdom) amid his initial foray into combat. As Emilio Bejel (2001) among others has argued, masculinist language and imagery were embedded in Martí's nationalist writings as the rhetorical basis for a redemptively liberated cubanidad.

This mythification of the guerrilla-as-national-subject, to borrow from Antoni Kapcia (2000), finds an ever-enduring form in the masculine image of Ernesto "Che" Guevara and his celebrated ideal of the "new man" as the über-revolutionary protagonist (Guevara [1965] 1970, cf. Saldaña-Portillo 2003). Elaborating on cultures of machismo long integral to Cuba and the broader Spanish Caribbean (de Moya 2004), this institutionalization of the masculine was therefore instrumental to the revolutionary imagination, one emphatically heteronormative if not homophobic in practice (Allen 2011; Arenas 1993; Bejel 2001; Fowler 1998; González Pagés 2004; Lumsden 1996; Saunders 2009). Revolutionary efforts to increase women's participation in the workforce coupled with broader gender equality promotion through institutions like the Federación de Mujeres Cubanas (FMC) and the 1975 Family Code (aimed at equitable labor in the domestic sphere) notwithstanding, male privilege and swaggering machismo remain durable fixtures of Cuban life.

While raperos' pursuits of self-crafting circulate within economies of the Cuban heteromasculine, it is notable that male MCs often differentiate themselves from other currents of black masculine performance conspicuous in Cuban popular music and culture. Surfacing during the 1980s and 1990s, Cuba's salsa-derived dance music timba emerged as another important site of racially charged music making and popular commentary amid Cuba's evolving neoliberal ambivalence (Perna 2005; Vaughan 2012). Eclipsing hip hop's fan base and rates of commercial production and revenue, timba's driving, often-frenetic cadence has long been dominated by black male artists who frequently appeal to sexualized play and lyric innuendo heavily centered on the gazed female body.

Echoing similar lines posed by U.S. black feminist critiques (cf. hooks 2003; Wallace 1979), Ariana Hernández-Reguant suggests such celebrations of hetero-virility offer symbolic currency through which young Afro-Cuban men exercise masculinist notions of power within a public sphere that otherwise affords few alternatives (Hernandez-Reguant 2005). Yet while these projections might contest revolutionary prescriptions of normative sexuality on some levels, they also reinscribe heteronormative privileging of Cuban machismo. Indeed, when articulated with race, such lines of practice may also reinforce enduring representations of Afro-Cubans—in both male and female form—as nonnormative sites of a primal hypersexuality (cf. Allen 2011; González Pagés 2004). The more recent phenomenon of Cuban reggaetón—to which I will return—that eventually usurped significant space and artistic talent previously occupied by hip hop as well as timba, draws on similar modes of black heteromasculinity channeled in important part through a sexualized bracketing of women's bodies (cf. Baker 2011).

By contrast, the spectrum of black masculinity displayed by many Havana-area raperos has tended to shy away from explicitly sexualized performance and lyric content. One possible mediating factor lies in varying sites of dialogue among artists that complicate monolithic claims of a black heteronormative male as the privileged subject of Cuban hip hop. Tomás Fernández Robaina and the literary critic Roberto Zurbano—long two of the most actively engaged of an older generation of Afro-Cuban interlocutors vis-à-vis local raperos—are either queer identified or queer conversant black men. The largely male ranks of Havana's MCs have therefore had to reckon with alternative frames of black masculinity that these men have brought to bear on notions of and conversations about afrocubanidad. In related conversation, the assumed stability of the heteromasculine within rapero circles was further disrupted when rumors circulated in 2003 that one highly respected old-school Havana MC was bisexual.[10] While potentially shattering a veneer of heteronormativity, in Tomás's view the episode failed to redress underlying homophobic currents within Cuba's hip hop community. As he explained to me on the heels of the rumor:

I would like to hear one rapero who's not gay, a man singing about the rights of gays, that they have the equal right to share space too. I think they all know that I'm gay, they accept and respect me, and that is something. But I don't know if the audience or gay raperos are prepared to speak publicly about their sexual orientation. That would be something important for the movement; it would be something that could really enrich the movement.

Tomás's scholarship on gender and sexuality via realms of Afro-Cuban religiosity is informative here regarding the privileging of the heteromasculine within broader Afro-Cuban vernacular spheres (Fernández Robaina 1996, 2005). Concerning gendered prescriptions within many Afro-Cuban religious communities, heterosexual men are often licensed within social hierarchies and ritual practice in ways that supersede if not exclude women and homosexual men altogether.

One salient expression of such scriptings is that of the Abakuá, a religious fraternal society with roots among black dockworkers in the ports of Havana, Matanzas, and Cardenas whose linguistic lineage can be traced back to similar all-male sacred societies among the Èfìk and Efu-speaking peoples of the Cross River delta region of Nigeria (Miller 2005; cf. Cabrera 1958; Ortiz 1950, 1951).[11] The Abakuá are noted to shun any expression of the effeminate among initiates, and homosexuality is largely prohibited (Fernández Robaina 1996, 2005; cf. Sublette 2007). Yet Tomás's work in the area suggests degrees of fluidity; sexual contact between Abakuá and other men may be cautiously permissible as long as the Abakuá maintains the dominant or active top position (Fernández Robaina 1996: 205).[12] Such flexibility resonates with Jafari Allen's discussion of the "macho" dominant self-designation among some same-gender-loving Afro-Cuban men who do not necessarily self-identify as homosexual (Allen 2011). In both cases, however, the performative semblance of the heteromasculine nonetheless remains largely intact.

Drawn from poor and working-class urban barrios, the Abakuá are often associated in the popular Cuban imagination with malevolent realms of *marginalidad* and appending claims of violent criminality grounded in enduring conceptions of an afro-primal (Ortiz [1906] 1973; cf. Maguire 2011; Miller 2005). Although highly secretive in ritual practice, the Abakuá do nonetheless garner degrees of admiration, if at times guarded, within urban realms of Afro-Cuban life, particularly with regard to working-class paradigms of respectable masculinity. Among such currents the Abakuá hold a notable resonance within cultural spheres of Cuban hip hop. At the everyday level of the vernacular, the expression "asere" that rapero men commonly use to greet and mutually mark one another is drawn from an Abakuá expression similarly used as a ritual salutation between initiates.[13] For instance, the now well-worn expression "¿Qué bola asere?" (roughly, What's up, brother?) has assumed proverbial status through its iconic association with raperospeak. While such mimetics suggest an intimacy of Afro-Cuban literacy shared by male raperos vis-à-vis the Abakuá and conjoined scripts of black working-class masculinity, the quotidian use of the address also engenders its own meanings of homosocial fraternity among Cuban MCs.

Rapero affinities with the Abakuá may articulate at more immediate levels as well. While in conversation a friend mentioned in passing that a mutual hip-hop-affiliated friend was an initiate of the Abakuá. While I had known this person for a number of years, I had never heard any reference to his membership by him or anyone else. Given the fraternal society's insular nature, I was not sure if it was appropriate to inquire about the rumor. In a later conversation I did in fact ask my friend if there was any truth to the claim. Without much hesitation, he affirmed, "Si asere, yo soy Abakuá, soy obonekué," intermingling the everyday Abakuá-cum-rapero address *asere* alongside the more esoteric *obonekué* for Abakuá initiates. When I asked how comfortable he would be if I commented on his membership, he responded that it would be fine, clarifying that while the society's sacred rites were indeed secret, one's individual membership as a ñáñigo—using a more widely used term for fraternal members—was not necessarily so.[14]

DJ Alexis D'Boys explained that although his family was not particularly religious, he had long felt pulled toward the realms of the sacred. It was, however, during a conversation amid a religious consultation with a babaláwo that sparked his curiosity regarding the Abakuá, leading him to seek out more information about the fraternity. Alexis recalled a particularly meaningful trip during this period to the municipality of Regla to attend a ceremonial funeral for a recently deceased Abakuá member. Describing his experience, Alexis explained:

> I went to the ceremony and saw a tremendous amount of discipline and closeness between all the brothers there. And I was like "wow," these brothers are very serious! For me this planted the idea of joining this community. But there are a number of things that must be shared about you before you can become part of the religion. So one day I presented myself to a group [of members] and said I wanted to become part of this secret community. They then took a year inquiring about me including visiting my family, because if your family doesn't agree you cannot become part of this religion. So they visited my grandfather's house and asked my grandmother about my family, because one of the requirements is that you have to come from a family with a good father.

We say "*Buen padre, buen hijo, buen hermano y buen amigo!*" (Good father, good son, good brother, good friend). Being a good father and a good son is fundamental, this is very important in this religion. . . . So they came to my house to meet my family and my parents were a bit nervous. They had heard that this religion was violent, that they killed and murdered people, what have you. When my grandmother asked me if I was sure I wanted to be part of this religion, I said, "Yes, I'm sure," and I was eventually invited to join. So I along with fourteen other brothers were initiated on December 4, 1994—a date I will never forget.[15]

Despite family concerns, the Abakuá's promise of sacred fellowship, fraternal discipline, and embedded ideals of respectable masculinity apparently resonated with Alexis's own yearnings for belonging as a young Afro-Cuban man. Similar echoes of admiration find artistic form in "Abakuá," a composition by Obsesión's Alexey Rodríguez released on the group's 2011 album, *El Disco Negro*. Something of a tribute to the Abakuá and by extension Alexey's home barrio of Regla as a central locale, as mentioned, of Abakuá tradition since the mid-nineteenth century, the track opens with a sample of an iconic Abakuá *enkame* or ritual call-and-response chant. For an interesting and indeed resonant comparative note, interpretations of this same enkame are performed by Dizzy Gillespie in the opening to his classic "Swing Low, Sweet Cadillac" (1967), the diasporic syncretics of which grew from Gillespie's collaborative history with Afro-Cuban *rumbero* and Abakuá member Chano Pozo.

In Obsesión's rendering, the opening enkame melds into a background of melodic hip hop beats inflected with a sparse fusion of conga phases and Cuban guitar chords, as Alexey riffs:

"Abakuá"

Una de las mayores virtudes que puede tener un hombre es la
descripción . . .
Pero Abakuá es q'manda, oye!
Siempre será una buena oportunidad para ofrecerle mi respeto y no
ofenderle a Abakuá
En Regla se fundó la primera sociedad, cosa de la que estoy orgulloso,
yo soy de allá!

Muchos tabúes y alrededor de esta linda religión, primero invito a
conocer antes
de dar opinión
Buen padre, buen hijo, buen esposo, buen
amigo!
Esto es pa' lo que la llevan de verdad, los que no distorsionan su
verdadera esencia . . .
El Abakuá no es malo, lo hacen malo
las personas
Respeta para que te respeten . . .

One of the greatest virtues that a man can have is how he defines
himself . . .
But Abakuá is in charge, hey!
It will always be a good opportunity to offer my respect and not offend
the Abakuá
In Regla the first society was founded, something that I'm proud of,
I'm from there!
A lot of taboos surround this beautiful religion, first I invite you to
know it before you offer your opinions
Good father, good son, good husband, good friend!
This is for those who truly carry the truth, not the ones who distort its
true essence . . .
The Abakuá are not bad, it's people who make it bad
Respect so they'll respect you . . .

Amid a tone of veneration and repeated calls for "respect," Alexey offers redress to what is viewed as distorted popular understandings of the Abakuá.
Countervailing odes to the fraternal society as disciplined exemplars of a
respectable masculinity resonate throughout.

Cultural layerings between raperos and the Abakuá need, however, to
be viewed within broader histories of Abakuá interface within realms of
Cuban popular music (León 1991; R. Moore 1997), a particularly intimate
expression of such being Afro-Cuban rumba (Acosta 2003; Miller 2000;
Sublette 2007). In addition to syncretic inflections of Abakuá drumming,
dance, and vocal styles, rumba traditions reflect a highly heterogendered
performance structure that similarly privilege men as *congueros* (drummers)

and broader practitioners of rumba song and dance (Knauer 2008). Drawing on such legacies, artists such as Chano Pozo, Arsenio Rodríguez, and Ignacio Piñeiro[16]—all translational figures of Afro-Cuban musicality into the wider Afro-Atlantic—were notably also initiates of the Abakuá. Might raperos then be elaborating on similarly gendered histories and musically articulated routes of the Afro-Cuban? Clearly, currents of black working-class heteromasculinity that resonate at the levels of music making and everyday social practice are integral elements of a fraternalism that undergirds much of the social fabric of Havana's hip hop community. Or at least this may appear to be the case for those who are male and performatively straight.

Black Feminist Queerings

Cuban hip hop's masculinist leanings are of course far from free of gendered complications. The participation of women within, and in close conversation with, the movement has worked in various ways to decenter and ultimately queer the community's otherwise male-centric focus (cf. Fernandes 2006, 2007; Saunders 2009). As cited earlier, the all-female trio of Instinto were among the key pioneers of women's involvement in Havana hip hop. Although the group's members, Doricel Agramonte, Yudith Porto, and Yanet Díaz, moved to Spain around 2002 and later disbanded, I recall their music fusing harder-edged riffs over R&B-styled background vocals. While placing black-women-centered narratives at the heart of their temas (see Pacini Hernandez and Garofalo 2000; West-Durán 2004), Instinto often employed sexualized play and innuendo as featured theatrical tropes. Often donning formfitting outfits for shows, the trio used sexual provocation as a mode of social commentary and critique along intersecting lines of race and gender. Yet such stagecraft seemed in the end to conform to, rather than complicate, conventional Cuban representations of heteronormative female sexuality.

With the increased participation of Cuban women in hip hop over the years, the performative style and range of female voices expanded as well. An important marker of this growth was the proliferation by the early 2000s of concerts and other events in Havana dedicated to the evolving vitality of raperas (female raperos) within the movement. In addition to female soloists such as MCs Yula and Mariana,[17] a number of all-female groups arose during this period including Explosión Femenina, Sexto Sentido, and La Positiva, many of them evocative of Instinto's sexualized play though with a seemingly more deliberate eye toward a commercial draw. The spoken-word vocalist Telmary Díaz, formerly of the hip-hop-fusion band Free Hole Negro, and later Interactivo collective, also emerged amid this period as a dynamic performer both within and beyond Cuban hip hop. A few pioneering women, moreover, eventually ventured into DJing, key among whom was DJ Leidis Freire, a longstanding member of the Vedado-based Diez y Diecinueve crew.

One individual active in supporting the growth and development of female artists was the African American political exile Nehanda Abiodun. With firm commitment and intellectual grounding in U.S. black feminist thought and practice, Nehanda often sought to foreground dimensions of gender and sexuality through her engagements with artists and Havana's broader hip hop community. Interminglings of gender and sexuality via wider frames of black liberatory struggle were, for instance, recurring themes of discussion during her informal class gatherings. Although less intimately involved, her fellow exile Assata Shakur has also long been a present and highly admired figure within rapero circles. These women provide living exemplars of black radicality rooted in female subjectivity and broader black womanist traditions of revolutionary activism. Nehanda and Assata have in this sense helped expand and varyingly decenter the largely male-focused vistas of black radical imagination among Havana-area raperos.

Such gendered queerings assumed important resonance among many female MCs. One evolving current among some artists involved interwoven critiques of gendered, sexualized, and racial forms of power in ways that challenged hip hop's otherwise masculinist orientation, while confronting broader domains of raced patriarchy in the Cuban everyday. Yet rather than simply reflecting forms of consciousness and ways of being sui generis, such voicings emerge in conversation with black womanist subjectivities that found animated evolving form through the expressive space of hip hop. Commenting on an apparent shift among female artists away from earlier, more conventional displays of female sexuality, Nehanda explained: "What has evolved since then are women who haven't negated their sexuality but are very sexy in their own right. I mean they are not pumping with sex. These are beautiful women, not sexy but beautiful women who are very secure in their ability to handle their own and not falling into the trap of being, you know, the ultra-sexy rapper, but real women who are rappers and saying, 'We have something to say as well!'"

Indeed, when considering women's space and intervention within rapero circles, a pioneering artist who deserves important recognition is Magia López of Obsesión. As mentioned, Magia's subjectivity as a black woman became an increasingly vocal and politicized component of her music and public persona. While her artistic partner Alexey has been long the primary scribe and producer of many of Obsesión's temas, Magia has over the years assumed a more active role in asserting her creativity within the duo's music-making process while critically developing her own artistic voice as a woman. Here a central and elaborating theme in Magia's work targets racialized frames of gendered discourse and practice historically ascribed to black and darker-skinned Cuban women. By way of Afrocentric clothing and flamboyantly natural hairstyling, Magia celebrates an unapologetically black womanhood in her own terms. In doing so, she offers a performative counterpole to prevailing norms that privilege the lighter-skinned mulata as the celebrated and highly sexualized object of a racially transculturated Cuba.

Yet wider economies of sexuality as interstitially lived with those of race, gender, and class remain critical concerns of redress. Magia's artistic growth along these line finds eloquent expression in her solo tema "La llaman puta" (They call her a whore), in which she gives an impassioned account of the struggles of young women involved in Cuba's tourist-driven sex trade. Although race is not referenced explicitly, it is evoked allegorically as Magia interweaves her narrative with choral chants in ritualized Yoruba to Ochún, the female orisha most strongly associated with feminine sexuality. Sung to the polyrhythmic play of the sacred batá drums of Ocha-Lucumí ceremony used to invoke the orishas, the tema opens as follows:

"La llaman puta"

La llaman puta
para todos no es más
que una mujerzuela
disfrutando el hecho de ser bonita
¡Loca! Carne que invita
que provoca . . .
¡Cuantas no van por ese camino!
Y entonces la llaman puta . . .

They call her whore
for everyone she is no more
than a loose woman
enjoying the fact of being pretty
Crazy woman! Flesh that invites
that often provokes . . .
How many don't take this road!
So for that they call her whore . . .
Forced to do what you don't want to
you avoid the idea,
But misery has an ugly face even if you don't believe it . . .
Your body assumes the responsibility and
they call her whore . . .
Society throws the hook and you
bite the bait . . .

Magia's empathy with the narrative's protagonist and circumstance is poignant. The bleak scenario painted here of female sex work is largely one of structural victimhood in which women are not only "forced to do what you don't want to," but are shunned for doing so. With few other alternatives, the body is seen as an exploitable resource within globally inflected markets of sexual consumption. While the suggestion "society throws the hook and [they] bite the bait" could be read as undervaluing questions of agency, Magia is singing against more dominant Cuban representations of jineteras (female sex workers) as joy-seeking materialists whose participation in sex work is steeped in pathologies of moral compromise (cf. Cabeza 2004; Fusco 1998). Alternatively, Magia offers an image of these women as social casualties of Cuba's neoliberal turn afforded few other means through which to access the island's life-essential, globally pinned currency.

While melancholic refrains to Ochún are employed to call on the orisha's feminine presence and aid in defense of these women, the intimacy of Magia's appeal to Ochún is mediated through her own subjectivity as a black woman. Although Magia is not herself a practitioner of Ocha-Lucumí, she chooses to invoke the female orisha in liturgical Yoruba to ground her woman-centered narrative within a language of Afro-Cuban sacred life. Magia's performative affinity with both female sex workers and Ochún is thus rooted in a confluence of gendered, racial, and class constraints that bind all within and against broader fields of patriarchal power.

As one of the most active and accomplished MCs transcendent of gender lines, Magia's tenacious work over the years has garnered considerable, if at times complicated, respect within Havana's hip hop community and broader island-wide movement. Yet despite an increasingly independent voice and organizational autonomy, as one long identified with her artistic partner (and now former husband) Alexey Rodríguez, Magia has had to negotiate perceptions of her artistic identity as one indebted to a male-female coupling.

Following on the heels of Magia, a later generation of all-women groups and female soloists arose during the early 2000s whose collective efforts have further intervened within hip hop Cubano's fraternal space. One influential set of female voices to emerge and representing a relatively radical challenge in this regard was Las Krudas. Garnering significant scholarly attention over the years (Armstead 2007; Fernandes 2006, 2007; Guillard Limonta 2005; M. Perry 2004; Saunders 2009, 2010; West-Durán 2004),[18] Las Krudas, or "the raw ones," are a lesbian trio of Afrocentric vegetarian feminists who entered Havana's hip hop scene around 2001. Prior to their involvement in hip hop, the highly creative trio of Olivia "Pelusa" Prendes and sisters Odaymara "Pasa" and Odalys "Wanda" Cuesta were active in street theater, most notably as members of a colorful troupe of stilt walkers who regularly performed in the heavily touristed area of Havana Vieja. Within a few months after Krudas made their hip hop debut, Pasa described the group's orientation to me in this way: "We're a female trio of new hip hop with a new consciousness, a new understanding about the role of women within this movement of hip hop. We classify our music as superground. So I am here with Pelusa and Wanda fighting, writing, and working to have our music heard to help, to open the mentality and the consciousness of this movement. We feel it's very important that they listen to our words."[19]

Pasa's reference to the trio's music as "superground" plays upon the U.S.-derived expression "underground" commonly used by raperos to distinguish between what is viewed as commercially compromised pop hip hop that predominates U.S. markets and the less adulterated, politically oriented forms that remain true to hip hop's socially committed roots. Less accessible or popular, the latter is thus deemed underground. The expression has in fact been central to ideological debates within rapero circles

4.2. MC Odaymara "Pasa" Cuesta of Las Krudas. Photo by the author

regarding the evolving challenges and future directions of Cuban hip hop writ large (cf. Fernandes 2006). The pivotal issue revolves around whether individual artists—if not ultimately the movement as a whole—would "sell out" their political convictions to an ever-encroaching Cuban marketplace.

As a discourse of authenticity, to remain underground implies a resistance to processes of commercial cooptation viewed as corruptive of hip hop's utopic promise. Such positions are hence implicitly rooted in critiques of consumer capitalism. Indeed, working from the figure of Mickey Mouse as a metaphor for the social vacuousness and commercialism associated with U.S. popular culture, many Cuban MCs express derision for what they see as the "miki miki" (i.e., Mickey Mouse) tendencies in much of commercial hip hop in the United States. As I discuss in the following chapter, such critiques and their underlying anxieties unfold with a particular urgency as hip hop artists have had to compete with the rise of Cuban reggaetón.

Reminiscent of linguistic word-play strategies that Jamaican Rastafari employ to subvert standard English phrasing (Pollard 2000), Pasa's allusion to Krudas as superground further underscores the overtly political, in-your-face nature of their feminist-directed intervention, an intervention targeted at expanding the movement's largely male-centered "mentality and consciousness." Commenting further on the group's inspiration, Pasa continues:

> This is my race, this is my color, this is my people, and yet the movement greatly lacks female representation. The community is made up of both black women and black men, and so we have to represent black women.[20] So we're supporting the movement, particularly the women because we share different realities. Some [in the movement] may think that we are all the same, no. There are different realities, different truths, different experiences that women have given their sex and their gender.

Pasa's concern over a dearth of black women's representation within Cuban hip hop recalls similar challenges leveled by U.S. black feminists regarding the male-centric leadership and masculinist character of the U.S. black freedom movements of the 1960s and early 1970s (E. Brown 1993; Wallace 1979). By foregrounding the particularities of black female subjectivity and experience through the differentiated ways that racial oppression is both gendered and sexualized, Pasa, like black feminists before, contests the heteromasculinist claims of a unified subject of struggle on which Cuban hip hop—if not the Cuban revolutionary and broader national project itself—is largely predicated. Conversant with an analytics of intersectionality (Collins 1990), Pasa explained: "I feel that it is an impossibility to talk about racism without talking about machismo. [In the past] machismo was a facet of slavery, understand? It's also a form of oppression. And so our *temas* talk about these things."

Claiming a black lesbian-feminist vocality within the movement's largely masculinist and heteronormative lines in this way renders critically audible questions of sexuality and homophobia in addition to those of race and gender. Such interventions evoke earlier challenges by black lesbians and other feminists of color in the United States who worked to decenter both black liberation and white feminist movements through a radical, often sexualized politics of difference (cf. Combahee River Collective 1986; Moraga and Anzaldúa 1981).

A queering poetics of identity is itself signified in the very name the trio have chosen for themselves. As the artists described it, the name Krudas—again, the female "raw ones"—was initially chosen to mark the group's adherence to vegetarianism (i.e., raw food), which they view as an important political facet of their alterity as raperas. At the same time, the artists refer to an unadulterated female "rawness" that they and their lyrics embody; theirs is an assertive in-your-face performance style that refuses to conform to patriarchal framings of Cuban women as objects of heteromasculine gaze. Pasa explains: "I think we also call ourselves Las Krudas because our image is a bit difficult to qualify under established classifications. Within the culture of hip hop it seems that our image is very powerful. Because in reality women that I have seen tend to be delicate, very refined, and passive—women for men, as usual, understand? So we are another type of thing. We are not niki, chiki, nor miki."

Indeed, Krudas, with their dreadlock-adorned full-figured bodies, uncompromising women-centered lyrics, and highly theatrical performances, represented a fairly radical departure from the dominant images of the Cuban feminine—"women for men, as usual"—as well as the standard masculinist hip hop fare. Afrocentric adornments of black womanist identity, moreover, are performatively inscribed by the women in the form of tattooed images of West African cowrie shells and renderings of the Egyptian ankh symbol associated with creative female energy, all of which stand in bold contrast to conventional racial and sexually normative gendered practice by way of "niki, chiki, [or] miki."

Pelusa recalls that Krudas' early performances were often greeted by fellow raperos and attending audiences with silence, mouths wide, eyes glazed. There did indeed seem to be an initial coolness among many male MCs I knew toward the trio when they first began performing in the early 2000s. When asked about Krudas, one prominent rapero commented along the lines, "Ellas no tienen ningún tipo de flow" (They don't have any type of flow), referencing the all-important verbal dexterity or "flow" that MCs exhibit in performance. It was notable that rather than citing lyric content, attention was paid to Krudas' supposed lack of technical proficiency or "skills" as the means of dismissing their artistic if not broader political significance as performers.

Yet there clearly was no avoiding Las Krudas' spectacular stage presence and provocative, womanist-centered message propelled through theatrical plays of music and performance style. As illustration, one of Krudas' signature temas, "Eres bella" (You are beautiful), recorded on their debut 2001 CD, Cubensi, offers a biting assessment of sexualized gender oppression vis-à-vis Cuba's neoliberal malaise. The tema opens with the following salvo:

"Eres bella"

Cantarte, tema dedicación
Dedicado a todas las mujeres del mundo
A todas las mujeres que como nosotras
están luchando
A todas las guerreras campesinas urbanas
A todas las hermanas
Especialmente a las más negras
Especialmente a las más pobres
Especialmente a las más gordas . . .
Artificios de risas y postizos son
Continuación del cuento colonialista
No te cojas pa' eso
Deja esa falsa vista . . .
¿Qué nos queda?
Prostitución, seducción
Esto es sólo una costumbre de edad para
Ayudar a nuestras gente económicamente
En este mundo tan material
No somos nalgas y pechos solamente
Tenemos cerebro, mujer
Siente, siente . . .

Sing, dedication song
Dedicated to all the women in the world
To all the women like us who
are fighting
To all the urban peasant guerrilla women
To all the sisters
Especially to the most black
Especially to the most poor
Especially to the most fat . . .
Fake laughs and implants are
a continuation of the colonialist tale
Don't buy it
Move away from that false point of view . . .

What is left for us?
Prostitution, seduction
This is only a tradition of our times
to help our people economically
In this very material world
We are not only breasts and ass
We have brains, woman
Feel, feel . . .

The tema thus begins in celebratory homage to a universal notion of women's militancy and struggle within which the trio locate themselves. Promptly, however, a more immediate affinity is claimed with those women black, poor, and, yes, fat. Herein lies a central line of critique within the song's text—the patriarchal objectification and normative conditioning of black Cuban women's bodies and forms of subjectivity (cf. J. Butler 1993). While the refrain "Fake laughs and implants are a continuation of the colonialist tale / Don't buy it" speaks to such disciplinary effects, it draws lines of articulation between these practices and fields of colonial governmentality in ways that historicize black female subjugation via broader histories of anticolonial/anti-imperialist struggle—narratives on which the Cuban revolutionary national project is itself grounded.

Such maneuvers evoke radical black feminist Jacqui Alexander's call for critical "pedagogies" aimed at deconstructing historical linkages between colonialism, citizenship, and intersecting realms of gender and sexualized oppression (Alexander 2006). Yet Krudas' cautionary "Don't buy it" implicates a certain market rationale within these economies of power as currently lived. Krudas, in turn, call for a rejection of such self-objectifying gendered prescriptions, celebrating alternatively their full-figured bodies in oppositional stance as a key performative facet of their queering interventions. The trio's later composition "La gorda" (Fat girl) takes on female body aesthetics front and center as a queer(ing)-feminist salutation to nonnormative fatness, one that triumphantly declares in its chorus hook, "¡La gorda ha llegado!" (The fat woman has arrived!).

Such queering alterity recalls what José Esteban Muñoz has termed a politics of disidentification employed by U.S. queer performers of color as a means of decentering heteronormative economies of aesthetic value and desire. As a "phobic object," to borrow from Muñoz's discussion of the performance artist Marga Gomez's use of feminine masculinity, fatness in this sense is "reconfigured as sexy and glamorous, and not as the pathetic and abject spectacle that it appears to be in the dominant eyes of heteronormative culture" (Muñoz 1999: 3). Krudas' efforts in this sense seek to performatively disidentify with and thus transgressively challenge normative truth claims rooted in both whiteness and heteronormativity through an alternative "worldmaking" as black lesbians (Muñoz 1999: 200). The temas' rhetorical query as to whether racism operates within a "maldita y machista sociedad" (wicked and macho society) underscores those articulations of racism and sexism as subjectively lived by Afro-Cuban women. In declaring "No hay verdadera revolución sin mujeres" (There is no real revolution without women), emancipatory projects—including those of national revolutionary struggle—are deemed hollow without the critical recognition and active participation of black women.

As narrative foil, "Eres bella" evokes the condition of Cuba's female sex workers, who represent some of the most acutely targeted subjects of racially imbricated forms of sexual objectification in a monetized Cuba. Possibly more directly than Magia's "La llaman puta," Krudas' identification with these women and their circumstances is grounded in the first person: "Yo también como tú he hecho cosas mezquina / Yo también como tú he fregado por dos pesos que sonaban en cualquier esquina / Yo también como tú he sido forzada y llevada sin mi voluntad a fornicación" (I like you have paced street corners for two pesos / I like you have been forced and taken against my will to fornicate). Such are the material conditions in which a raced female sexuality becomes a key if not sole source of exploitable capital for these women.

"What is left for us?" they ask. "This is the only tradition of our times / To help our people economically in this very material world." Departing from such market-driven interpolations, black women's self-redemption lies in the recognition that "We are not only breast and ass / We have brains." Indeed, rather than corporal sites of phallocentric consumption, Las Krudas call on women to simply "feel" who they are for themselves, melding otherwise juxtaposed realms of affect and intellect in an embodied realization of female subjectivity.

When asked about their openness about their sexuality when they first entered the hip hop scene, Pelusa explained that although they harbored some caution regarding public identification as lesbians, it was apparent from the very start that they were queer. While the trio may have experienced some coolness from other artists at the onset, their vigorous involvement and evolving presence ultimately garnered them space and significant respect among many quarters of Havana's hip hop community. Indeed, Las Krudas eventually collaborated with and/or shared performances with a range of Havana's most established male artists. Their first album *Cubensi* (2007), moreover, involved artistic partnerings with producer Pablo Herrera and MCs Michael Oramas and Andy Yensy Oruña of Junior Clan. Collaborative exchanges of the kind suggest lines described by U.S. cultural critic Mark Anthony Neal in his call for new hip-hop-informed scriptings of black masculinity that both confront and move beyond heteropatriarchal privilegings (Neal 2005).

Such transgressive aspirations have resonance beyond hip hop. Drawing on extensive work with Las Krudas and broader realms of black lesbian life in Havana, the U.S. sociologist Tanya Saunders suggests that despite recent openings by the Cuban state and its institutions to more public recognitions of nonnormative sexualities, Cuban lesbians of color struggle for public space and affirmation while negotiating added challenges of racial and gendered marginalization (Saunders 2010). Such limitations, Saunders argues, tend in the end to (re)produce queer privileges along male and white-racial lines, while reinforcing heteronormative modes of femininity and accompanying lines of sexual morality. Las Krudas' asserted visibility and vocality thus seek to engage and expand upon nonnormative spheres of race, gender, and sexuality within Cuba's wider everyday.

Krudas' feminist-centered queerings did not always resonate uncomplicatedly with other female artists, however. I recall tension, for instance, arising during a 2006 workshop on women in hip hop as part of a hip hop symposium organized by Magia López and Alexey Rodríguez of Obsesión. During one exchange, Pasa suggested that the domestic sphere of childrearing and heterosexual partnering constrained the liberatory possibilities of straight women as both artists and activists. Implicit in her charge was a privileging of queer female subjects as agents of more radical kinds of creative undertaking. At this juncture Magia chimed in, voicing discomfort with the idea that straight female artists were in effect compromised politically by their sexuality. Pasa responded by affirming her respect for Magia and her work as a central figure and pioneering woman in the movement. She did, however, add that as a performer partnered with her then-husband, Alexey, Magia could not be seen as occupying a fully autonomous position as a female artist.

Although I had been aware of tensions arising between Magia and Las Krudas in the past, I was also mindful that Magia and Alexey's success (and strategic agility) in navigating institutional state-run structures and resources engendered political costs among some in the hip hop community who were more wary of state collaborations. While there may indeed have been additional issues informing this particular exchange, a queer critique of heteronormative confines was clearly at the center of Pasa's commentary.

Another related set of intrafemale dialogues occurred around 2005. As part of Las Krudas' ongoing work within Havana's hip hop community, the trio were instrumental in helping form a performance collaborative of female hip hop artists dubbed Omega Kilay, aimed at promoting women's participation and visibility within island hip hop.[21] In addition to Krudas, the collective included the long-active member of EPG&B MC Magyori "La Llave" Martínez, the graffiti artist Yanelis "Nono" Valdez, and DJs Leidis and Yaribey "Yary" Collia. As DJ Yary explained, it was during an all-female concert amid an annual state-sponsored Cubadisco Awards that a consensus emerged among performing artists to "shoot for something new, something more powerful, a union of strength. So we decided to focus in one direction and say, 'Let's create a project among us women who rap underground, because there're already others who do commercial fusion music.' As we were the most prominent underground artists, we decided to join together. We defended more or less the same interests, the same rights; we had the same aspirations and everything was good and flowing well and solid."[22]

Along these lines, a summary of Omega's stated goals involved calls to:

- reflect the sociopolitical experiences of "Third World" Latinas;
- encourage the development of Cuban women;
- search for peaceful ways to liberate women; defend women's rights; and eradicate machismo, domestic violence, and social, sexual, and racial forms of discrimination;
- promote the development of festivals and events dedicated to Latin American female rappers;
- promote the expansion of hip hop in Cuba and throughout the world;
- educate the public on themes of sexuality; and
- obtain greater incorporation of women within Cuban hip hop.[23]

While advocating a kind of Third World feminist praxis and transnational citizenship (Alexander 2006; Mohanty 2003; Uma 1997) by way of hip hop activism, there may have been some divergences among Omega members around more individuated levels of difference. During a 2006 interview with MCs Magyori and Nono and DJ Yary, who were performing largely as a trio at the time, the artists expressed some ambivalence regarding the centrality of gender and feminist critique in relation to their work and self-identity as artists. As Nono elaborated: "Our songs reflect everything, not just feminism, it is not so important. What's important is to give our mission to our music. Each one of us has our own message, but the main message is for us to be seen as artists, equal to all, not just women artists, but like a normal artist—we are all equal."

Magyori added that she had a long history of working closely with male artists as the sole female member of EPG&B, a space in which she claimed to have felt neither compromised nor constrained artistically as a woman. DJ Yary clarified in turn that she did not consider herself a feminist, implying that such a belief would invoke a separatist position she claimed not to embrace. All three women stressed the notion that they had garnered respect from their male peers and broader public through hard work, dedication, and artistic talent rather than as women per se. Speaking of the collective's membership, Yary explained:

The fact that we all belong to Omega Kilay shows that we are all here together and agree in many respects. The very fact that we were all together means that there is a tie between all of us as artists and that we all respect each other. Our purposes and intentions are largely similar though the only difference is that Las Krudas are inclined toward the stronger side of feminism here in Cuba. Being Third World, black, and overweight has influenced them and they have fought hard. My story would not be that, right? I talk about other things because, well, I have not suffered the same ways as they have. Everyone has experienced different things, each one has our own experience and we always translate them into positive messages.

Though not referenced directly, Yary's comments suggest varying locations among Omega's members along differential lines of sexuality. Embedded, for instance, in the commentary above of Yary and the other women is an apparent tendency to associate feminism with a lesbian subject position, from which all three women seem to distance themselves. While offering a possible misreading of feminist epistemology, these women nonetheless illuminate an evolving range of self-reflexive conversation both about and through questions of gender and sexual difference—ones that no doubt owe much to Las Krudas' work. Krudas' interventions in this sense have been productive in introducing vocabularies of nonnormativity into spheres of Cuban hip hop otherwise largely devoid of such critical grammar. Their ability to forge alliances with both male and other female artists across lines of gender and sexuality testifies to the queering effects of their work—precisely the kind of disruptive intervention that Tomás Fernández Robaina advocates above. It is hence through multivocal claims to inclusive citizenship at overlapping levels of the national and transnational that new, critical understandings and ways of being Afro-Cuban come into active focus. Hip hop is in this sense instrumental in aiding such self-refractive undertakings.

Chapter 5.
Racial Challenges and the State

Late one night following a local hip hop concert in the barrio of Vedado, I sat with a few friends in a nearby park reminiscing about the evening's events while sharing a few cajitas (small packaged boxes) of Los Marinos Paticruzado rum. Amid our musings, I noted my companions, Sidney Anson, DJ Alexis D'Boys, and MC Michael Oramas of Junior Clan, were adorned with an interesting collage of Afrodiasporic imagery. In succession, the trio sported T-shirt portraits of Jimi Hendrix, Bob Marley, and the Black Panther Party accompanied by an assemblage of cowry shells, an Ethiopian Coptic cross, and red-, black-, and green-beaded necklaces and wristbands. Attached to DJ Alexis's hat sat a small pin of Africa awash in the same nationalist triad of colors given celebrated form by Marcus Garvey and his call for black redemption through African repatriation. All stood in syncretic harmony with a set of mini-stereo headphones dangling around Sidney's neck (see figure 5.1). This Afro-Atlantic bricolage suggested a kind of black and expressly masculine cosmopolitanism in which these young men participated and literally stitched themselves within as contemporary Afro-Cubans. As discussed, black Cubans have long engaged transnational circuits of cultural commerce in the crafting of black social imaginaries and lines of political affinity (Acosta 2003; Brock and Castañeda Fuertes 1998a; Childs 2006; Fernández 2006; Guridy 2010; Jacques 1998; J. Moreno 2004). This, of course, is not new.

5.1. Sidney Anson, DJ Alexis D'Boys Rodríguez, and MC Michael Oramas.
Photo by the author

For my friends and many of their peers, however, hip hop offered a global
expansiveness that both reflected, and was responsive to, the imperatives
of a Cuban present formed at a shifting, racially imbricated confluence of
history, nation, and an expanding market economy. The ways these young
Cubans choose to self-identify and define themselves as black per se were
rooted in social meanings fashioned in part through embodied style and
musical practice. These men thus participated in their own transnational
markets of racial consumption, yet ones directed toward particular affective
ends. Indeed, to be negro/a in this context is not simply the result of being
materially interpellated as such, but rather self-ascribed positions and politically marked possibilities from which to move and act.

The political grammars through which raperos refashion blackness in
and of themselves, moreover, threaten the very stability of Cuban nonracialism long central to the island's nationalist projects both past and present. Recalling the nonracial groundings of José Martí, black Cuban identity
claims with the slightest of political implications have been viewed as a
counternational peril to the enshrined integrity of nation before race. Such

perceived defiance carried real political consequences in both pre- as well as post-1959 Cuba, with the 1912 state-sponsored massacre and dissolution of the Partido Independiente de Color embodying the most violent of historical expressions. One need not be familiar with rapero lyric allusions to these legacies to recognize the ways these artists evoke similar calls for full, non-self-negating inclusion and citizenship within the Cuban nation.

Raperos' explicitly modern claims to a black cosmopolitan globality, moreover, also disrupt nationally bound narratives like those of state-promoted folklore that tend to mark blackness, when recognized, as a "traditional" cultural holdover of an earlier moment—one autochthonously rooted in Cuba's racially transculturated and therefore ultimately de-raced national past. The diasporic amalgam of black signifiers that my drinking companions donned on that post-concert evening clearly superseded in the most celebratory of terms such national-temporal constraints.

Yet beyond the immediate circumstances of their making, what impacts and kinds of articulations might these practices and their broader interventions animate within wider spheres of Cuban life? Or in a more politically direct sense, what has been the revolutionary state's position vis-à-vis Cuban hip hop and its racially situated voicings? To what extent might raperos' critical affirmations of black difference complicate in both form (identity) and function (lyric-based critique) utopic claims of a Cuban postracial exceptionalism that would otherwise seek to silence social difference for the greater revolutionary and national good?

State Maneuvers

As previously noted, the revolutionary state and its institutions have occupied an ambivalent and often shifting role in relation to hip hop's development on the island. By varyingly restricting and facilitating access to U.S. popular music, while providing fragmentary support during the transitional growth of la moña into hip hop Cubano, the revolutionary state's early engagement can generally be seen as one of cautious tolerance. As alluded to earlier, it was the state-run Asociación Hermanos Saíz (AHS) that eventually took the lead as institutional liaison with the island's hip hop movement. The increasingly active role of AHS in successive hip hop festivals after 1999, however, signaled a strategic shift in state involvement. To recall, Grupo Uno, the hip hop collective headed by Rodolfo Rensoli that launched the first Cuban hip hop festival in 1995, approached AHS in 1997 with the aim of securing institutional support for subsequent festivals held in Alamar's amphitheater. While this move ultimately extended Grupo Uno's organizational leadership of the festival for a few additional years, it also marked the beginning of an escalating governmental stake in the evolving space and future direction of island hip hop.

A key figure in this early confluence of interests was Roberto Zurbano, an Afro-Cuban writer, literary critic, and then vice president of Hermanos Saíz, whom Rensoli first approached regarding governmental support for the festival. In conversation with Zurbano he recalled that part of Grupo Uno's initial appeal from an institutional standpoint was the collective's proposal to expand the local festival to a province-wide event. Zurbano added that it was a subsequent invitation by Rensoli to meet with local raperos in Alamar, however, that sparked his interest in hip hop at a deeper personal level. Although he had no previous exposure to rap and had found the Alamar scene somewhat disorganized, Zurbano told me he was intrigued by what he experienced during his visit:

> Right away I found that I had a strong affinity with these young people. I understood what they wanted, what they were saying. They brought some music to me and I began to hear their lyrics and their music. As a matter of principle, when I take something on I do it thoroughly, and so I wanted to inform myself about rap. So I began searching for literature on rap and read some bibliographic materials though unfortunately not much because there's very little on rap, at least here in Cuba. And then somehow I eventually became involved in the organizing committee for the event.[1]

The event to which Zurbano refers was the 1997 Cuban hip hop festival in Alamar, which marked AHS's entree into hip hop as a collaborative organizer of the annual festival alongside Grupo Uno. From that point on, La Asociación—as it became known to members of Havana's hip hop community—became the principal and increasingly invested site of institutional contact between the revolutionary state and the island's evolving hip hop movement. As a key initial mediator of this engagement, Zurbano's curiosity and affective "affinity" with local raperos extended well beyond institutional concerns. Through a range of intellectual activities including scholarship (cf. Zurbano 2004a, 2004b, 2006, 2009) and eventual editorial directorship of the state-run hip hop publication *Movimiento*,[2] Zurbano became a pivotal interlocutor and advocate for Havana's hip hop community, frequently acting as intermediary between the movement and varying state-run cultural institutions.

As one of an influential handful of Afro-Cuban intellectuals who would foster important relationships with Havana-area raperos, Zurbano's evolving institutional positionality—with AHS, the Union of Cuban Writers and Artists (UNEAC), and his former directorship of the publishing wing of Casa de las Américas—while largely respected, also drew ambivalence from some of the movement's younger, more institutionally cautious members. Such circumspection spoke of a broader ambivalence of positionality Zurbano occupied as an institutionally situated Afro-Cuban and intellectual progeny of the socialist revolution whose efforts, while potentially transcendent of institutional functionality, remained to an extent circumscribed by state interests. These tensions, as discussed in chapter 6, eventually gave rise to an episode of political fallout that once again underscored the political stakes of antiracist advocacy amid ongoing Cuban legacies of regulatory nonracialism.

Reflecting on the earlier moment of state engagement with hip hop, AHS's mission, in Zurbano's words, was aimed at integrating "new cultural forms within enduring frameworks of the nation, and national and political culture, opening up utopian possibilities and new forms of expression" (Zurbano 2009: 144). Regarding Cuban hip hop, this translated into "identifying talented rap artists, legitimizing their activities, improving their social recognition, supporting their initiatives, and incorporating them into more established cultural spaces" (Zurbano 2009: 145). To again paraphrase Fidel Castro's oft-cited "Inside the Revolution, everything. Against the Revolution, nothing," the operational subtext of AHS's engagement with hip hop thus seemed one aimed at incorporation. Although such an agenda may indeed have been on the horizon in the late 1990s, successive hip hop festivals continued to be organized by Grupo Uno on the most meager of resources, provided in large part through local municipal sources (Hoch 1999). Hence despite AHS's official cosponsorship of the festival, state commitments to hip hop remained in practice more akin to guarded tolerance than active support. Whereas raperos would continue to struggle for official recognition and greater access to state resources and space, the revolutionary state's view of the movement generally remained that of a faddish, inorganic cultural phenomenon that would eventually fade.

A critical shift in perspective, if not implicit strategy, occurred in May 1999. Cuba's then-influential minister of culture Abel Prieto called a meeting in Havana with representatives of both rapero and rockero communities to convey the state's official recognition of rap and rock music as legitimate forms of Cuban cultural expression. One individual present at the meeting was Pablo Herrera, who remembers harboring apprehension about the shift in position. Recounting an exchange during the meeting, Pablo recalls:

> What I told Abel Prieto [at the meeting] was, "Senior Ministro [*laughs*], you and I know that the minute you decide to stop Cuban hip hop you can, like an electrical switch, just shut it down. You can just stop the current from going there—stop the whole thing and shut it down." The president at the time of Hermanos Saíz, Fernando Rojas, said to me that I was being a bit apocalyptic. And when the minster decided to close the meeting he referred to my question and said that in the past, "We [the state] have had to power down certain things because we felt like they were not viable with the agenda that we have as a government."[3]

In a public ceremony held just a few weeks later, Prieto reportedly declared: "We have to support our Cuban rappers because this is the next generation of Cubans and they are saying some powerful things with this art. I am responsible for giving this generation the freedom to claim their power culturally" (Hoch 1999). From this point on the state took a conspicuously active interest in hip hop, with the Ministry of Culture under the direction of Abel Prieto serving as the central coordinator of efforts to incorporate hip hop within institutional realms of revolutionary national culture.

Another meeting later that same year involving Minister Prieto that may have also played into the state's pivot on hip hop was attended by a visiting Harry Belafonte (cf. Baker 2011; Levinson 2003). An important difference, however, was that this gathering involved Fidel Castro himself. A bit of background here. Sharing a history with Cuba predating the 1959 triumph of the revolution, Belafonte's artistic work as a performer and Caribbean-born native found fertile grounding in the vibrancies of Afro-Cuban music making.[4] At the same time, a life of progressive activism spanning U.S. and international involvement provided Belafonte a perspective on the post-1959 period that helped frame a history of critical engagement with Cuba's revolutionary project (Belafonte and Shnayerson 2011). It was during a trip in December 1999 to attend Havana's annual International Film Festival that

Belafonte first came into contact with local raperos, an experience that apparently left a mark and shaped the terms of a subsequent conversation with Castro and Prieto.

As Belafonte recounts in his memoir, while at lunch at the stately Hotel Nacional:

> I noticed a group of blacks who told me they were rappers. I said I hadn't known that Cuba had rappers. After all, rap is in your face, by definition. How could they be true to rap's spirit in Castro's Cuba? They couldn't perform in Havana's clubs, they acknowledged; to the country's elite, they didn't even exist. But they did perform underground, often for hundreds of people. That night, [my wife] Julie and I went to hear the ones we'd met. We were amazed. Of course we didn't understand every word and idiom; rap is hard enough to follow in English, much less in a second language. But a translator helped us follow the gist, and I fully appreciated the passion behind what I was hearing.
>
> The very next day, Julie and I had lunch with Fidel, along with his minister of culture, Abel Prieto, a tall, very handsome, very Spanish-looking hippie with long hair and blue eyes. We started talking about blacks in Cuban culture, which gave me the opportunity to bring up the black rappers we'd heard the night before and what a pity it was that they could only perform underground. I could see that Castro had only the vaguest idea of what rap and hip-hop were, so I gave him a crash course in how they'd swept the planet, how they not only dominated the international music industry but had so much to say about the social and political issues of the day. For Castro to be unaware of how much Cuban rappers were adding to that conversation was truly a pity—not least because I could see how a U.S.-Cuban cultural exchange in rap and hip-hop might start a dialogue between the two countries. Fidel turned in some bafflement to the minister of culture. "Why are these artists afraid to perform in Havana?"
>
> Prieto had to admit he didn't know much about rap or Cuban rappers, let alone black ones. To Fidel, free speech wasn't so much the issue as racism; if black artists in Cuba were being repressed, that undermined Castro's no-prejudice policy. Lunch was over, so we stood up to take our leave. "Where are you going?" Fidel demanded. I suggested we might head back to our protocol house. "No, no, no. I want you to come with

me and tell me more about these rappers." (Belafonte and Shnayerson 2011: 360–61)

In Belafonte's understanding, questions of race were front and center in the exchange as well as a potential factor in a political disconnect between Cuba's leadership and local raperos. Reflecting similarly on the episode, Nehanda Abiodun recalls:

> The first thing [Belafonte] did was meet with them in the Hotel Nacional, and it was an open forum—all rappers were invited, it wasn't a select group. [This was 1999?] Yes, this was '99 in December. And to the credit of the rappers they didn't hold back. And Harry just listened, he just listened to it all. The next thing he did was attend this small concert and party that was held just for him. But after Harry listened to the music of the hip hoppers he had a meeting with Fidel. And he said that what started out to be just a lunch with Fidel turned out to be a ten-hour meeting, and a large part of the discussion was on hip hop. [Ten hours?] Yes, ten hours![5]

In a subsequent return to Havana in 2002 Belafonte again met with local MCs, though this time the assemblage was hosted by the newly inaugurated state-run Agencia Cubana de Rap (ACR). Parts of this exchange are documented in a 2004 article, "Encuentro entre amigos," published in the Agency's *Movimiento* magazine, where themes of race and blackness serve as central points of national and generational translation between Belafonte and a score of Afro-Cuban raperos. Thus an official shift did indeed appear to occur yet one involving multiple players, but let us avoid getting too far afield.

Returning to that 1999 juncture, Hermanos Saíz eventually assumed full administrative control of the Cuban hip hop festival, usurping the previous leadership of Rensoli and others in Grupo Uno. While there were reported charges of financial improprieties on the part of Rensoli and Grupo Uno as the basis for their state-sanctioned removal as festival organizers, it seemed fairly apparent to many at the time that the driving motivation behind AHS's administrative takeover of the festival was political. By 2001 a new public face of the festival emerged during a high-profile press conference held in a swanky lounge bar atop the Teatro Nacional (National Theater). On the podium, bookended by Pablo Herrera and Ariel Fernández Díaz, sat a collection of institutional figures including Hermanos Saíz's then vice president Fernando León Jacomino. As La Asociación's key liaison with Havana's hip hop community at the time, Jacomino had established a fairly respectable reputation among many MCs. Fairly quickly, though, Jacomino disappeared from the scene. His position was filled by Alpidio Alonso, Hermanos Saíz's new national president, who had recently been transferred to Havana from the eastern city of Santa Clara. The shifting of responsibility from the vice presidential to presidential rank of AHS represented a further ratcheting up of the state's engagement with hip hop, one now led by a unfamiliar outsider. Assuming a direct and fairly aggressive hands-on approach, Alpidio eventually established working relationships with a number of key figures in Havana's hip hop community. In the end, however, many of these associations were marked by tension if not distrust.

When I asked about the evolving role of the state with regard to Cuban hip hop, Alpidio explained that the responsibility of Hermanos Saíz was to help incorporate raperos and their work within institutional structures that would support and channel their creative energy more directly within the revolutionary process. He spoke of raperos as among la vanguardia (the vanguard) of the revolution, explaining that hip hop was in many ways "in front of the institutions" in terms of their social vision regarding Cuba's current challenges. As such, he concluded, the institutions—and by extension the revolutionary state—needed to pay greater attention to what raperos were voicing through their music. Somewhat echoing this position, in response to an interview query as to whether AHS saw itself as providing official space for hip hop, Alpidio responded: "I would prefer if the question was asked directly to the raperos themselves. But yes, Cuban rap has found through AHS a space to speak, to be part of the Revolution. And it spreads a revolutionary message and committed one, because their texts express it this way" (Mantienzo 2004: 1). Despite Alpidio's expressed concern about not speaking for raperos, it became apparent that Hermanos Saíz's newfound interest in hip hop was tied to managing the public face—if not the organizational character—of the movement. The official press conference for the 2002 hip hop festival stands here as a vivid case in point.

Held in Havana's International Press Center in the commercial heart of the thoroughfare of Calle 23, a small collection of middle-aged white men—once again sandwiched between the younger and darker Pablo Herrera and Ariel Fernández Díaz at either end—sat on the stage before a packed audience. At the center, Alpidio directed the proceedings while Pablo and Ariel appeared less as active participants than perfunctory window dressing for the event. The dozen or so MCs who showed up for the press conference lined the back wall, looking on rather detached at the unfolding spectacle onstage. This disconnect was later noted by Pablo, who commented on how telling it was that one of the purported authorities on hip hop, an older white man whom no one seemed to recognize, repeatedly mispronounced the names of the artists slated to participate in the upcoming festival. Following the press conference, Ariel put it to me this way: "black music, white people, same ol' shit." Apparent inconsistencies between these statements and Pablo and Ariel's actual participation (or at least the official semblance of such) in the press conference spoke again to a certain tenuousness they now maneuvered as members of Havana's hip hop community with institutional access. As I explore momentarily, Ariel's evolving positionality as one betwixt and between the movement and the state carried a particularly charged set of complexities.

A tone of paternalism presided over much of the press conference in which Alpidio and company seemed set on conveying the message "These are our Cuban youth [as silent(ced) as they are], and the state is here to provide." In line with moves that denied autonomous voice to Cuban MCs, any mention of race was conspicuously absent from the press conference. Such omissions became standard practice in practically all official references to hip hop by the Cuban state and its institutions. An incorporative discourse of "our youth" was deployed strategically in state pronouncements, thus avoiding any public acknowledgment of the racial currents that underpinned much of the movement. To do so would expose the present urgencies of race and Cuban nationhood, a subject the revolutionary leadership remained reluctant to openly address. Official couchings of raperos as "our youth," moreover, were reminiscent of state paternalism directed at black Cubans during the earlier revolutionary period (cf. de la Fuente 2001). Here the post-1959 canonization of Nicolás Guillén's poem, "Tengo," as a celebrated ode of indebted black gratitude to the revolution assumes added levels of resonance—ones nonetheless challenged by Hermanos de Causa's revisionist interpretations (see chapter 4).

The state's institutional ante vis-à-vis hip hop was raised considerably, however, with the establishment of the Agencia Cubana de Rap (ACR) under the Ministry of Culture in late 2002. Prior to this moment the only institutional outlet available to a select few raperos was membership in the previously mentioned state-run empresa Benny Moré, an "auto-financed" agency designed to promote and provide a minimal wage to performing artists associated with popular dance music (cf. R. Moore 2006b: 91–92). As one of the few MCs associated with ACR, Magia López of Obsesión recalled her early experience with the empresa:

> So in 2000 after many battles, four [rap] groups managed to enter the empresa Benny Moré and were recognized as professional. But in reality we were without work and wages for a long time, because this empresa did not know how to promote or market our work. They had over twenty years of marketing primarily popular and traditional music and we [raperos] were basically a quite different thing.[6]

Dedicated explicitly to hip hop, La Agencia, as it became known within rapero ranks, assumed the responsibility of representing a select number of hand-picked rap groups with whom it coordinated performance activities such as concerts and tours. The initial ten groups incorporated into ACR's portfolio were Alto Voltaje, Anónimo Consejo, Cubanos en la Red, Cubanitos, Doble Filo, Eddy-K, Free Hole Negro, Obsesión, Papo Record, and Primera Base. Appointed to head ACR was Susana García Amorós, a black woman in her early forties who had previously worked as an institution-based researcher with a specialization in Afro-Cuban literature. Although her appointment as a black woman appeared strategic, many noted that she had no background in music administration, let alone familiarity with hip hop. In this light Susana was viewed by some as not much more than a *funcionaria* or state functionary within Cuba's larger bureaucratic apparatus. As Ariel Fernández Díaz mused in conversation: "I mean, you need to ask where did Susana come from, the communist party. So when Susana had a decision on the table that needed to be made, something that required she'd have to choose between the hip hop movement and the communist party, she would choose the communist party."[7]

In describing the objective of ACR, Susana explained that the agency was formed to promote and commercialize hip hop talent within its portfolio. It was generally understood that a key criterion used in identifying artists for inclusion was tied to their perceived commercial viability, a mandate read critically by some. As a designated *auto-financiado* (self-financed) state organ, ACR was designed to draw on the potential revenue of its talent pool to finance its operational costs. As Pablo Herrera suggested to me at the time, the formation of ACR in his view was ultimately linked to state interests in farming out Cuban hip hop to an international marketplace. He likened such moves to state efforts to "pimp" hip hop for commercial gain. Arrangements of the kind had already occurred with the ever-growing numbers of Cuban musicians now traveling abroad in the wake of an international boom in Cuban music since the mid-1990s following the Buena Vista Social Club phenomenon. In some of these early scenarios the Cuban state was reported to have garnered upward of 50 percent of artists' overseas earnings (Watrous 1997).

Those in decision-making positions were, moreover, no doubt aware of the commercial potential of Cuban hip hop given the international success of Orishas, a French-produced rap group of Havana expatriates, including two former members of the pioneering hip hop trio Amenaza, whose debut album A lo cubano (2000 Universal Latino) surpassed the platinum mark in Europe and sold over 50,000 copies in the United States.[8] The collaborative brainchild of the Paris-based hip hop producer Nicolas "Miko" Nocchi and the Cuban MC Flaco Pro Nuñez, a key factor in the album's international appeal was the astute coupling of identifiably "Cuban" musical elements such as son, rumba, and traditional Cuban vocal styles with rap lyricism and hip-hop-informed beats. In dialogue with au courant packagings of Cuban blackness, however, economies of race were also central to the project's commercial branding from inception. From the savvy choice of "Orishas" (gods), to the stylized incorporation of Yoruba-derived chants of Ocha-Lucumí and Afro-Cuban percussive lines, to a graphic darkening of the artists' portraits on the album cover, a cultivated "Cuban" aesthetics of blackness was integral to the group's international marketing strategy.

An ubiquitous sonic presence in the streets of Havana immediately following the album's debut, Orishas returned to Cuba in December 2000 and January 2001 for a series of sold-out concerts. The explosive nature of the events and broader commercial possibilities of Cuban hip hop no doubt caught the attention of the revolutionary leadership. While most Havana-based raperos I know were generally critical of what they viewed as Orishas's overtly commercial nature, many also respected, if not envied, the high-end production qualities of their music. Some, moreover, acknowledged that Orishas's commercial success may have opened new commercial prospects for them both at home and abroad.

When I spoke with the ACR director Susana García Amorós about the significance of hip hop in Cuba, she made the repeated point to distinguish island hip hop from its originating cousin in the United States. Susana emphasized that raperos had begun developing their own style of dress, gestures, and textual thematics that reflect a distinctly Cuban sensibility. Throughout she referred to raperos as *los jóvenes* (the youth) who, she suggested, were contributing to a deepening of understanding of Cuban society, "pero," she added, "en una forma constructiva" (but, in a constructive way) within the revolutionary process. When asked about racial dynamics within the movement, Susana responded: "Here in Cuba you can speak about pigmentation or coloration, but you cannot talk about 'the races' because in reality we are all mixed."[9] Her response seemed to me a bit incongruous at the time given her previous research background in Afro-Cuban literary themes.

Susana then qualified that in terms of skin color, yes, the majority of raperos are darker skinned but, she emphasized, there are also those "*más claro*" (lighter skinned). I added that in my own experience with the community, race appeared to factor into hip hop beyond simply questions of skin color, pointing out the salience of black racial identity themes and self-practice within the movement. At that she let the issue rest without further comment. While Susana may have had cause to be cautious with me as a yuma (foreigner) and a Yankee at that, her avoidance of racial complexities seemed telling. Thus in noted contrast with the commercial packaging of Orishas, race seemed largely expunged from La Agencia's official discourse on hip hop.

One of the early projects Susana undertook in her new role as director of ACR was to accompany Magia López and Alexey Rodríguez of Obsesión along with MC Edgar González of the hip hop duo Doble Filo during a 2003 U.S. tour. Doble Filo's other artistic half, MC Yrak Saenz, was denied the required permission to travel by Cuban immigration. While no official reason was given, one possible factor may have been a concern that the artist might refuse to return to Cuba at the conclusion of the tour. Such anxieties were heightened given the previously mentioned rapero "defection" episode during a 2001 tour to New York City. Although the 2003 tour was organized and funded entirely through a collaboration of Miami- and New York–based arts organizations,[10] the Cuban Ministry of Culture negotiated Susana's inclusion as official state chaperone. Susana's addition did indeed put an official face to (and within) the tour, while establishing a new degree of institutional coordination of hip hop as a whole.

While Obsesión as one of the most accomplished of Cuban hip hop groups was officially represented by La Agencia, many other talented, more critically postured groups in Havana conspicuously were not. I recall one exchange in particular that exposed some related tensions around ACR's operational nature. During a discussion at a public colloquium organized in 2003 as part of the now state-run Cuban hip hop festival, MC Soandres del Río of Hermanos de Causa took the floor to challenge what he saw as ACR's exclusionary nature. The critique was directed at Alpidio Alonso, who earlier that day had defended La Agencia against other charges given Susana's noted absence from the colloquium, the first held during her new tenure as director. Alpidio responded by arguing that it was impossible for the agency to represent all groups, suggesting it was ultimately a question of resources. Soandres countered by asking Alpidio if he knew his name or to what group he belonged, which Alpidio conceded he did not. At this, Soandres concluded that institutional claims to "represent and support" hip hop were at best woefully out of touch, if not in the end implicitly suspect. Soandres's charge reflected a broader disillusionment and distrust shared by many in the community toward the new rap agency and broader institutional efforts to engage island hip hop. Even Magia and Alexey, who were among the celebrated "stars" of La Agencia, soon grew critical of the office's workings.

In truth, the revolutionary state and its institutions held resources that raperos long sought, resulting in something of a paternal relationship (if episodic and largely strategic) between the Cuban state and hip hop artists. In the immediate years following its establishment, ACR, in conjunction with Hermanos Saíz and the Instituto Cubano de la Música, organized a range of hip hop concerts throughout Havana alongside the first national hip hop tour involving Obsesión and Doble Filo in 2004. During this period raperos and their music, long invisible in state-run media, began appearing—albeit within certain constraints—on television, radio, in print, and on the Internet. Under Hermanos Saíz auspices, between 1999 and 2003 the annual hip hop festival expanded from a three-night event in Alamar to a five-day, multisited program throughout greater Havana involving colloquia and art exhibitions in addition to music performances. The concurrent rise of weekly shows at Café Cantante and La Madriguera marked a further expansion of Havana-based raperos' access to officially sanctioned space and resources.

An increasingly central player in this elevated state engagement was Ariel Fernández Díaz. In addition to holding court alongside Pablo Herrera as DJ Asho at Café Cantante's Saturday afternoon showcases and evening peñas at La Madriguera—both under AHS's auspices—Ariel assumed a position within Hermanos Saíz in 2000 as hip hop events coordinator and official state liaison with the movement.[11] Although bringing a minimal peso salary, this move catapulted Ariel, already something of an organic intellectual figure within the hip hop community, into an official state capacity. Ariel later described his new position as a move from "the margins to the center," one broadly analogous in this sense to state incorporations of Cuban hip hop as a whole. Among his new responsibilities, Ariel became the lead person for leasing state-owned audio equipment for hip-hop-related music events.

One case in point in late 2001 involved the informal Vedado street venue of Diez y Diecinueve, during which the hip hop collective EPG&B organized an afternoon concert with a local assortment of invited artists. As the man of the hour, Ariel coordinated the event's audio needs, which in classic Cuban fashion arrived a couple of hours late. Yet unlike previous times when police forced the street crowds converging at this intersection to disband, officers were conspicuously absent amid the public spectacle of black bodies and music. This scenario reflected a new level of state tolerance and material support for hip hop, a development in which Ariel now played an informative role.

In addition to promoting music-related events including those in his role as DJ Asho, Ariel's institutional position afforded him new intellectual outlets and resources as an impassioned advocate for hip hop in Cuba. A major undertaking along these lines was his editorial directorship of *Movimiento*, a glitzy state-financed magazine dedicated to Cuban hip hop published under the auspices of ACR and the Instituto Cubano de la Música. Launched in 2003, the project pulled together an eclectic array of hip-hop-affiliated individuals, the vast majority of whom were Afro-Cuban. Among those involved were journalists, photographers, intellectuals, graphic designers, and hip hop artists who collectively exercised fairly open editorial control over the magazine's content.[12] Under Ariel's directorship through 2005, *Movimiento* published four issues encompassing a wide range of articles and imagery relating to island hip hop. As a journalist, Ariel also contributed a broad selection of articles and other material to the magazine. The project as such

5.2. Journalist, DJ, and events producer Ariel Fernández Díaz.
Photo courtesy of Ariel Fernández Díaz

represented an important moment of critical triangulation between the hip hop movement, Afro-Cuban intellectuals and artists, and state resources via an institutionally facilitated medium.

In conversation about his new position with Hermanos Saíz, Ariel acknowledged that his thinking had recently shifted with regard to his longstanding distance from the state and "the revolution." Now, he implied, he saw things somewhat differently. When I asked whether he shared a greater level of identification with the state given his new involvement, Ariel responded:

Of course, completely. [What changed?] I don't know, my thinking is deeper, my struggle is deeper, my political understanding is more profound. Before, when I started, the only thing important was that rap could be in Cuba, that it could be heard in Cuba. Now I'm interested in what role rap can have in the political life of the country, no? . . . Many people complain about the state but there are things that the state does that may harm five or six people, but benefit many. It's very complicated, understand? It's very complicated to understand.[13]

During the years I knew Ariel, his thinking and positionality seemed to be constantly evolving in ways that often involved wresting with conflicting tensions. In describing his newfound responsibilities working with Hermanos Saíz, the internal seeds of some of this discord were apparent.

My mission is to be an artist, to be human—think for it, work for it. This is the same mission of the movement itself. I am fighting to be a messenger between the Cuban institutions and the artists, understand? I arrived at the Cuban institutions—the Minister of Culture, Asociación Hermanos Saíz—because raperos wanted that. I am there to fight because raperos want concerts, discs—for these kinds of things. [Like a bridge?] Yes, like a bridge. I do not desire that people create an identity for me apart from the movement, no. I think that people intend for me to have a role within the movement. I don't want people to think that I want to be a "mogul" like Russell Simons. Sincerely, if I'm a leader or the face of the movement about many things, I always have to respond to what the movement itself wants.

Although on the surface these remarks may suggest otherwise, Ariel's comments betray an ambivalence that he occupied as a middleman caught between hip hop and the state. Ariel's need to repeatedly assert his fidelity to the movement reflected the potentially compromising position he now occupied. While Ariel and, to a lesser degree, Pablo Herrera have served varyingly as intermediaries between the state and the hip hop movement, their positionality as advocates and artistic producers grew organically out of long-term engagements within Havana's hip hop community. Most raperos I knew highly respected Ariel and his tireless, if at times seemingly obsessive, efforts over the years to promote the cause of island hip hop. This, however, did not mean that Ariel's (or for that matter Pablo's) relationship with Cuban MCs and others affiliated with the movement was free from complexities and tensions.[14]

While many recognized the instrumental role Ariel played in securing needed state-related resources, this did not translate to unguarded trust of the Cuban state and its institutions. Ariel in turn seemed cognizant of how he, as an employee of Hermanos Saíz, might be implicated by concerns regarding state modes of intervention. Indeed, one well-positioned person within the movement once playfully likened Ariel to "a house negro" in Hermanos Saíz. In truth, over time Ariel grew increasingly conflicted about his position. He often complained about the frequent arguments he would wage with the Hermanos Saíz's leadership over the direction of his work and the movement itself. Ariel eventually expressed frustration and mounting misgivings about continuing his involvement (i.e., employment) within AHS, including his desire to break from Hermanos Saíz and organize his own hip-hop-related projects independent of the state. The challenge, of course, was how and with what resources. Although he gradually created distance between himself and AHS and would eventually resign from his position, for that moment in the early to mid-2000s Ariel was caught at the epicenter of an ongoing dance between hip hop and the state as both grappled with a rapidly changing Cuba.

Shapings of a Black Public Sphere

It is important to consider the interplay between Cuban hip hop and the revolutionary state in light of a set of confluences beginning in the 1990s that gave rise to an *apertura* or "opening" on the part of the Cuban state to a wider public range of social and artistic expression along with broader recognitions of social difference (cf. Dilla Alfonso 2002). The revolutionary state's relatively more tolerant position on homosexuality, though clearly with limitations (see Saunders 2010), stands as one example of such openings during this period (Bejel 2001). Many cite the Third Congress of Cuba's Communist Party in 1986 as something of a watershed event in this direction (de la Fuente 2001; N. Fernandez 2001).[15] Signaling a measured reopening of public discussion of race after long silencings,[16] Fidel Castro acknowledged the persistence of racial discrimination during the congress's closing, pointing to the scarcity of blacks, women, and youth within the party's leadership. His call for redress eventually gave rise to a two-fold increase of nonwhite membership in the party's Central Committee following a purge of older committee members (de la Fuente 2001; Dilla Alfonso 2002; C. Moore 1989).[17]

The party's Fifth Congress in 1997 drew renewed attention to the continued scarcity of blacks in the party's ranks, again raising questions of racial exclusion within Cuba's political structures (Pérez Sarduy and Stubbs 2000). Although a decade apart, these declarations occurred during significant periods of economic anxiety, the first involving a national effort to "rectify" recent market reforms and their social impacts,[18] and the second amid an ambivalence regarding neoliberal expansion and the very moment and circumstances under which the Cuban hip hop movement was finding its footing.

Recalling state broachings of the topic of racism in the early years of the revolutionary period, Alejandro de la Fuente observes that black intellectuals played an important role in pushing public terms of debate on the issue (de la Fuente 2001: 260). Within this more recent historical frame, I suggest that raperos played a similar contributing role in reopening public dialogues on race and blackness in the early 2000s. Here a dialectic play of sorts occurred between hip hop as a new space of racial articulation in both form (racial subjectivity) and practice (race-based critique), and the Cuban state in its efforts to manage the terms of such expansive contest. What then in a more explicit sense were the working dimensions of this interface, and in what ways might raperos' and other aligned actors' efforts align with periodic openings and subsequent retreats of state-sanctioned space (cf. Cabezas 2009; Corrales 2004)?

I suggest that black and darker-skinned raperos were in fact active in shaping a nascent black counterpublic at the millennial turn rooted in a black political difference and antiracist advocacy within an otherwise nonracial national imaginary. Taking a lead from Michael Dawson (1995), I draw on Nancy Fraser's notion of subaltern counterpublics as competing sites of social and political expression vis-à-vis the often marginalizing effects of official public spheres. For Fraser, such counterpublics frequently challenge "exclusionary norms of the bourgeois public, elaborating alternative styles of political behavior and alternative norms of public speech" (Fraser 1990: 61). While conventional notions of a public sphere associated with liberal democratic societies (Habermas 1989) may not operate as such within revolutionary Cuba, where domains of public engagement have been largely channeled and regulated by state-run institutions, this does not mean that alternative modes of public expression and dialogue do not exist. Indeed, the recent rise of a relatively cantankerous Cuban blogosphere is illustrative of such expanding alterities to state-mediated realms of public discourse (see Duong 2013). Efforts to give Cuban voice to an emergent black counterpublic have similarly required alternative, nonformal means of public engagement and redress.[19]

Integral to this new moment of Afro-Cuban parlance, Cuban hip hop can be seen as operating precisely in this sense as an alternative site of black public enunciation. Here raperos' voicings and attending modes of black self-crafting have been instrumental in pushing critical discussions of race and class into realms of Cuban public discourse. Where else in revolutionary Cuba, for instance, might one stand before upward of three thousand black youth and engage publicly in critiques of racial exclusion and racially directed police harassment? Perhaps Cuban timba and more recent reggaetón, whose artists and fan bases also draw heavily from Afro-Cuban youth, may also offer public sites of social critique via realms of popular music (cf. Baker 2011; Hernández-Reguant 2004; Perna 2005; Vaughn 2012). While these genres represent vibrant locales within an expanding field of racially inflected expression—ones in varying conversation with hip hop themselves—neither timba nor reggaetón articulate the explicit racial claims or antiracist advocacy found in hip hop.

Black-identified raperos as such maneuvered in somewhat vanguardist terms vis-à-vis Cuba's spectrum of racial politics at the millennial turn, occupying critical ground within a broader unfolding present of Afro-Cuban political articulation. The evolving lines of this confluence have been noted by others (Fernandes and Stanyek 2007; M. Perry 2004; Saunders 2009), including historian Alejandro de la Fuente, who, citing raperos among key agents, has likened such developments to a "new Afro-Cuban cultural movement" that encompasses "musicians, visual artists, writers, academics and activists shar[ing] common grievances about racism and its social effects" (de la Fuente 2008: 697; see also de la Fuente 2010).

An important marker of hip hop's weight in this dialogic mix involved a growing interest in raperos and their art by a small but active Havana circle of Afro-Cuban intellectuals, a particular current of which was composed by an older generation. The filmmaker Gloria Rolando was among such interlocutors who, in addition to other involvements, collaborated with Anónimo Consejo in developing her film *Raíces de mi corazón* (Roots of my heart) and its exploration of the Partido Independiente de Color. The social psychologist Norma Guillard Limonta, whose research centers on black women via overlapping dimensions of race, gender, and sexuality, also shares an important history of engagement with hip hop. Guillard Limonta has been particularly interested in the role of women within the movement and has published scholarly articles along these lines including a piece in *Movimiento* magazine (Guillard Limonta 2005). The ethnomusicologist Grizel Hernández Baguer, with the Cuban Center for Investigation and Development of Music (CIDMUC), has similarly taken a long-term scholarly interest in island hip hop (Hernández Baguer, Casanella Cué, and González Bello 2004), as has the journalist Joaquín Borges-Triana (2004). The Afro-Cuban poet and literary figure Victor Fowler, for his part, has also made frequent contributions to *Movimiento* in the form of brief reviews of recent Cuban publications on racial issues (Fowler 2004a, 2004b). *Movimiento* in this sense was instrumental not only as a forum for documenting hip hop's Cuban rise, but also as an emergent space for Cuban conversations on race through the organizing frame of hip hop itself.

A more intimate level of intergenerational engagement involved Tomás Fernández Robaina and Roberto Zurbano, who, in addition to their collaborative involvements with the movement, have published scholarly commentary on island hip hop (Fernández Robaina 2002; Zurbano 2004a, 2004b, 2006, 2009). Sharing some thoughts amid a conversation about hip hop's Cuban relevance in 2006, Zurbano elaborated:

> Issues of race, gender, class, and notions of sexuality are being reflected in hip hop here in Cuba in terms of making a series of projections, not only in the fields of aesthetics and the arts, but also in the ideological

field. . . . Hip hop is subverting ideas, critiquing a way of life in which a new Cuban economy creates a lot of marginal subjects and spaces—a new economy where there are mutually exclusive terms, excluding spaces, excluded subjects. In this sense they are producing discourses that are not only artistic but also social. They have taken a social discourse and rearticulated revolutionary values within which they have been trained and educated.

These are the utopic horizons for possible rescue that they are fighting for. And in this sense I find they are a vanguard not only because of the social critique embedded in the text of their songs, but also how they live a discourse that is a critique of the social ills of today, Cuba today—a global society. The most interesting thing is that the social criticism that they are making is shared by many who feel oppressed in other parts of the world such as other black people, the poor, the oppressed, those crushed under the culture of neoliberal capitalism.[20]

Zurbano's comments underscore an appreciation for hip hop's vangardist possibilities not only in terms of seeking "rescue" of the revolutionary promise in the face of the exclusionary challenges of the neoliberal moment, but possibly more so regarding raperos' globally expansive revisionings of utopic possibility.

Another individual of note echoing similar lines of appraisal is Gisela Arandia, a prominent Afro-Cuban researcher and journalistically trained scholar of contemporary black issues affiliated with the Union of Cuban Artists and Writers (UNEAC). Gisela was instrumental in launching UNEAC's previously mentioned "Color Cubano" project in 2001 as a forum for writers and artists—the majority of whom were Afro-Cuban—to reflect upon and debate issues of racism, black media representation, and the role of Afro-Cubans in revolutionary society. The project drew its name from Nicolás Guillén's famed yearning for a postracial Cuban future embodied in the celebrated verse "Algún día se dirá: 'color cubano'" (One day it [Cubanness] will be known as: "Cuban Color") from his 1931 poem "Songoro cosongo." In revisiting the theme, the forum was illustrative of recent institutional openings to relatively more public discussions of race,[21] openings in which Afro-Cuban intellectuals again played an active role. Reflecting on hip hop and its relevance to broader conversations on race in Cuba, Gisela explained to me:

In this sense debating the issue [of race] is where we are at this moment. This means we have to advance the issue beyond the taboo—the subject starts to speak and voices begin to emerge. In this context the rap movement is extremely important because it allows us to look at very specific things and recognize the problems. If you were always told before, "Here there is no racism," and then a rap song tells the story of police in the streets asking you 15,000 times for your ID card while not stopping some other white boy, right then and there the specifics are condemning.

Now, what is important is that raperos make alliances with people and seek a broad spectrum. Of course they elect their own leaders and I'm not pretending to be incorporated into the movement because, of course, there is a tremendous distance between us, principally generational and intellectually. But of course they deserve support because they are a front in the fight against racism. This is important because in essence they introduce an antiracist discourse.[22]

For Gisela, a key space of exchange with raperos and others around hip hop occurred during a series of annual colloquiums organized as part of Hermanos Saíz's expansion of Cuba's hip hop festival. Unlike earlier years when the event drew an informal gathering of no more than a handful of raperos, since 2000, when I first participated, the colloquium grew into a multiday program drawing Cubans and foreigners alike around commentary and analysis of hip hop as a new Cuban phenomenon. In addition to Hermanos Saíz, participating state organs included UNEAC and El Museo de la Música (The Museum of Music), reflecting increased institutional recognition of hip hop as well as ongoing efforts to frame its official terms of debate. These public forums were often charged grounds for exchange around issues like racism, identity, and questions of citizenship—all read against the social backdrop of hip hop. Whether intentional or not, the colloquium's shift toward a more formal academic exchange in the end tended to marginalize raperos as participants. While MCs filled the seats listening to others, including myself, pontificate about *them* and *their* music, they were rarely if ever on the podium themselves. This did not, however, inhibit many from making their voices heard.

During a panel organized as part of the 2002 colloquium, Ariel Fernández Díaz—who himself played a key role in organizing the colloquium in his official capacity with AHS—offered a rather blistering critique of racial representation used in print advertising packaged for the foreign tourist market. Using imagery culled from this media, Ariel underscored the invisibility of black Cubans within much of the promotional literature or, when present, framed in racialized caricatures reproductive of folkloric or "colonial" portraiture. In juxtaposition, Ariel offered a collection of Cuban rap lyrics exemplary of the movement's black political currents. His tone was unapologetic and represented something of a milestone at the time in its public voicing of hip hop's racial orientation. In spite (or precisely by way) of his institutional capacity, Ariel contributed to a shattering of the official silence around hip hop's racial dimensionality, an issue that at the time still remained largely outside sanctioned state discourse and acknowledgment.

Discussions of this kind provoked an interesting set of exchanges. At one point a middle-aged black man from the audience addressed a panel, complaining about what he viewed as a misguided emphasis by raperos on issues of racial identity and racism. He suggested that Cuban MCs were merely, and uncritically, reproducing discourses prevalent in U.S. hip hop that were largely inorganic to Cuba. His concerns, however, failed to resonate with the audience, the majority of whom where themselves raperos who had long affirmed their Cubanness as artists.

On another colloquium day, Sekou Umoja of Anónimo Consejo addressed the colloquium from the floor, complaining that the enduring invisibility of Afro-Cuban figures compelled black youth to look elsewhere for "our heroes," citing the examples of Martin Luther King and Malcolm X. In Sekou's view, blackness had in essence been disenfranchised from Cuba's national narrative. Building on themes of racial disenfranchisement, Sekou continued by citing his inability as a "Cuban" to travel freely "dentro mi propio país" (in my own country) following the recent implementation of travel restrictions to regulate internal migration on the island.[23] While these laws were primarily designed to limit in-migration to Havana from eastern provinces at a time of growing regional inequality, such regulation often involved racially coded surveillance and policing of darker-skinned *palestinos* (or others filling the bill), as immigrants from the eastern Oriente region are commonly termed. Shortly after his remarks, Sekou was pulled aside by the president of Hermanos Saíz, Alpidio Alonso, who chastised him for his comments. During their exchange, Alpidio could be heard reminding Sekou not to forget the heroics of José Martí and Antonio Maceo and their martyred struggles for a nonracial Cuba, the tone of which seemed to suggest that Sekou should simply be thankful.

Additional voices active during this period of expanding dialogue included a small group of young Afro-Cuban intellectuals and artists, some of whom first came into contact with raperos while attending Tomás Fernández Robaina's "El Negro en Cuba" class in the Biblioteca Nacional. Coming of age amid the same ambiguities and frictions of the period, many among this emerging generation of thinkers and cultural producers shared with their rapero peers a similar set of critical perspectives on race and social power as lived in the current everyday.

One such member of this generational cohort was Yesenia Sélier, a thirty-something social psychology–trained researcher from Havana's Centro Juan Marinello whose work at the time centered on race and racial identity in Cuba. A key focus of Yesenia's scholarship—and one in conversation with Sekou's challenge above—addressed absences of historical memory vis-à-vis race on the part of both Afro-Cubans and Cuba's broader national imaginary. She suggests that such gaps, far from being incidental, are actively produced through the ideological workings of national discourse (see Sélier 2002). Not surprisingly, Yesenia's work eventually drew her to hip hop. Rather than a detached researcher, Yesenia's involvement with Havana's rapero community ranged from coauthoring an academic article with Pablo Herrera on hip hop for the prestigious Casa de Las Américas (Herrera and Sélier 2003), to performing poetry alongside a collection of female MCs during a Havana hip hop concert in 2003.[24] On more overtly artistic grounds, the photographers Diamela "Ife" Fernández, Ariel Arias Jiménez, and Javier Machado Leyva have all shared relationships with Havana-area raperos. Their involvement in documenting moments and broader ongoing elaborations of island hip hop have included contributions of images and production skills to *Movimiento* magazine.

Among this peer group of hip-hop-conversant intellectuals and artists, Roberto Diago Durruthy, known professionally as Diago, stands as a particularly high-profile figure.[25] As a relatively young, internationally renowned Afro-Cuban painter who has exhibited extensively in Cuba and abroad, much of Diago's work explores contemporary themes of race, racial identity, and racism, often fusing Afro-Cuban religious motifs and racially marked text in ways some have likened stylistically to Jean-Michel Basquiat (Mateo 2003).

Diago had been a key figure in the groundbreaking 1997 group show *Keloids*, organized at Havana's Casa de Africa by the visual artist Alexis Esquivel, examining Cuban themes of race and racism. Building on subsequent *Keloids* shows in 1999 and 2010, an updated rendering of the exhibition that also included Diago's work *Queloides/Keloids: Race and Racism in Cuban Contemporary Art*, curated by Alejandro de la Fuente and Elio Rodríguez Valdez, traveled to the United States accompanied by a handsome, essay-laden catalogue (de la Fuente 2010). Underscoring the resonance of hip hop in the dialogue, Hermanos de Causa's Soandres del Rio was invited to perform during the exhibition's 2010 U.S. opening in Pittsburgh.[26]

My first introduction to Diago was in Tomás's class, where he was often a highly engaged participant in discussions. Like Yesenia Sélier, it was in this setting that Diago initially came into dialogue with raperos. Although never coming to full fruition, there was talk at the time between himself, raperos, and others in class about organizing a collaborative presentation around the course's racial thematics. When later interviewed by a Cuban journalist regarding the centrality of racial critique in his work—which was framed by the journalist as exemplary of a new generation of black intellectuals— Diago responded by drawing parallels between himself and raperos in terms of a "carga agresiva" (aggressive charge) that characterized the kind of in-your-face challenges and unapologetic claims to black racial subjectivity central to both locales of artistic work (Mateo 2003: 25).

At the same time, Diago became something of a celebrated son of Cuba's new openness to overtly "black" forms of artistic expression, securing a highly coveted solo show in 2002 at Havana's new, relatively palatial state-run Museo Bellas Artes. In conjunction with the show, a well-attended symposium was coordinated around his work's racial thematics, drawing a high-profile assemblage of Afro-Cuban intellectuals including eminent cultural historian Rogelio Martínez Furé and celebrated poet Nancy Morejón. The symposium was officiated by the then cultural minister Abel Prieto, who, among a new generation of institutionally groomed intelligentsia arising in the 1990s,[27] had been something of an early advocate for greater state openness to more plural, antidogmatic forms of cultural production (see Davies 2000). Strategic as it may have been, this policy apparently extended to raperos, given Prieto's key role in mediating the state's institutional shift regarding hip hop.

Yet overtures to a relatively more tolerant climate toward cultural expression and the arts again corresponded with an increasingly commodity-driven national landscape, one heavily dependent on the commercial packaging of identifiably "Cuban" (and often racially marked) cultural forms and bodies. Diago's rise and accompanying state responsiveness may in this sense speak to an articulation of global markets, emergent sites and forms of black social expression, and the Cuban state's seemingly strategic recognition and institutional opening to both.

In the case of hip hop, the widening of institutional space and resources within which raperos operated after 1999 did not occur simply through a benevolence of state paternalism. Rather, these openings emerged within an evolving confluence of factors, including raperos' own labors to win space within an elaborating moment of Afro-Cuban enunciation coupled with market expansions that carried their own assimilative logics. By accommodating the critical arts, the Cuban state may have sought to manage potential challenges to the nonracial status quo by incorporating hip hop within the structural and discursive folds of revolutionary national culture while at the same time hedging on possibilities of its commercial draw. Although such efforts may have had restrictive effects, it is also evident that raperos along with allies were able to exploit openings to pose critiques and expose contradictions in both discursive and material realms of everyday Cuban life. Yet how sustainable, in the strategic end, was this negotiated balance?

Chapter 6.
Whither Hip Hop Cubano?

This is my life, my life is hip hop, hip hop's my culture, I am hip hop! This is my culture, the culture of my family and culture of all my brothers. And for all the brothers who are ready to fight for hip hop, I'm at your side. Hip hop's my life, wherever I am, until I die. Hip hop will continue here in Cuba. And they'll kill me for saying it but hip hop here in Cuba will never die.[1]
—DJ Alexis D'Boys

Robin Moore has documented the ways Cuba's *nueva trova* movement of the late 1960s and 1970s underwent transformation from a youth-centered music steeped in social commentary to a prominent state-sanctioned symbol of national revolutionary culture. In ways analogous to raperos albeit of an earlier generation, *trovadores* were inheritors of a revolutionary history and culture who, while embracing many of the ideals of state socialism, questioned the ways and extent to which such ideals were addressed during the early revolutionary period. Initially the Cuban state was not particularly receptive to such query, launching a period of intimidation directed at a number of the movement's key figures, including Pablo Milanés and Silvio Rodríguez (R. Moore 2006b).

By the early 1970s, however, a shift occurred that culminated in the formation of the Movimiento Nacional de la Trova (The National Trova Movement) under the Ministry of Culture in an effort to integrate a previously autonomous artistic movement within institutional folds of the state. While such developments provided nuevos trovadores much-needed access to state-controlled resources like performance venues, studio time, and distribution networks, Moore notes that the arrangement impacted the movement's independence of voice. Artists' work was now under tighter scrutiny; if one did not tread lightly one faced the possibility of losing state favor. As Moore explains, "*Trovadores* thus walked an ever more delicate line between fidelity to a government that now supported them and fidelity to themselves and their own points of view" (R. Moore 2006b: 157). The example of nueva trova hence begs the question as to whether raperos faced similar challenges regarding their evolving relationship with the Cuban state and its institutions. When considering such comparisons, two interwoven factors distinguish hip hop in historically significant ways. Unlike nueva trova of the previous moment, raperos' mediations of state power were complicated by the ascendancy of the Cuban marketplace as well as the (related) political salience of race among many leading artists.

In a pioneering 2000 article, "¿Poesía urbana? O la nueva trova de los noventa" (Urban poetry? or The nueva trova of the nineties), published in Cuba's youth-oriented periodical El *Caimán Barbudo*, Ariel Fernández Díaz similarly evokes parallels between hip hop and nueva trova. In the piece, Ariel offers a spirited defense of the cultural legitimacy of hip hop in Cuba, while underscoring raperos' revolutionary engaged role—like nuevos trovadores before—as critical commentators on the complexities and ambiguities of Cuba at the millennium's turn. While in his words raperos "make revolution with their texts, and educate with their poetry," they remain "misunderstood, censored despite carrying the truth in their hands" (A. Fernández Díaz 2000).[2]

In advocating for official space and recognition for hip hop, Ariel may not have foreseen the range of implications such moves ultimately engendered. What did become clear for many early on, however, was that a patronage-based relationship with the state required compromises and degrees of dependency that threatened autonomous music making and artistic control. In reality, what limited resources the Cuban state and its institutions did provide were far from adequate for meeting raperos' most basic production and performance needs. Given the limitations at both the political and material levels, many Cuban MCs sought entrepreneurial means to develop alternative, non-state-related strategies for production, performance, and distribution of their music. The crafting of background beats and voice tracks in makeshift home studios became increasingly possible through the proliferation of personal computers and an evolving range of consumer-based production software like Pro Tools, Cakewalk, and Fruity Loops. Such technological developments were critical given the lack of access to state-run recording studios and the prohibitive cost of private or quasi-private facilities such as Silvio Rodríguez's Abdala Studios in Havana. Coupling these home studios with CD-burning capacity, growing numbers of raperos were able to distribute music through informal channels at concerts and eventually the Internet. Collaborative projects were pursued as well. In 2005 a hip hop collective dubbed El Cartel, composed of a handful of Havana's most celebrated "underground" artists, released an independent CD project produced by Pablo Herrera.[3]

Obsesión's Magia López and Alexey Rodríguez along with their then-producer Yelandy Blaya collaborated with the duo Doble Filo in an independent venture labeled La Fabri-K. Ventures undertaken under the moniker included a 2002 CD release, a series of domestic and international tours,[4] and the 2005 launching of an annual multiday Hip Hop Symposium that combined workshops with nightly performances by MCs from both Cuba and abroad. Although the creative impetus and organizational energy behind La Fabri-K was largely independent, a number of early projects under its auspices remained dependent to some degree on state resources or institutional collaborations.

By 2004, however, it was apparent that the Cuban state's expansion of support for hip hop after 1999 was clearly on the wane. An early indication of this move was the abrupt postponement by the state-run Asociación Hermanos Saíz (AHS) of the tenth annual hip hop festival just a few days prior to its August start. The western portion of the island had recently suffered heavy damages from Hurricane Charley, and all public resources were said to be directed toward the recovery effort. While the postponement may have been justified under these circumstances, many within the hip hop community cried foul, sensing politics rather than material circumstances as the underlying rationale. Such sentiments found voice in the 2006 documentary *East of Havana* by the U.S. filmmakers Jauretsi Saízarbitoria and Emilia Menocal, which focused on the lives of three Cuban MCs in preparation for, and ultimate resentment over, the canceled August festival.[5] The film vividly captured a growing moment of disillusionment and frustration these and other artists felt regarding the Cuban state and its declining support for hip hop.

6.1. DJ and events producer Alexis D'Boys Rodríguez. Photo by the author

While the festival was eventually held that November, the shift in timing and resources led to a marked reduction compared to past levels of organization, attendance, and participation among Cuban MCs and invited artists from abroad. Again breaking from the long-standing August tradition, the 2005 festival, held again in November, also paled in comparison in size and scope with previous years. More significantly, the 2005 festival represented the final year of the state's support for the annual event. The anticipated festival for 2006 was abruptly canceled, again with oblique references to resource limitations due to seasonal hurricanes, and no alternative plans in the end were offered. Many read this move as a definitive signal that the Cuban government was no longer invested—to the extent and under the terms it had been—in a patron-based relationship with Cuban hip hop.

It was during this period that another effort emerged to carve out alternative space for island hip hop in a small open-air amphitheater in Parque Almendares—a lush green oasis on the sleepy banks of the Almendares River dividing Havana's barrios of Vedado and Miramar. Initially launched in 2003, project Almendares Vivo (Almendares Live) was hosted by DJ Alexis "D'Boys" Rodríguez, who, along with the venerated Afro-Cuban musician

Gerardo Alfonso, conceived the venture as an alternative festival for local MCs denied competitive entrance to the larger state-run festival.[6] By 2006 the multiday event drawing local MCs and a small collection of foreign artists ran in lieu of the canceled state-run festival, and was billed as an "autonomous" (that is, authentic) expression of hip hop's underground talent on the island. While the project initially operated with the nominal support of the Cuban Ministry of Culture, a significant part of the event's funding was provided by sources external to the island. As DJ Alexis explained in 2006 while in preparation for the upcoming festival:

> The institutions don't provide funds for this kind of event, they're not interested in supporting us so we have to do for ourselves. They do not want hip hop culture nor do they have any interest in hip hop culture. What they want is to eliminate it. You know it's like being treated like a child; they say "you cannot do this."
>
> So what we are doing here is to show them that we have discipline, that we are not undisciplined, that we have awareness and knowledge of music, culture, and respect for humanity. We are not, as they say, "la calle" [the street]. We are *of* the street, but people with respect and discipline, and they have to recognize this and eventually pay attention. So we're fighting and everything planned for the upcoming festival will happen. And for those who say, "There isn't going to be a Havana hip hop festival because there is no hip hop," forget about it! This will happen! My work this year has been about showing there's indeed a hip hop movement and that hip hop here in Cuba is very disciplined. Forget about it, my brother, pa'lante! [forward!], we can no longer sleep. You can try to shut the mouths of people but we will not allow hip hop culture here in Cuba to be exterminated, that's impossible! What we have to do we'll do, brother. We will continue fighting and this will not stop.

Elaborating on the festival's organizational nature, Alexis added:

> Many thanks to all international artists and activists who are coming to participate and help us not only in terms of money, but also with materials to support the movement here in Havana and to make this event an educational expression of hip hop. For it is not only a marathon of MC performances—we have conferences, workshops, and documentaries. This is not just a festival but more an educational encounter. Anyone

interested in knowing about graffiti, you will see a space for them, the history of graffiti. Anyone who wants to know how to be a DJ, you'll see a person who teaches DJ workshops and the history of DJ culture. This is a big project, so big it's going to last for four days from August 17 to 20. But all the background, all the help and labor has been from Toronto, the United States, San Francisco, Venezuela, and Europe.[7]

Thus in the absence of state support—at one time both circumstantial and likely strategic—Alexis underscores the instrumentality of extranational resources in enabling Almendares to operate, enterprisingly so, as autonomous space of Cuban cultural production. These comments bring again to focus those global circuits of cultural and material exchange so vital to raperos' crafting of alternative modes of both identity and maneuver. Yet Alexis's remarks also speak to a disparaging paternalism he attributes to institutions and the broader Cuban state in their dealings with hip hop. His reference to a pejorative labeling of raperos as "la calle" (the street) again indexes racialized discourses of marginalidad that have long positioned black Cubans outside the normative parameters of a modern euro- or racially transcultured Cuba. Such claims as discussed are often hinged to enduring notions of cultural primitivism and urban criminality mapped onto Afro-Cuban bodies, and subsequent calls for rehabilitative intervention by the revolutionary state (see chapter 1). For DJ Alexis, the realms of music making provided a critical means and space through which to mediate such institutionally translated materialities of race.

Indeed, in conversation one afternoon following a hip hop rehearsal at Parque Almendares, Alexis recalled his introduction to the violin as a young Afro-adorned boy by his great uncle, Rafael Lay Apesteguía, bandleader of Cuba's famed Orquesta Aragón. Enamored with the instrument, Alexis pursued it with such fervor that he eventually gained entrance to Havana's prestigious Escuela Nacional de Arte (ENA, or National School of Art). Alexis explained that during his training one of his (white) violin instructors advised him to switch to percussion because, as he was told, "violins were for white people, while blacks were naturally better at percussion." Alexis cites this incident along with others at ENA as experiences that eventually pushed him away from the violin and into hip hop's fold as a break-dancer, then DJ, and ultimately an events producer.

It was, however, another more recent encounter at the convergence of race and music that appeared to carry additional pained costs for Alexis. During the closing day of a 2003 reggae festival in Parque Almendares celebrating Bob Marley's birthday that drew large numbers of Cuban Rasta, uniformed police and undercover officers raided the crowd for alleged marijuana use. Scores of young black men were arrested, many targeted for wearing dreadlocks. During the melee police reportedly mocked and taunted attendees with racially charged language (Fontanar 2003). While tied to a wider state government crackdown on marijuana use in 2003,[8] the raid aligned more broadly with market openings and expanded state efforts to police and regulate its citizenry in often racialized ways amid the flux. In the raid's immediate aftermath Alexis, who was one of the organizers of the festival, and a number of other young black men sheared off their dreadlocks to avoid future bouts of racial targeting. The fact that one of Alexis's close peers, the brother of a prominent rapero, was picked up in the raid and imprisoned for an extended period carried particularly charged resonance for both him and Havana's wider rapero community.

As discussed, the recent cultivation of dreadlocks by young black men and more limited numbers of black women was used as a style practice to mark and performatively embody Cuban blackness in new globally conversant and indeed Afrocentric ways. Regimens of state policing sought to regulate such black self-fashionings by reining them back within secure national bounds of racial conformity. Although emotionally distressing, Alexis explained that the cutting of his and others' dreadlocks was tactically necessary given the heightened moment of racial surveillance and targeting. Resonances abound; this episode recalled a previous moment of racial regulation in the 1960s when the Cuban state banned Afro hairstyles (C. Moore 1989), the era's celebrated aesthetic of black power and beauty made globally conversant—rather ironically in Cuba's case—by the likes of Angela Davis and others.

It is therefore not surprising that early encounters like those of his schooling and ongoing grievances of raced policing informed a distrust Alexis held for the Cuban state and its institutions, one that no doubt found expression through his commitments to hip hop. In this light, Alexis's repeated call for the need to demonstrate raperos' disciplined character operates on at least two overlapping levels of vindictive defiance. In an immediate sense, asserting raperos' capacity to move in an autonomously organized fashion legitimizes it as a viable, self-sustaining cultural movement in the face of what Alexis describes as state attempts to exterminate it. Yet at a broader discursive level, raperos' ability to organize apart from state institutions challenges those claims and related state paternalisms that relegated black Cubans to the margins as uncultured wards of a grand Cuba in need of intervention and guidance (cf. de la Fuente and Glasco 1997; de la Fuente 2001). For Alexis and others, Almendares promised not only an autonomous space for hip hop's creative self-fashioning but also emancipatory possibilities for a vindicated black alterity.

Rise of Reggaetón

By 2006 an additional unease voiced by Alexis and others in relation to retreats of state support coupled with the island's ongoing marketization involved an emerging, and increasingly competitive, space of music making, reggaetón.[9] While I had been familiar with the broader Spanish-Caribbean phenomenon for some time (see Rivera, Marshall, and Pacini Hernandez 2009),[10] it was in Santiago de Cuba in the eastern province of Oriente that I first encountered Cuba's emerging reggaetón scene in 2001. I had been spending time at the Ateneo Cultural Antonio Bravo Correoso, a municipal cultural center on Calle Felix Peña near Santiago's popular (and touristed) Parque Céspedes. Ateneo's open-air patio hosted a weekly peña in which local MCs performed before a modest audience of devoted hip hop heads. A small equipment room doubling as a rehearsal space and video screening room served as a central gathering point for area raperos. The project was overseen by Luis Gonzales, who, while not an MC himself, was an instrumental figure in Santiago's hip hop community, one smaller and significantly more resource strapped in comparison to Havana's given its distance from centers of tourism and circuits of capital and cultural trade. As was the case with hip hop's early formation in Havana, Santiago's hip hop scene evolved out of local rectos competitions, an improvised street-level variation of U.S. breakdancing (César Jiménez and Tissert 2004).

A central concern resonating through the Ateneo at the time related to the recent rise of reggaetón artists who were accused, rather resentfully, of siphoning away what limited resources and fan-base local raperos had struggled to build. Historically indebted to the Afro-Caribbean by way of circulatory labor immigration and commerce between Haiti, Jamaica, and Barbados (Carr 1998), the port of Santiago and the broader Oriente region have long been celebrated (or alternately scorned) as the more *caribeño*—read darker—region of the island. Given this, it is no surprise that reggaetón's Caribbean arc first found receptive grounding in Santiago. Exemplified in the work of pioneering *santiaguero raperos* such as Café Mezclado, Regimiento, and Chucho SHS, reggae-infused rhythms and vocal styling were a common facet of Santiago hip hop, marking a regional sound distinct from that of Havana to the west. Many artists grew up with reggae as an everyday staple of their musical landscape, its presence fed by AM radio broadcasts from neighboring Jamaica given Santiago's relative proximity.

One pioneering group of note that embraced such *caribeñida* was the trio Crazy Man. Formed in the late 1990s, Crazy Man's MCs fused the frenetic lyricism of Rubén Cuesta Palomo with the beat-box skills of Omar Planos Cordoví, alongside Aristey Guibert, whose *raggamuffin*[11] vocal style and lyric sprinklings of English reflected his familial roots in Jamaica by way of Guantánamo. As Aristey mused in conversation, "Cuba y Jamaica, Jamaica y Cuba, es lo mismo" (Cuba and Jamaica, Jamaica and Cuba, it is all the same).[12] In something of a coup, in 1999 Crazy Man were the first hip hop artists to perform in Santiago's otherwise folklore-centered Festival del Caribe (also known as Festival del Fuego). A narrow and ultimately exclusionary focus on Afro-folkloric music, dance, and religious practice within the state-run festival was in fact a long-standing grievance among Santiago raperos. Reflecting on this disparity, Crazy Man's Rubén explained: "Here in Santiago rap is not considered part of our tradition, and it seems [the institutions] don't want to stray from tradition. But time passes, music changes, and young people don't want to be limited to tradition. In the end, though, the government wants to restrict the influence of what they see as foreign music."

Within an institutional privileging of "traditional" formulations of Afro-Cuban expressive culture, hip hop's extranational claims to a black global cosmopolitanism are indeed disruptive of such nationally framed, temporally delineated constraints. Yet for Rubén it was ultimately by way of reggaetón—that hybridized Spanish-Caribbean melding of reggae and hip hop—that such regulatory prescriptions were eclipsed.

Around 2001 MC Rubén left Crazy Man to launch a solo career under the name Candyman, playing a pioneering role in what would become Cuba's reggaetón explosion that soon swept west toward Havana. Responding to those who would argue that his sound was somehow foreign or inorganic to the island, Rubén early on countered: "Listen, reggae is part of the culture of

Oriente. I've been listening to reggae since I was very young. I'm Cuban and I have my own message. And I like to deliver my message with melody, with swing [*con swing*]. And because of this I choose to express myself through reggae, the message for me is more direct with reggae."

Beyond questions of style, Rubén's departure from Crazy Man—and in essence from hip hop more broadly—marked in his words an end of an era, one signaled in important part by a shift in performative focus. Unlike the self-consciously political language of social critique central to many of his rapero peers, Candyman's entrée to Santiago's nascent reggaetón scene drew heavily on themes of sexual play and heteromasculinist grammars of pleasure centering on body and dance. I recall hearing of local authorities' efforts to regulate Candyman's public performances, which were attracting growing numbers of highly enthused dancing teenagers, for his perceived lewd and lascivious content. It is not surprising that once he broached the space of state-run television, Rubén is reported to have altered his lyrics for broadcast (González Bello, Casanella Cué, and Hernández Baguer n.d.), a negotiation not unfamiliar to many a rapero (cf. Fernandes 2006). Articulating with gendered lines first laid and globally popularized by Puerto Rican reggaetón artists (Jiménez 2009; A. Moreno 2009), sexualized celebrations of the heteromasculine thus emerged as a key performative facet of Cuban reggaetón from inception.

While signaling an apparent shift from hip hop's more overt emphasis on politically centered lyricism, appeals by Candyman and other early *reggaetoneros* to the sexualized body were not necessarily devoid of embedded critique. The ethnomusicologist Geoffrey Baker suggests that reggaetoneros' attention to body-centered pleasure and celebrations of the material can be read in part as a generational counterpoint to eroding socialist ideals of labor and productive citizenship, ones reflective of a broader disenchantment with revolutionary ideology among Cuban youth in light of expanding market conditions (Baker 2011). Somewhat similar claims, as discussed in preceding chapters, have been made in relation to Cuban timba regarding the music's exaltation of black heteromasculine prowess by way of a phallocentric eroticism and material flamboyance (cf. Hernández-Reguant 2005; Perna 2005; Vaughan 2012). Yet as potentially contestive of revolutionary convention, such performances as I have suggested may in the end reproduce rather than undermine dominant representations and hierarchies of gendered and racial difference.

Analytic tensions aside, or possibly precisely through them, it is clear that reggaetón tapped into a particular resonance among large numbers of Cuban youth at the millennial turn, the vast majority of whom were incidentally black and brown. The music's emphasis on dance rhythms and the moving body was undoubtedly an important facet of its youthful appeal, one channeled largely through sexualized modes of corporal pleasure. As scholars of the Afrodiasporic condition have noted, the play and politics of pleasure have been central to the ways Afro-descendant communities have sought transcendent celebration of human resilience and freedom, both through and ultimately beyond the body (Cooper 2004; Davis 1999; Gilroy 1990; Kelley 1997; Reed 1998, cf. Lorde 1984). At the same time it is unquestionable that market logics were also key to the rise and rapid spread of reggaetón on the island.

Shortly after my return to Havana from Santiago in 2001, I had a conversation with Osmel Francis, a business savvy forty-something Afro-Cuban who had recently returned to Havana after living in Spain for many years. Osmel was the creative force behind the recently formed Cubanos en la Red, a commercially minded hip hop group in which he, flanked by a collection of significantly younger MCs, performed a somewhat comic self-parody as an elder rapero. Osmel expressed excitement at the time about the idea of bringing Rubén, or Candyman, to Havana for a series of performances as a way to introduce habaneros to the energy of Santiago reggaetón. His entrepreneurial read was that the music would explode in Havana's larger music-crazed market, and he wanted to be sure to be part of it. It was shortly thereafter that Candyman made his first wildly received tour of Havana, launching him as one of Cuba's most successful and enduring reggaetoneros. His music, however, had preceded him by informal routes of circulating CDs and audio cassettes that had found their way to Havana.

It was a relatively short time before Santiago reggaetón worked its way into the fabric of Havana's streets, enabled in part by the city's enterprising networks of bicitaxis (three-wheeled bicycle taxies) whose strapped-on boom boxes eventually carried reggaetón throughout Havana's urban interior (see Baker 2011; González Bello, Casanella Cué, and Hernández Baguer n.d.). In this sense reggaetón's westward march echoed early waves of lore emanating westward from Oriente—the celebrated launching point of both Cuba's nineteenth-century independence struggle as well as its revolutionary Movimiento 26 de Julio led by the Castro brothers and others. Some within Havana's hip hop scene had already experimented with reggaetón-esque fusions. S.B.S (Sensational Boys of the Street), an early commercially oriented, internationally marketed trio with a party-centered vibe, were possibly the first to do so. Numerous others in Oriente's wake would follow.

Splintering off the pioneering hip hop trio Primera Base in 2002, Cubanitos 20.02 embraced the reggaetón wave and rode it to relative commercial gain with their 2003 album *Soy Cubanito*. Not surprisingly, Cubanos en la Red also adopted a reggaetón-focused sound around the same period. Both Cubanitos and Cubanos en la Red were, moreover, among the initial artists incorporated into the newly formed state-run Agencia Cubana de Rap (ACR), charged with the commercial promotion of Cuban hip hop domestically and abroad (see chapter 5). Among the ten original members of ACR, three sets of hip hop artists—Eddy-K, Alto Voltaje, and intermittently MC Papo Record—shifted their focus (or, in the minds of some, "jumped ship") toward the increasingly popular and ultimately more commercially lucrative reggaetón. Eddy-K emerged as one of the island's preeminent reggaetón groups, frequently performing abroad in Mexico and Europe with the crew's lead MC, Eduardo Mora, and DJ José Antonio Suarez eventually leaving Cuba to settle in Miami.

Although this pivot toward reggaetón was by no means limited to members of ACR,[13] this did not preclude the play of strategic interests on the part of the Cuban state. While it may indeed be true that the state viewed reggaetón, as it once did hip hop, with uneasiness as a music genre culturally antagonistic to revolutionary ideals (cf. Baker 2009; González Bello, Casanella Cué, and Hernández Baguer n.d.), reggaetoneros did eventually gain visible institutional footholds in state-run radio and television. For its part, ACR, long viewed by many a rapero with varying degrees of caution, was by 2006 commonly perceived as abandoning hip hop altogether in favor of the more commercially promising—and possibly less politically menacing—reggaetón. Sanctioned space and resources once occupied by hip hop, limited as they might have been, now seemed to shift in the direction of reggaetón in ways that aligned with the island's broader market turn.

In the wake of such developments, DJ Alexis D'Boys offered this analysis of the state's swing:

Folkloric music and culture have become a commercial trade, and the [state] institutions themselves have become commercial. They provide space, but these spaces are in commercial places. As a result this culture has lost a lot of its roots, at least here in Havana much has been lost. And now the same thing is happening to hip hop. The [Cuban Rap] Agency has participated in this and I always knew it intended to exterminate hip hop by commercializing it. And that's what's happening now to hip hop in Cuba. It's not dead, but it's missing a lot of talent, and it's lost the cohesion it once had in the '90s until, say, 2002 because of this institution, and it's partly to blame for this. Many raperos are now doing reggaetón because of the Cuban Rap Agency, so they're destroying the culture of hip hop by commercializing it.

When I asked specifically what he thought of reggaetón's rise in Havana, Alexis offered:

Compadre, look, for me, I'm not against reggaetón. For me reggaetón is dance music, a popular music for dancing. Reggaetón is a music that's now in fashion, it's for people to dance, to forget problems, prejudices, and things, and think a bit more about materialism—it's made for this. They [reggaetoneros] are people who have no interest in changing the world. The problem here in Cuba is that reggaetón is a product of the despair of hip hop artists who have neither space nor attention, they aren't respected as musicians. So what's happened is that they have gone for the easy way, for reggaetón, where they're given space. The music is commercial and they're not talking about political issues or situations. What they talk about is "the party," and people have gone for that because the institutions have opened their doors and they're paying people to perform in those places.

The Cuban Rap Agency has ten groups that used to do hip hop, but only two now remain. My respect to them, Anónimo Consejo and Obsesión, but all of the other groups are doing reggaetón. They're sent to work outside Havana in tourist and commercial places and are paid for it. That's their salary, they benefit from this. For me, it's a reggaetón agency, not a rap agency, at least that's the way I see it, and my respect goes to Anónimo Consejo and Obsesión, who, though involved, are struggling.[14]

Alexis's reading offers a cogent critique of state moves toward reggaetón as those tied to the market and aligned interests to undermine the salience of hip hop on the island. In particular, he suggests that an articulation of state and commercial forces engendered new economies of exchange (e.g., tourism, commercial zones) within which long-excluded raperos could now participate by way of reggaetón. To a dedicated hip hop purist, such commercialization represented a fragmentizing anathema to a collective sense of revolutionary commitment long sacred to many within the hip hop movement. To Alexis the ultimate goal of this seemingly calculated state strategy was the dissolution of hip hop all together.

Reflecting back on the moment from a distance, Ariel Fernández Díaz echoed a similar understanding regarding the state's shift toward reggaetón, explaining: "Reggaetón exploded in this country and came into a Cuban social narrative that had nothing to do with it. But people felt motivated to make more easy music—not to talk about social issues, you know what I mean?" When I asked if he thought the state played a part in the equation, Ariel responded: "Definitely, I mean it was completely orchestrated. If the government needed to choose between a movement that talks about issues we have here in the country, the social issues and social difference that we have, or people who talk about 'shake yo ass'? It's easier and more comfortable for the government to deal with people who care about making money and shaking booties. There're people who're trying to challenge the status quo and intellectually challenge the government policies and political party, you know what I mean?"

Regarding the commercial nature of the Agencia Cubana de Rap in particular, Ariel added:

> One of the policies of the groups [in the ACR] is to make money. They have to reach a certain amount of productivity and success, especially financially; if not you can't be a member of la Agencia—you need to make money and entertain people. So la Agencia was not trying to create space to promote or spend resources on you because you're addressing issues that need to be addressed. No, they're really not going to promote what we were talking about because it was not in support of the policies or politics of the revolution that they wanted people to have access to.[15]

Beyond simply an outcome of state interests, however, both Alexis and Ariel suggest that artists harbored their own motives in gravitating toward reggaetón, ones also tied, in short, to "making money." Such moves were accompanied in their view by a depoliticization of the music and broader movement as a whole in ways concurrent with the shifting focus of both the state and the national economy. Amid this commercial flux, "the party" has seemingly displaced "the revolution" as a central driving motif. Moreover, as Geoffrey Baker notes, in the artistic turn toward reggaetón many former raperos "deprioritized their own blackness by eliminating explicit racial discourse and aligning themselves with a broader musical culture in which latinidad overshadows negritud" (Baker 2011: 281). Yet rather than a corrective restoration of a purported nonracial orientation as suggested, might such realignments and political deprioritizations of blackness articulate with evolving conjunctures of the state and marketplace? Is the exalted underground that many raperos often spoke of indeed now in peril?

Deferring questions of race for the moment, to couch raperos' tack toward reggaetón purely in terms of economic exigency or as the result of manipulated guidance from state institutions may fail to capture the range of strategies some artists have fashioned within an economy of shifting opportunities. Many may undoubtedly have made rational decisions in light of new markets for popular Cuban music and the performative black body itself.[16] Scenarios of this kind evoke a certain neoliberal rationale of self-directed individualism moving in entrepreneurial pursuit of personal gain, analogous to the concurrent rise of state-promoted *cuentapropismo* (self-employment schemes) amid an ever-receding socialist state. As Wendy Brown aptly suggests, neoliberal forms of governance tend to figure "individuals as entrepreneurial actors in every sphere of life," engendering them "as rational, calculating creatures whose moral autonomy is measured by their capacity for 'self-care'" (Brown 2003: 15).

In this light, raperos' prioritization of individuated market pursuit stands in juxtaposition to more collaborative modes of political cohesion and solidarity, precisely the kind of nostalgic loss Alexis laments with the rise of reggaetón. Such self-invested individualism similarly emerges in tension with a collective ethos of racial affinity and antiracist contest long instrumental among Havana raperos and their self-defined movimiento. Indeed, if one can in essence individually "opt out" of the structural limitations brought by racial positionality through market maneuver, then why not?

Departures to Diaspora

Flights to a more commercially viable reggaetón were not the only individuated strategy available to enterprising raperos. Another factor impacting social cohesion, and ultimately racial orientation, of Havana's hip hop community from the mid-2000s was a growing exodus abroad of many foundational members. Among Cuba's rich spectrum of artistic and athletic talent there has long been a draw to leave the island in search of greater, more lucrative professional possibilities *afuera*. This has increasingly been the case since the economic shifts of the early 1990s. Consider for one the rash of Cuban baseball players (or similarly, professional ballet dancers) who in recent years have defected to the United States. In the case of hip hop, the morphing of Havana's pioneering hip hop troupe Amenaza into the international commercial sensation Orishas after members' relocation to France in the late 1990s stands as a particularly poignant example of such early moves among raperos. It was, however, the decision by MC Julio Cardenas of Raperos Crazy de Alamar (RCA) not to return following a 2001 tour to New York City that seemed to resonate most deeply within Havana's tight-knit rapero circles (see chapter 2). I recall many at times conflicted conversations regarding the incident, ranging from criticism of Julio's decision as a self-interested move that could complicate future tours, to those empathizing with his move.

By the mid-2000s, mounting frustration and disillusionment with waning state support coupled with the broader deterioration of economic conditions led to truncated artistic and social aspirations for many in the hip hop community. Like many of their generational peers in Cuba, they too imagined and sought the promise of new opportunities that life afield might offer. One was Yaimir "Pitit" Jiménez of Grandes Ligas and EPG&B fame, who in 2003 immigrated to Sweden, where he continues his artistic career as a commercial MC. It was by way of a foreign fiancé visa that Pitit managed (and likely financed) his emigration. As mentioned, fiancé visas were the primary means by which male hip hop artists in particular were able to leave the island, a reality often linked to wider monetizations and corresponding strategies of racially informed exchange (see chapter 1).

One of the biggest blows during this period was Ariel Fernández Díaz's decision to immigrate to New York City in 2005. To recall, Ariel, aka DJ Asho, rose to prominence as one of the most influential members of Cuba's hip hop community, eventually garnering a position as official hip hop liaison within the state-run Asociación Hermanos Saíz. A committed fighter for Cuban hip hop by way of radio, journalism, and events promotion, Ariel's decision caught many by surprise. In a conversation shortly after his move, Ariel's tone was sharp as he spoke critically about what he viewed as the Cuban state's manipulative dealings with the movement. His position had thus evolved and shifted significantly since his earlier involvements, as ambivalent as they may have become, with Hermanos Saíz (see chapter 5).

In short order a growing list of key Havana artists followed in exodus, including Los Paisanos, Las Krudas, Pablo Herrera, and Alexis D'Boys, to name a few. Rather than signaling an end to their artistic commitments, many have continued to pursue their music and broader engagements with Cuban-centered hip hop in often enterprising ways. Many have also managed to maintain active connections with MCs on the island while developing vibrant networks of hip hop community in the diaspora. In addition, among movements of artists between Cuba and abroad as well as among those living within the United States, Canada, and Europe, electronic technology has played an important role in enabling artistic exchange and virtual networks across spatial divides.

Artists have been particularly resourceful in mobilizing the Internet and social media as a modes of organization in dispersal. There is an ever-growing plethora of media sites like YouTube, SoundCloud, and Facebook where raperos and their increasingly global supporters maintain ongoing dialogue via trafficking of videos, images, and digitized music. Such creative use of information technology is analogous to a kind of diasporic "bridge building" championed at an earlier literary moment by a group of Cuban writers (Behar 1996), whereby the global reach of electronic media is now employed plank by cybernetic plank in forging transnational dialogue and community. A difference here, however, is that rather than efforts to mend long-standing cleavages between mainland and Cuban American *exilio* communities, these current *puentes* are about diaspora in-formation enabled in important part through subjectivities of hip hop. In light of descriptive gazings by academics, journalists, and a growing host of foreign-produced documentaries,[17] many artists now employ digital technology to globally circulate their own work and self-imagery.

Émigré life of course was far from struggle free. As with most global South-North migrations, many found the transition to new lives fraught with challenges. Notions that working-class Afro-Cuban MCs could simply rely on their artistic talents in the commercial markets of the United States, Canada, and Europe were quickly dispelled. The realities of being poor, racialized immigrants with often limited resources, levels of formal education, and English-language skills meant that many had to work at low-wage jobs to make ends meet. For instance, MC Julio Cardenas, formerly of RCA, found employment as a restaurant delivery person in New York City while honing his acting skills and developing a play drawn from his experiences in Cuba. Former Obsesión member Roger Martínez, who immigrated to the Los Angeles area in 2002, eventually attained trade skills as an electrician while building a small in-home recording studio in his labored pursuit as a hip hop producer and performer. The challenge often pitted dreams of artistic success against the market-driven competitivism of the North.

Ariel Fernández Díaz struggled for a number of years in search of gainful music-related employment following his arrival in the New York City area, despite a depth of experience and extensive contacts within local hip hop and Latino music and activist circles. In the end Ariel has been successful in piecing together an enterprising range of projects under the moniker Asho Productions, including giving academic-targeted talks on Cuban hip hop, hosting monthly music events at the Bronx Museum, having ongoing Afro-Cuban-centered DJ gigs, and most recently helping coordinate U.S-based Afro-Cuban-focused cultural tours to Havana.[18] Alternatively, Cuba's vanguard hip hop producer Pablo Herrera left the island for Scotland in 2005 on a scholarship to pursue a master's degree in sound design at the University of Edinburgh. Despite distance, Pablo has sought to remain in dialogue with Cuban hip hop via his academic work and blogging, including collaborative work with Cuban artists in the diaspora such as the Madrid-based fusion band Habana Aberita, as well as MC Randy Acosta, formerly of Los Paisanos, who now resides in Barcelona pursing an active performing career. Pablo has also maintained spiritual ties to Cuba, a connection perhaps carrying added significance given the unfortunate recent passing of both his parents. This connectivity, Pablo shared, is fed through his recent mentioned initiation into the sacred rites of Ifá divination during repeated trips to Cuba.

Among Cuban MCs, Las Krudas have been particularly resourceful in translating and expanding their work abroad. Long based in Austin, Texas, following a circuitous route through Russia, the all-female trio has astutely

6.2. MCs Randy Acosta and Jessel "El Huevo" Saladriga of Los Paisanos.
Photo by Sahily Borrero

tapped into womanist, LGBT, and college performance circuits across the
United States, Puerto Rico, and Latin America. Krudas have been especially
savvy in using social media, video, community radio, and informal media
such as hand-printed T-shirts as promotional vehicles for their music and
broader queer-feminist advocacy. In addition to collaborative projects with
other Cuban MCs in the United States, the artists have maintained a level
of involvement with islandside raperos by way of hip hop colloquia, workshops, and performance events in Havana. Regarding émigré communities,
Oakland, California, emerged as something of a hub for emigrating raperos.
One notable figure in the mix is Leidis Freire, who has established herself
as a dance-music DJ with a strong hip hop and internationalist flair. Leidis
has also been instrumental in helping organize Bay Area performances for
touring island artists including Obsesión. Also among Oakland's scene are
MC Magyori "La Llave" Martínez of Omega Kilay and MC Miki Flow (aka Michel Hermida Martínez), formerly of Alamar's Explosion Suprema, who has
remained a relatively active performer. The operative term here is relative.
With the possible exception of the French-produced Orishas, no Cuban hip

hop artist to my knowledge has yet to sign with a commercial music label or secure much by way of a lucrative career as a performer. A select few who made the crossover to reggaetón long ago, such as Eddy-K now in Miami, also stand here as anomalies. In a word, the lucha (struggle/hustle) remains a defining facet of life for many émigré MCs.

Raperos' diasporic terrain is far from limited to the United States. Free of U.S. travel restrictions, Canada has long been an important interlocutor with the island's hip hop community, with Montreal and Toronto serving as key nodes of intersection. One pioneer along these lines has been the Montreal-based hip hop collective Nomadic Massive, whose multiracial/lingual collection of MCs and musicians hailing from immigrant backgrounds reflects Montreal's mélange of new multiculturalism.[19] The collective's Cuba connection stems from the founding member MC Lou "Piensa" Dufleaux, who befriended Obsesión members Magia López and Alexey Rodríguez while living in Havana in the late 1990s. Piensa's artistic directions as a MC and hip hop producer are in turn deeply indebted to his engagements with Havana-area raperos. Performing first alongside Obsesión during the 2000 Cuban hip hop festival, Piensa returned to the 2004 festival with a group of Montreal artists including Haitian Canadian MC Vox Sambu. This second foray provided the creative impetus to the founding of Nomadic Massive, and the collective has subsequently made repeated trips to Havana to perform alongside Cuban MCs in addition to organizing a series of Canadian tours for Obsesión and others.

Concerning routes of emigration, however, rapero émigrés have tended to favor Toronto, which boasts Canada's largest concentration of migrant Cubans. Histories of artistic exchange with Toronto-based artists such as Jamaican-born spoken-word artist Debbie Young, moreover, have helped Cuban MCs find a receptive home within the city's music scene and broader Afro-Caribbean topography. A key individual amid the vibrancy has been Alexis D'Boys Rodríguez, who emigrated from Havana in 2007. Alongside a day job at a computer recycling center, Alexis remains active as a DJ and music promoter specializing in hip hop. Settled in a neighborhood near the intersection of Oakwood and St. Clair Avenues long associated with immigrant communities of Italians, Jamaicans, and more recently Latinos, Alexis tells of his early years in an apartment block he playfully baptized "Hotel de Cuba" given the stream of Cubans cycling through over the years. Among those sharing early domicile was Telmary Díaz, rapera and spoken-word artist formerly, as mentioned, of the innovative fusion bands Free Hole Negros and Interactivo. A native of Alexis's Vedado barrio, Telmary has had noted success as a solo recording artist and touring performer across Canada, Europe, and more recently the United States.

In addition to periodic peñas with local artists, Alexis participated in the 2011 Toronto leg of the commercially oriented Havana Cultura Tour. Launched in 2009 as the brainchild of the British DJ Gilles Peterson and sponsored by Cuba's quasi-corporate rum distillery Havana Club,[20] the international touring project involving young Cuban musicians served as a global marketing venture for Cuban culture and tourism. The project's glitzy English-language website, billing itself as "a global initiative to promote contemporary Cuban culture,"[21] offers flashy videos and profiles of numerous Cuban artists, including a collection of raperos such as Anónimo Consejo, Obsesión, Doble Filo, and Telmary Díaz. Along with an assemblage of reggaetoneros, many of these artists are featured in a 2009 *Havana Cultura* CD compilation recorded in Havana's state-run EGREM studios and a subsequent 2011 *Havana Cultura: Remixed* album.

Globally attuned commercial interests in Cuban hip hop were not limited to domestic state-private ventures, however. For a number of years Havana hosted a national freestyle hip hop competition, the Batalla de los Gallos (Cock fight), sponsored by the energy drink giant Red Bull. The Australian-based company, which has built a multibillion-dollar global brand through sponsorship of spectacular youth-centered competitions like extreme sports and urban music contests,[22] apparently recognized the potential marketing value of Cuban MCs. With the winner to represent Cuba in Red Bull's crowning Batalla of finalists from Latin America and Spain, a number of old-school raperos served as judges with Doble Filo's Edgaro González playing lead host. In addition to their advertising worth, videos of the lavishly staged one-on-one battles have garnered tens of thousands of hits on YouTube, helping to promote individual artists (and Cuban hip hop) within the global marketplace. Thus despite potential posturing otherwise, a confluence of state and market interests aligned in ways that continued to claim hip hop, at least in part, as a globally trafficable form of Cuban cultural capital— an economy within which Alexis and other hip-hop-affiliated Cubans, both home and abroad, were apparently actively conversant if not adept.

Los Aldeanos

In what ways has the flight of so many established raperos alongside Cuba's monetization and the competing rise of reggaetón impacted the character and vitality of Havana's hip hop scene? Some pioneering old-school artists like Anónimo Consejo, Obsesión, and Hermanos de Causa's Soandres del Río[23]—despite the loss of his artistic partner Alexis "el Pelón" Cantero to Spain—long "held it down" or continue to do so in Havana while taking advantage of occasional opportunities to perform aboard. The moment, however, has clearly given rise to a new generation of artists who fashion themselves as inheritors of Cuban hip hop's underground urgency. Front and center among these are artists Bian "El B" Oscar Rodríguez Gala and Aldo "El Aldeano" Roberto Rodríguez Baquero of the highly provocative duo Los Aldeanos (The Villagers). Since forming in Havana in 2003, Los Aldeanos have built a reputation via live performance and a prolific range of independently produced albums and videos as among the most critically outspoken of MCs on the island. Such efforts have involved collaborative work with allied artists such as the hard-edged rapero-cum-hip hop producer Papá Humbertico (see chapter 1), who, through his home-based studio known locally as Real 70, has helped produce a number of the duo's albums.

Yet unlike an earlier generation of artists who often chose more mediated tones of critique, Los Aldeanos have embraced (and very much celebrate) a more cynical and ideologically adversarial tone vis-à-vis the Cuban state. Claiming a mantle as "revolutionaries," they view the revolutionary state largely in irreverent terms as an autocratic, often-repressive regime and principal progenitor of a range of social hypocrisies that mark the current Cuban everyday. In one of their signature temas, "El rap es guerra" (Rap is war), Los Aldeanos declare: "Always on the offensive / In defense of the lives that nest wounded / Rap is war / The fight is not lost / Free the captive truth / Do not stand idle / Rap is war / They want us to fill our demos with upbeat songs / But they forget that rap is war."[24] This combative ethos finds visual form in a matching set of large tattoos reading "El rap es guerra" that adorn the forearms of both heavily tatted MCs. To further effect, in their tema "Libertad" (Liberty), Aldeanos evoke enslavement as a metaphor for contemporary life and citizenship in Cuba where all are beholden to the state as master. Under such a regime, one is held a "slave to your nationality, identity, and issues . . . a slave of a fucked and slow agony . . . a slave of your duties, a slave of your rights," and ultimately "a slave struggling endlessly without finding happiness."[25]

Not surprisingly, Aldeanos' provocations—and an additional set of eventual circumstances, to which I will return—drew government attention. The Cuban state's approach to the artists had generally been one of apprehension, variously restricting their access to state media, performance space, and international travel. One particularly notable incident occurred in 2009 when police reportedly entered the home of MC Aldo, briefly arresting him and confiscating his computer along with its trove of music compositions. The official charge for the seizure was lack of ownership papers, a circumstance common to most computer owners in Cuba. Yet the episode contributed to the duo's already-celebrated status among some circles as a new voice of generational dissonance challenging state censorship and restrictions on public speech, issues the artists themselves address critically in their music. For one, the ever-vocal Havana-based journalist Yoani Sánchez closely chronicled and championed Los Aldeanos' cause in her multilingual blog "Generación Y" (see Sánchez 2009).

The transnational dimensions of such animus have been complicated. During a 2010 Miami performance tour with the allied MC Silvito "El Libre" Rodríguez, the artists were inundated by local journalists angling for public denunciations of the Castro leadership and broader revolutionary government (Hanken 2010). A similar scenario played out in 2002 during a Miami tour involving members of Obsesión and Doble Filo, yet in both cases the artists were fairly adroit at sidestepping incitement. Aldeanos' Miami reception nonetheless remained couched by some within the Cuban exilio-attuned media along lines examplified by a *Miami New Times* journalist who wrote: "In the face of Cuba's pathetic, failed socialist experiment is a new revolution, a cultural one, led by the youth of the island. It's nonviolent, it's artistic, and a rap group called Los Aldeanos stands at the forefront" (Katel 2010).

While the duo have been vocal in their criticism of Cuban reggaetón for its viewed commercial frivolousness and lack of political engagement (Baker 2011), like many of their reggaetonero peers the artists come from an emerging Cuban generation disillusioned with the incongruencies of the revolutionary project at this expanding neoliberal moment. The degree of irreverence that Aldeanos hold for state authority can be seen as reflective of growing cynicism with the revolutionary state in its efforts to police and regulate, in often autocratic ways, a new Cuban reality shaped evermore by the terms of global capital. While Aldeanos may stake out a radically juxta-posed position vis-à-vis reggaetoneros, both can be seen as generational manifestations of the same historical juncture. Indeed, though the duo has long contended with (and in many ways capitalized on) their outlaw status with regard to limits of artistic freedom, reggaetón artists have also been subject to state bannings from radio and television in apparent response to a deemed offensiveness of sexually explicit lyrics (de la Hoz 2012). Ambigu-ities linger. Despite Aldeanos' acclaimed dissonance, for instance, they long remained coveted marketing tender of the state-private promotion venture Havana Cultura.

A counterfoil to Los Aldeanos' antiestablishment posture can be seen in the example of Magia López of Obsesión, who assumed directorship of the Agencia Cubana de Rap (ACR) in 2007.[26] To recall, under the leadership of the former director Susana García Amorós, the ACR had acquired a poor reputation among many raperos due in part to the expansion of reggaetón artists within its fold. In conversation with Magia two years into her ten-ure as director, she echoed Ariel Fernández Diaz's earlier read in under-scoring that part of ACR's shift toward reggaetón was tied to the agency's auto-financiado (self-financed) nature, which obliged it to raise much of its operational budget via the more commercial route of reggaetón.[27] In line with a broader neoliberal turn, such entrepreneurial strategies spoke again to the quasi-privatization of Cuba's public institutions in light of a withering socialist state. Similar scenarios had long been in place for many state-run research centers that sought alternative revenue streams through mandated affiliation fees for foreign researchers like myself. More immediately, this shift again underscores the linkages between economic expediencies and political contingencies regarding the Cuban state's divergent dealings with hip hop and more commercial, presumably less contestatory reggaetón.

Noting that there were currently only three reggaetón groups on the agency's roster, Magia explained that one of her priorities as ACR direc-tor was to recenter the institution's focus on and promotion of hip hop. To such ends, she sought to push the agency toward a more participatory model akin to her previous work under the collaborative umbrella project La Fabri-K. Through the now-official auspices of ACR, Magia expanded in both scope and institutional form the annual Hip Hop Symposium that she and her artistic partner Alexey Rodríguez launched under La Fabri-K around 2001. Occurring in a number of subsequent years through 2011, the retitled "Simposio Internacional de Hip Hop Cubano," involving local and foreign participants, continued to offer evening performances along with daytime workshops, discussions, and audiovisual presentations. The challenge here, Magia acknowledged, was walking an often tricky line between independent and institutional parameters.

When in 2011 I asked whether her relationship with folks in that wider hip hop community had changed since her institutional move, Magia replied, "*Claro!*" She explained that there were many expectations about what she could and/or should do in the position, as well as presumptions that much could be accomplished immediately. "*Pero no es posible*" (But it's not possible), she offered, adding that an institution cannot easily be turned around after five years under someone else's direction. Magia confessed that she was having a challenging time getting things done administratively, finding the institutional workings "terribly rigid and structurally inflexible," and concluded, "*Es una lucha*" (It's a struggle).[28] Indeed.

When asked about the rise of Los Aldeanos, Magia underscored that the artists represented a new generation of raperos, implying that they drew from a different historical moment within the movement. While acknowledging the duo as highly talented and critically voiced MCs, Magia pointed out that the two reside in the relatively affluent barrio of Nuevo Vedado, suggesting that the artists were relatively more privileged than many within the movement, affording them greater access to resources. Los Aldeanos have indeed been remarkably savvy in terms of music and video production, much of which now circulates globally on the Internet by way of YouTube, Facebook, and a range of web pages and sites. An extensive selection of the duo's music can now be downloaded commercially on iTunes and amazon.com.

This global exposure, and ultimately commercial marketing, of Aldeanos' music and particular brand of posturing has brought significant international attention along with a notable following abroad. El B's famed freestyle skills receive worldwide attention via YouTube videos of his bouts as Cuba's two-time national champion of Red Bull's Batalla de los Gallos competition. Aldeanos' renegade status was in turn enhanced by reports that El B's travel permission to attend the international finals of the Batalla was twice denied by the Cuban state. These events were captured in the widely circulated 2009 biographical documentary *Revolution* by the Havana-based filmmaker Mayckell Pedrero. A subsequent documentary, *Viva Cuba Libre: Rap Is War* (2013), by the Los Angeles–based Jesse Acevedo, also profiles Los Aldeanos with a notably more sensationalist and unabashedly anti-Castro flair. A third documentary, by the Havana-based filmmaker Alejandro "Iskander" Moya, who similarly characterizes the duo as "virulently antigovernment and explicitly anti-Fidel" (Katel 2010), is reportedly in production as well. Such efforts have undoubtedly helped amplify Aldeanos' international stature and popular draw as flamboyant young voices of Cuban discord. A prominent figure in Aldeanos' mix of global promotion has been Melissa Riviere of Emetrece Productions, an audiovisual production and entertainment company run between Minneapolis and San Juan, Puerto Rico. A PhD graduate in anthropology from the University of Minnesota whose dissertation research dealt comparatively with Cuban and Puerto Rican hip hop, Riviere had been until fairly recently an early and key advocate in championing the duo internationally through a range of media projects.

In conversation, Magia López questioned the level of international attention bestowed on Los Aldeanos, citing Riviere's involvement in particular as an example of the duo's external networks of patronage. Her query seemed twofold. The degree of foreign support for the artists on both political and material levels raised questions for Magia as to the extent of Aldeanos' claimed marginality within Cuban society as the grounding for their critical posture. At another level, she wondered about the extent to which their foreign support might itself be feeding—in provocative if not potentially manipulative ways—the duo's adversarial stance toward the Cuban state. This second concern no doubt carried its own implicative challenge for Magia, given her recently assumed role as director of the state-run ACR. For Magia, Los Aldeanos' claim to the critical underground stood in tension with their artistic practice, one she ultimately positioned as "*buen comercial*" (solidly commercial). Yet at the same time Magia's own position as a rapera-cum-head of a state institution charged with the commercial promotion of island hip hop was clearly fraught with its own loaded set of complications.

In hindsight, however, these conversations may have had unexpected foresight. Recent revelations reported by the Associated Press suggest that the United States Agency for International Development (USAID) during this period engaged in covert provocateur efforts within Havana's hip hop movement as part of a broader program to actively support and implicitly encourage dissonant elements within Cuban society (D. Butler et al. 2014b).[29] In addition to a Serbian contractor working through a Panamanian front company,[30] those implicated in the scheme were in fact Los Aldeanos, who reportedly received resources and forms of support. Regardless of the details of the circumstances, the duo were eventually pressured to leave Cuba and now reside in South Florida.

Whither Race?

The mercurial rise (and subsequent fall) of Los Aldeanos is reflective of another more recent shift within Cuba's broader hip hop movement, one characterized by a marked decentering of race and black racial subjectivity once pivotal to the work and lives of many pioneering raperos. To recall, the British ethnomusicologist Geoffrey Baker has suggested that black racial currents within Cuban hip hop were chiefly expressions of foreign, particularly U.S., cultural influences and political interventions by U.S. hip-hop-affiliated individuals, academics, and resident African American exiles (Baker 2011). Key here is Baker's contention that with the 2003 close of the U.S.-based Black August collective's annual participation in Havana's hip hop festival, an implicitly inorganic grounding of black identity and discourse among Havana-area raperos waned as well.

While I have addressed the role of Black August as well as the salience of racial orientation in hip hop prior to the collective's Cuban involvement (see chapter 3), it is largely true that black identity expression and accompanying antiracist challenges long integral to hip hop's rise in Cuba have receded since the mid-2000s. As the most visible of today's new face of Cuban MCs, El B and El Aldeano of Los Aldeanos—who would phenotypically speaking fall respectively between mestizo and white racial categories in Cuba—do not in fact foreground racial identity, analyses, or themes in their music. The same can be said of MC Silvito Rodríguez, son of composer Silvio Rodríguez and another leading figure within Havana's new generation of hip hop artists.

An undeniable factor informing this shift has been the mentioned outflow of so many pioneering figures of Havana's hip hop community abroad, many if not most of whom centered black subjectivity and antiracist intervention in their music and artistic lives. Regarding his experience working with Los Aldeanos during his Almendares Vivo project and production of the related 2004 L3Y8 compilation disc,[31] DJ Alexis D'Boys recalls:

> Los Aldeanos were part of a project of mine because they had tremendous talent, and I had invited them to hold a concert in Almendares. I had a lot of interest in them, I gave them a lot of attention, and we did a lot of business together. And they understood a lot about black culture and its presence here in Havana. But after I left Cuba, everything fell apart. They started to do their thing apart from that movement—they believed more in themselves and less in the hip hop movement. In the end it became a movement of *raperos blacquitos* [little white rappers], and this affected the rest of the hip hop movement. . . . After I left Cuba everything changed; today the movement is completely white. After 2006 all the black artists left Cuba, and now all the raperos are white. These people are not aware of the roots of this culture in Cuba.[32]

In a conversation with Obsesíon's Magia López and Alexey Rodríguez, they echoed a similar theme regarding what they view as an ideological disjuncture that emerged between a now largely émigré cohort of pioneering MCs and a new generation of artists who arose in the vacuum. With this break in discursive continuity, they argued, the torch failed to be passed. Speaking to what he described as "this generation's disconnect with Cuba's history, including Angola," the producer Pablo Herrera characterized the shift as one akin to a de-racializing slide from "Afro-Cuban hip hop to Cuban hip hop."[33]

Some have suggested that there may have been additional factors in the mix informing hip hop's waning black origination, in particular those involving state interests. Recalling the moment from his then home in Newark, New Jersey, Ariel Fernández Díaz implied that there was a deliberate effort on the part of the Cuban state to undermine the movement's black leadership, claiming that some were in fact pushed out of positions, if not ultimately out of Cuba itself:

> The truth behind why black identity discourse has slowed down and been stifled within hip hop is that it was a designed attack on the black leadership within the movement to cut off this thing that was going on—it was the attack on Rensoli,[34] the attack on me, the attack on Pablo. So there's

a certain way the leadership of the movement or the intellectual leadership of the movement—Rensoli, Pablo, me—were completely cut out of the equation, you're not going to have the presence of those individuals pushing for discussion and debate within the movement. . . . So the truth is that it was an institutional plan and an organized attack precisely to cut out this element within hip hop. I also think the coordination of the Cuban Rap Agency (ACR) helped with that; I mean, you're trying to make the leadership look to the commercial aspect of the music and not the social-political aspect of the music, you know what I mean?[35]

Here again Ariel alludes to the promotion of reggaetón through the ACR as an illustration of the linkages between commercial expediency and the Cuban state's interest in defusing the political salience of race within hip hop. Commenting on his and others' departures from Cuba, Ariel added: "We were pushed to leave the island. I never wanted to leave Cuba. I wanted to live in Cuba but I could not live without support. And the basic institutional strategy was to shoot me down and destroy the moral space, and whatever respect I earned through the years of my work here was really put in danger with different political and institutional tactics used to try to set the movement against me, you know what I mean?"

Reflecting on the period in conversation from his home in Edinburgh, Pablo Herrera ultimately questioned the strategic wisdom of those in the hip hop community claiming status as a movimiento. As artists, Pablo argued, raperos never had a clear or unified project or strategy when dealing with the Cuban state, and as such pitted themselves against an institutional apparatus with whom they were woefully unprepared and outmatched. Using the metaphor of a ball game, Pablo mused, "I think a lot of people who wanted to make hip hop into a movement have basically committed suicide, have basically thrown [hip hip] against the wall and basically killed it," adding:

The minute we said that we're a movement—I take responsibility for that as well—the minute people said that we're a movement then they said, "We have to get you guys out, ok, you guys are out," and that was it, you know what I mean? The minute we asked for that much power, we were speaking the language of the government, the language of cultural policy, of cultural politics. And as soon as we started speaking to that we were completely out of bounds with being able to know what we were doing. Because we were playing with tools that are not natural to us as artists. Now we are in *their* court, *they* have the ball, you know what I mean? They have the rap of exactly how to play us. From being players we became a ball. And they knew exactly how to play it, so they could shut down what we were doing.[36]

During the exchange Pablo repeatedly professed in a reflective tone of certitude, "I'm a person that's about cultural longevity, not political martyrdom."

Among those cited by Ariel and Pablo as being forced out of leadership was Magia López, who left her post as ACR's director amid controversy in 2012. As a result of mounting tensions between her and an assortment of old and new Havana raperos, including Los Aldeanos, a letter was submitted to Cuba's Minister of Culture Abel Prieto in late 2011 while Magia and Alexey were abroad touring Canada and the United States. The letter listed grievances about Magia's directorship including allegations of self-promotion and reported financial mismanagement, ultimately requesting that she be removed from her position. A version of the letter, signed by a prominent (all-male) collection of older-school MCs, found its way to the blog *Penúltimo días* run by the Barcelona-based dissident writer Ernesto Hernández Busto, who, among other accolades, has been celebrated by the George W. Bush Institute's "Freedom Collection" as a "recognized authority on technology and democracy."[37] Under duress, Magia was forced to vacate her directorship and was replaced by her longtime artistic colleague Roberto Rosell Justiz of the hip hop duo Hermanazos. Obsesión subsequently departed from ACR's artistic portfolio.

While the incident brings to focus a complicated set of converging factors, a central and persistent element in the mix relates to long-standing internal tensions and fragmentation within Havana's hip hop community. It had certainly been my experience over the years that, despite the artistic depth and politically charged focus of much of the music, the rapero community often seemed beleaguered by internal antagonisms and competitive, at times ego-centered politics that hindered possibilities for more unified organizational efforts. All said, citing concerns beginning with Rodolfo Rensoli's 1999 removal as lead organizer of the annual hip hop festival and running through Magia's 2012 forced exit from ACR, both Ariel and Pablo suggested the hand of a divide-and-rule strategy by the Cuban state. In Pablo's words, folks had their "tops blown off as a result of people not knowing how to play the system, or play within that system. This is what I meant by being a ball rather than a player. Someone else is holding the racket. You're not in your court."

Although the extent to which Cuban institutions may have fanned or possibly exploited fractional dynamics is difficult to ascertain, Pablo's critique of the community's strategic shortcomings (or naïveté?) in dealings with state apparatuses may hold some validity. On his role during the period, Ariel confessed in hindsight:

> I definitely feel that I didn't succeed at what I wanted to, we didn't succeed. I mean my idea of the hip hop movement was to create a type of coalition. My idea was to create a type of Abakuá society, a really tight brotherhood-sisterhood. That didn't happen because of us [leaders], it happened because people within the movement didn't want to come into this view, or the egos didn't allow them to do so. I might have made mistakes in the process, definitely. But I think I can prove that I took different actions and steps to try to bring everybody to the table, and tried to really put everybody on the same page. . . . Through the work that I did with the movement, through writing articles, creating Café Cantante, creating the [Movimiento] magazine, I really wanted to create a sociocultural coalition because I thought that was what the movement was calling for. It didn't make sense to me to talk for ten years about how police treat you without coming to the point when it's time to take action that goes beyond the stage.[38]

Recognizing such limitations does not, however, deny the significance of hip hop's rise as a critical lens into, and an active player within, Cuba's evolving fields of racial articulation and life during a period of historic flux. While hip hop's racial orientation and politically directed focus may have undergone change, the terms, struggles, and potential consequences of black antiracist expression and activism in Cuba clearly continue.

One need only consider the recent controversy surrounding Roberto Zurbano, the Afro-Cuban intellectual and long-standing interlocutor with Havana-area raperos who assumed directorship of the state-financed Movimiento magazine following Ariel Fernández Díaz's 2005 departure from Cuba. In the wake of a 2013 New York Times op-ed piece published in English translation that addressed the persistent and evolving nature of racial inequality in Cuba (Zurbano 2013a), Zurbano found himself demoted from his position as director of Casa de las Américas' literary press. For Zurbano, a key issue in the mix was his charge that the *New York Times* had manipulated the tone of his essay through a (deliberate) mistranslation of his original title, "El país que viene: ¿Y mi Cuba negra?" (The country to come: And my black Cuba?), to "For Blacks in Cuba, the Revolution Hasn't Begun." A broader concern for Zurbano, however, was his subsequent state censorship for broaching Cuba's current dilemmas of race within a highly visible international (and in particular a U.S.-based) forum. In his defense, Zurbano penned an open online response titled "Mañana será tarde: Escucho, aprendo y sigo en la pelea" (Tomorrow is too late: I listen, I learn, and I'm still in the fight), which opened:

> If a conservative left in and outside of Cuba thinks that a black Cuban revolutionary shouldn't make critiques of the Revolution, they do not understand the role blacks have played in this [Revolution], nor what a truly revolutionary process is. At the core, at the heart, in the base and on the shores of this process has been black support. We claim the moral right to criticize it as a duty to defend it, because what we have achieved is still insufficient in terms of what we have done and deserve. To renounce this critique is to renounce bettering the Revolution and embodying it more as our own.
>
> Combating racism is one of the major tasks of the century. This scourge did not arise in a particular country, but in a global context involving various nations and cultures marked by the colonial desire to divide the world and establish economic and political hierarchies that survive today. Contemporary racism is also a global phenomenon and the struggle against this goes beyond all boundaries. Renouncing the international debate is to reduce its impact to old nationalist concepts and disregard the process of unequal exchange generated by tourism, new information technologies, migration, and transnational culture. It is a debate about the persistence of racism in Cuba [and] on the paternalistic and sophisticated ways this degradation is reproduced or renewed and, especially, regarding how to recognize and address them in a new context. (Zurbano 2013b)

Zurbano's charge brings into pithy focus a similar range of Cuban tensions that many raperos have long confronted in their music. From validating a critical black subject of national and revolutionary history, to challenging the limitations of nonracial national formulations that deny such historicity, to the global fold of racialized power via the current market dimensions of racial inequality, struggles over Cuban complexities of race and national citizenship remain at urgent center. As discussed, the analytical lines of such appraisal arose in dialogue with raperos and can be seen as part of an emergent black counterpublic seeking to challenge a silencing of black antiracist struggle and attending forms of political subjectivity. To evoke Pablo Herrera's language, might Zurbano's dismissal from the directorship of Casa de las Américas' press be yet another instance of a prominent "top being blown off" by the state?

Amid such developments, Obsesión's Magia López and Alexey Rodríguez were among those who continued to pursue hip-hop-related projects, international travel, and local engagements organized around antiracist themes. Key among these has been their participation in the founding of a local Cuban chapter of the regional antiracist alliance Articulación Regional de Afrodescendientes de Latinoamérica y el Caribe (ARAC, or Regional Coordination of African Descendants in Latin America and the Caribbean). It was through correspondence with Magia in late 2012 that I first became aware of ARAC's evolving development in Havana.

Building on a decade of global antiracist forums, a group of activists from Colombia, the Dominican Republic, Puerto Rico, Costa Rica, Ecuador, and Venezuela along with an assemblage of Afro-Cuban intellectuals and others convened in Havana under the auspices of ARAC in September 2012. The gathering was organized to discuss collaborative efforts to address racism and racial discrimination against Afro-descendant communities in the region. As an outgrowth of the meeting, a Cuban chapter was launched in 2013. Claiming institutional autonomy as an organ of a nascent Cuban civil society while distancing itself from being viewed as a dissident organization,[39] ARAC's stated objectives sought to combat racism and racial inequality through dialogue with Cuban institutions and the national media (Companioni 2013). Among those Afro-Cuban intellectuals taking lead roles in ARAC's organizational impetus were Gisela Arandia, Tomás Fernández Robaina, and Roberto Zurbano—all of whom shared active histories of support and engagement with Havana-area raperos.

Quite timely, one of the early challenges faced by the newly formed collaborative was Roberto Zurbano's dismissal as head of Casa de las Américas's press. In response, ARAC issued a statement with a series of points, opening excerpts of which read, in English translation:

> Regarding the recent controversy in the national and international media concerning the problem of race in Cuba today, we wish to express the following:
>
> - The project of our civil society is still under construction and [we] recognize that radical antiracism is part of the very essence and the most genuine popular element of the Cuban revolutionary process.
> - [We] urge Cuba to eradicate all vestiges of racism, racial discrimination, colonialism, exclusion, social inequality and lack of respect for differences.
> - ARAC strongly supports and will continue to support the free expression of ideas for all of its activists, as part of the fundamental freedom of expression in our society as a whole.
> - ARAC thus opposes any institutional or individual process or method of an obstructive or repressive nature against any participant involved in such controversies who has elected to express his or her opinion or views.
> - We believe the deepening of controversy around issues that concern us is a good sign of our society's ability to solve challenges independently as actors in solidarity and with respect for diversity without interference from external powers. (ARAC 2013)

Adding a personal voice to the debate, ARAC member Gisela Arandia wrote an online response to the Zurbano affair, arguing that it exposed the "virulence" of Cuban racism to the world. She then went on to identify three obstacles to resolving racial inequality in Cuba—an absence of political will on the part of the state, enduring ideological claims that the revolution had resolved the "racial problem," and a lack of strategic unity among black Cubans themselves (Arandia 2013). A key concern voiced by Gisela was her contention that antiracist critique is often delegitimized in Cuba by bounded nationalist discourses that claim such orientations are inorganically influenced by the United States, in particular African American approaches to antiracism. Indeed, similar accusations as discussed undergird dismissals of racial critique and related subjectivity among Cuban raperos in light of transnational histories of engagement with North American interlocutors (cf. Baker 2011). ARAC's Cuban formation, Gisela counters, "is trying to challenge the myth of racism in a new political and economic reality by exposing the historical polarization of racism-poverty. In recent years this reality has unfortunately increased the gaps of access to better living conditions for large parts of the black Cuban population who remain in positions of great poverty and limited upward mobility. . . . By weakening the myth of silence there may creatively arise multiple collective proposals that carry the legitimacy that the matter requires" (Arandia 2013).

While the broader resonance and organizational longevity of ARAC and its interventions may be difficult to gauge at this point, the impetus for its formation are the same historical urgencies and tensions that helped shape the rise and critical voicings of Cuban hip hop. At the center of both are efforts to readdress Cuba's historically fought, and indeed complexly lived, ambiguities of race, national citizenship, and legacies of revolution amid unfolding uncertainties of the neoliberal present. The challenge thus raised concerns how to effectively both mediate and ground a sense of black revolutionary Cubanness in non-self-negating and meaningfully active ways through such flux. In what ways might struggles to expand the future Cuban terms of a nascent civil society via emergent claims to a black counterpublic in this sense occur in dialogue with broader global conversations and attending political affinities? While the arc of such inquiry may be in fluid play, it is clear that Cuban raperos have occupied a particularly animated role within this evolving moment, lending both artistic expression and popularly embodied voices to the charge.

For Havana's now-expansive émigré community of raperos and their affiliates in the diaspora, one might consider the life and work of the late, great Celia Cruz for generational comparison. A native of Pablo Herrera's barrio of Santos Suárez, during an international tour in 1960 Cruz refused to return to Cuba in defiance of the revolution's recent triunfo, settling in New Jersey and ultimately assuming U.S. citizenship. An enduring vocal critic of Fidel Castro and the socialist project, Cruz has long been considered a persona non grata by the revolutionary state. While her life's music and mention were effectively banned from official Cuban media, her voice remains ever resonant at the popular level of la calle through songs like the rather apropos "La vida es un carnaval." Yet during the span of her artistic career Cruz continued to celebrate her fidelity to Cuba by drawing heavily—as did Chano Pozo, Arsenio Rodríguez, and others—on Afro-Cuban secular and sacred currents of musical practice. Capturing the nostalgic complexity of her ambivalence, Cruz's "Por si acaso no regreso" (In case I don't return) laments: "Although time has passed with pride and dignity, I have taken your name; to the whole world over, I have told your truth" (Aunque el tiempo haya pasado, con orgullo y dignidad, tu nombre lo he llevado; a todo mundo entero, le he contado tu verdad). Indeed, many a rapero afuera could testify similarly.

Postscript

On a warm October afternoon I set out with Obsesión's Magia López and Alexey Rodríguez to attend a local Sunday second-line parade in a black working-class section of New Orleans. The two had arrived the night before for a weeklong program of performance and forums as part of a 2011 North American tour. This being their first visit to New Orleans, I could think of no more fitting introduction to the city's cultural cartography than a Sunday second-line parade. With the recent lifting of Bush-era travel restrictions on Cuban artists and intellectuals, Havana raperos were now again free to tour the United States after a long hiatus. Building on stints of international travel melding music and social activism—including participation in the 2006 World Social Forum in Caracas, Venezuela, and repeated invitations to Vancouver's Hip Hop for Peace Festival organized around antiwar and anti-imperialist concerns—Magia and Alexey were quite resourceful in exploiting the renewed opening. This would in fact be the first of two subsequent U.S. tours, the second unfolding in 2013 and involving artistic collaborations with émigré and local MCs alongside outreach in black and Latino communities regarding antiracist and antisexist themes.[1]

This Sunday's second-line was organized by Women of Class Social Aid and Pleasure Club, one of a handful of such female-centered clubs in New Orleans and seemingly all the more apropos given Magia's pioneering work as a rapera. Following the club members' flamboyant entrance from a local bar to the calls of an awaiting brass band, the second-line started at a slow gait. As the energy grew, however, Magia and Alexey found themselves enveloped in the moving mass of bodies and music as they danced their way along the second-line's three-plus-hour route of street parading. A certain *afrocaribeño* intimacy appeared in play as the two spoke of an affinity and embodied comfort with the second-line, drawing on their experiences of *la Conga*, Santiago de Cuba's massive carnival street parades that, akin to New Orleans' circum-Caribbean variation, weave through black working-class barrios of Santiago as community members follow in step with percussive *conga* bands. I too was reminded of the congas' shuffle-step procession, often of thousands marching in moving time with the bands' *clave* (key rhythm), as I worked to keep step with the second-line's rolling mass lest I trip and take down others, given the intimacy of the shared movement. The second-line's music and pace calls all into rhythmic communion as a mobile community, one in which Magia and Alexey seemed to find fellowship that New Orleans day.[2]

During our parading we noticed a sharply dressed, young Asian man dancing up front. In classic hip hop flair of baseball cap, warm-up jacket, baggy pants, and athletic shoes, the dancer exhibited a wonderfully playful sense of the second-line "footwork" as he improvised his way down the route with attendant focus on the other dancing parishioners. As Alexey and I admired his moves, I queried a woman photographing him. She informed me that his name was Ivan Stepanov, aka B-boy Forwin—a breakdancer from Siberia who had just arrived in New Orleans at the invitation of a local arts nonprofit. Like Magia and Alexey, it was his first second-line, and on the spot the two invited him to perform with them in one of their upcoming shows. The following Friday evening B-boy Forwin joined the duo alongside an assemblage of local artists including an Afro-Cuban percussionist, a Japanese bassist, a saxophonist, a DJ, and a Trinidadian-born MC—all in creative sync via converging currents of diaspora and hip hop that found innovative form that week.

As explored, transnational routes of musical communion have been similarly alive in the creative making and moving of Cuba's hip hop community. Amid legacies of racial disenfranchisement forged at the confluence of exclusionary national histories and ongoing market elaborations that have denied equities of presence and participation, Afro-Cuban raperos have sought a multivocality of black citizenship and antiracist critique through spheres of musical life. Here the now-global cultural terrain of hip hop offered both imaginative resource and creative recourse in crafting political claims and cosmopolitan belonging at simultaneous levels of the nationally and transnationally diasporic. Within this mix, raperos have had to navigate varying state strategies to manage their art and message in addition to the enduring constraints of a regulatory nonracialism, while contending with Cuba's unfolding complexities of neoliberal marketization alongside the competing rise of reggaetón. Rather than moving as isolated outliers, these efforts arose in dialogue with a range of social actors seeking antiracist redress to the ideological silencing and structural marginalization of Afro-Cubans from full livelihood within the Cuban nation. While this moment may indeed be one in ongoing flux, as is all in a rapidly transforming Cuba, it appears evident that the political urgency of such calls continue to resonate critically forward.

Coda: In November 2013, Alexey Rodríguez and his partner gave birth to their daughter, Nehanda Imani—her name a celebratory ode to their friend, African American political exile, and rapero mentor Nehanda Abiodun, coupled with Imani, Swahili for faith.

Notes

Introduction

1. *La escalera* (the ladder) refers to the practice of binding suspects to ladders for brutal interrogations that often involved severe whipping. This was a central method used against those allegedly involved in the 1812 conspiracy.

2. To this day this legacy privileges the white Dominican-born General Máximo Gómez of the independence forces as the supreme military hero of a liberated Cuban nation.

3. In this light, recently liberated blacks were figured in paternalistic terms as indebted wards of the independence movement, loyally indebted for their bestowed freedom.

4. Early Cuba's nonracial promise was complicated by U.S. interventionism following the Spanish-American War. Subsequent military occupations of 1898–1902 and 1906–9 secured U.S. capital expansion within the island's sugar economy, enabling U.S. firms to control upward of 75 percent of the island's sugarcane production by the mid-1930s (Jatar-Hausmann 1999: 11). Successive military administrations entrenched discriminatory hiring practices in Cuban state institutions (Helg 1995), while introducing ideologies of racial inferiority by way of Jim Crow–like segregation in U.S.-owned sugar facilities (de la Fuente 2001).

5. Here racialized terror, to borrow from Achille Mbembe, provided a way "of marking [black] aberration in the body politic [where] politics is read both as the mobile force of reason and as the errant attempt at creating a space where 'error' would be reduced, truth enhanced, and the enemy disposed of" (Mbembe 2003: 19).

6. Fidel Castro, "Revolución," March 26, 1959, cited in Fernández Robaina 1993: 103.

7. Calls for national unity assumed added urgency given escalating U.S. hostilities following the failed Bay of Pigs invasion (1961), the Russian missile crisis (1962), and imposition of the U.S. trade embargo (1963).

8. As David Theo Goldberg notes of analogous postracial projects, discourses of antiracism are often appropriated and collapsed into national "color-blind" discourses of official nonracialism, rendering antiracist avenues of contest debilitated (Goldberg 2009).

9. As will be elaborated upon in chapter 1, an important caveat to such racial erasure occurs in official realms of Cuban folklore, which tends to render blackness ahistoricized and incorporatively bound within the limits of nationhood.

10. Consider here Lisa Duggan's (2004) critique of the tendency in neo-Marxist/left circles of positing a valuative—and ultimately artificial—dichotomy between "class" and "identity" politics regarding their presumed efficacy as competing forms of social organizing.

11. Along these lines Baker also cites Fernandes 2006, though similar critiques are extended to de la Fuente 2008; Saunders 2008; and West-Duran 2004.

12. Between enduring poles of *negro* (black) and *blanco* (white) comprising Cuba's informal racial classification system, there is an expansive range of vernacular terms of graduated nonwhiteness given histories of racial mixing and attendant ideologies of mestizaje. Contingent on racial markers like skin pigmentation and hair texture, some of the more common terms include *jabao*, *trigueño*, *mestizo*, *mulato*, *indio*, and *moreno*.

Chapter 1. Raced Neoliberalism

1. The term *Regla de Ocha* or simply Ocha (a Spanish contraction of *orisha*) is commonly used by practitioners and aligned scholars for the syncretic Yoruba-derived belief system popularly known as Santería. The ethnically tied African cognate Lucumí is alternatively used in particular circles to privilege the religion's African cultural lines. While many simply refer to their religious community as *la religión*, I will generally use the term Ocha-Lucumí when referring to the religious tradition.

2. Following independence from Portugal in the wake of its War of Independence (1961–74), Angola's subsequent civil war unfolded from 1975 to 1991.

3. Established in 1997, this monthly per-rental-room tax was collected regardless of whether rooms were occupied.

4. Between 1990 and 1993 family food consumption fell 33 percent, accompanied by the rise of some neurological diseases tied to poor nutrition (Leogrande and Thomas 2002: 343; Hidalgo and Martínez 2000: 107).

5. The 1992 Torricelli Act designed to restrict third-country commerce with the island halted an estimated $768 million in annual trade, 90 percent of which involved imports of food and medicine (Leogrande and Thomas 2002: 355). For an extended

discussion of the U.S. trade embargo's impact on Cuba's public health system, see Hidalgo and Martinez 2000.

6. Escalating efforts to attract global capital included a 1992 constitutional amendment allowing up to 49 percent foreign control of joint ventures, a 1995 law guaranteeing foreign firms protection against expropriation and up to 100 percent ownership in certain sectors, and the establishment of free trade zones in 1996 (Leogrande and Thomas 2002: 343–44). Some early joint venture agreements, however, were reportedly later rescinded in favor of subsequent contracts with Venezuela, China, and Brazil (The Economist, March 24, 2012: 6).

7. In contrast with standing policy limiting foreign investment to joint-Cuban-owned ventures, Mariel's "Special Development Zone"—upgraded with financing from Brazil and operated by Singapore-based PSA International—allows 100 percent foreign ownership of ventures.

8. A proposal by Raúl Castro to phase out the libreta was met with resistance given that large numbers of poor Cubans remain dependent on its subsidized staples, as limited as they may be.

9. The largest medical personnel swap has been with Venezuela, recipient by 2005 of some fourteen thousand doctors (roughly equivalent to 20 percent of Cuba's physician force) in exchange for oil imports accounting for upward of two-thirds of Cuba's daily consumption (NewsMax.com 2005).

10. Rather, an autonomous mode of unregulated capital, neoliberalism, as Michael Hardt and Antonio Negri suggest, operates more akin to "a form of state regulation that best facilitates the global movement and profit of capital" (2004: 280).

11. Surveying the largest Cuban émigré population, the 2000 U.S. Census recorded 90 percent of naturalized Cubans and 84 percent of Cuban noncitizens self-identified as white (Tafoya 2004: 7). Black Cubans living in the United States, moreover, tend to be poorer, more recent immigrants in comparison to established networks of white Cubans concentrated primarily in the Miami area. Although some black Cubans may have closer immediate links to family on the island, their more limited levels of surplus income translate to fewer financial resources for remittances. For further discussion of racial disparities in remittances, see Blue 2004; de la Fuente 2008; Eckstein 2010; Espina and Rodríguez 2006; Sawyer 2005.

12. Tourism remained Cuba's principal source of foreign exchange through 2005 when it was surpassed by payments from international contracting of Cuban professionals abroad.

13. In ways reminiscent of similar practices in Brazil (de Santana Pinho 2010; Goldstein 2003), it has been suggested that darker-skinned Cubans are often excluded from tourism-related employment on the racialized grounds that they lack buena presencia, or "good presence" (de la Fuente and Glasco 1997: 65; see also Cabezas 2009).

14. The time allotted Cubans abroad prior to forfeiture of citizenship was recently ex-

tended to two years, while additional extensions can be applied for on an individual basis.

15. Examples of revolutionary state institutions dedicated to the study of Afro-Cuban cultural forms include the Instituto Nacional de Etnología y Folklore (est. 1961) and the Departamento de Folklore del Teatro Nacional de Cuba (est. 1962).

16. A key architect of Cuba's post-1959 cultural policy, Armando Hart Dávalos served as the revolution's first minister of education (1959–65) and influential minister of culture (1976–97), and wrote prolifically on the role of cultural production as revolutionary instrument.

17. See also the Conjunto's former artistic director Rogelio Martínez Furé's oft-cited distinction between "positive" and "negative" (i.e., primitive, irrational) aspects of Afro-Cuban folklore in his celebrated work *Diálogos imaginarios* (Martínez Furé 1979).

18. Like many Afro-hemispheric music traditions, rumbas are customarily held on Sundays, historically the day of rest and leisure for working-class Afro-Cubans dating back to enslavement.

19. Similar strategies among young black men have been observed by Katrin Hansing in the context of Cuba's Rastafarian community (Hansing 2001) and comparatively documented by Steven Gregory in tourism zones of the Dominican Republic (Gregory 2006).

20. Some of the state-related costs associated with Cuban travel, such as the infamous "carta blaca" (white card), have been recently curtailed under Raúl Castro.

21. For further discussions of the raced character of Cuba's sex-trade, see Cabezas 2009; N. Fernandez 1999; Fusco 1998; O'Connell Davidson 1996.

22. Denise Brennan (2004) and Steven Gregory (2006) have noted similar dynamics between white male tourists from the United States and female sex workers in the Dominican Republic.

23. Quoted from http://cuba-sex.com/cuba_prostitutes.htm, accessed May 4, 2004.

24. See, for instance, "US Stands by Cuban Sex Tourism Allegations after Castro Denials," *CubaNet*, July 28, 2004, accessed March 23, 2012, http://www.cubanet.org/htdocs/CNews/yo4/ju104/28e7.htm.

25. Jesús María, for instance, is host to one of Havana's largest communities of Abakuá, the secretive all-male Afro-Cuban fraternity that has been historically associated with a (black) criminality and related Afro-cultural archaisms (Miller 2000). References to the Abakuá are in fact ambivalently drawn in the subsequently mentioned film *De cierta manera*.

26. Following Gómez's untimely death in 1974, *De cierta manera*'s final cut was finished with the help of the fellow auteur Tomás Gutiérrez Alea and others.

27. All Spanish-to-English translations of song lyrics, interviews, and Spanish text are done by the author unless otherwise noted.

Chapter 2. Hip Hop Cubano

1. Antonio Eligio Fernández, aka Tonel, is an accomplished artist and art commentator from Havana now residing in Vancouver, British Columbia.

2. Fernández Díaz's 2000 article in the state-run, youth-targeted periodical *El Caimán Barbudo* touches upon many of the historical elements mentioned in our conversations.

3. Personal interview in English, January 10, 2002. All quotations of Ariel Fernández Díaz in this chapter are from this interview unless otherwise noted.

4. Personal interview in Spanish, August 2, 2002.

5. The song "Lo Negro" was eventually released on their 2003 self-issued album, *Paisanología*.

6. Initiates of Ocha-Lucumí are usually governed by one leading orisha, commonly referred to as their personal santo (saint).

7. Ifá deviation is traditionally mediated through *babaláwos*, or male "priests" of Ocha-Lucumí.

8. Personal interview in Spanish, July 31, 2006. All quotations of Alexis "D'Boys" Rodríguez in this chapter are from this interview unless otherwise noted.

9. Personal interview in English, July 20, 2012. All quotations of Pablo Herrera in this chapter are from this interview unless otherwise noted.

10. Personal interview in Spanish, September 29, 2012.

11. Personal interview in English, July 26, 2012.

12. Personal interview in English, July 26, 2012.

13. *B-boy* is a U.S.-derived hip hop term coined to refer to male breakdancers.

14. See introduction.

15. "We both speak African" is a simplified rendering of Gillespie's original phrasing, "bo peek African," which he used as an approximation of Chano's Cuban-inflected English.

16. Regarding the racial contours of Mario Bauzá's life and work, see J. Moreno 2004, and for Arsenio Rodríguez, see R. Fernández 2006 and García 2006.

17. Personal interview in Spanish, July 31, 2006.

18. Capoeira is a Central-African-derived, Afro-Brazilian dance/martial art form with some striking stylistic similarities to breakdancing.

19. Regarding state circulations of U.S.-produced media more broadly, North American film has long been a popular staple in revolutionary Cuba in theaters and on state-run television. Television broadcasts of *The Sopranos* and *Grey's Anatomy* are some of the more recent expressions of such diffusion.

20. La Piragua continues today to be an important official locale for music performances.

21. The hijacking of a Havana–Regla ferry on August 4, 1994, was in fact the third of a series of similar ferry hijackings within just over a week.

22. This frenetic moment is captured in Charles Bosch and Joseph Maria Doménech's

Oscar-nominated 2003 documentary *Balseros*, produced for Spanish television channel TV3. New York–based photographer Janis Lewin has also documented the moment through her exhibited collection of photographs of the episode.

23. Other early Cuban la moña DJs included two associates of Adalberto's, Randell Villalonga Davalos and Miguel Caballero.

24. Personal interview in Spanish, July 4, 2002.

25. Freestyle refers to the practice of improvised rapping, often occurring in a group setting or cypher.

26. The Asociación Hermanos Saíz is named after the brothers Luis and Sergio Saíz, celebrated urban youth activists of the Movimiento 26 de Julio (the revolutionary guerrilla force led by Fidel Castro). The brothers were killed by Batista's police in 1957 outside a movie theater in western Pinar del Río.

27. Personal correspondence, August 9, 2009.

28. Primera Base's *Igual Que Tú* album was released in 1997 on the Panama-based label Caribe Productions.

29. Personal interview in English, August 5, 2003.

30. Personal interview in Spanish, August 1, 1999.

31. *Cruzao* is a Cuban term most often used in religious contexts to refer to the syncretistic fusion of African-derived religious forms in everyday religious practice.

32. The competition component of the festival was phased out in succeeding years.

33. Original Spanish text by Joel "Pando" Heredia, as cited in Pacini Hernández and Garofalo 2000. English translation by the author.

34. The former Black Panther and journalist-activist Mumia Abu-Jamal is serving life imprisonment for the alleged murder of a Philadelphia police officer in 1981. Supporters and various human rights organizations maintain that he is a political prisoner and have coordinated a long-running international campaign for his release.

35. References to Mumia Abu-Jamal can be found in the lyrics of foundational groups such as Obsesión, Los Paisanos, Anónimo Consejo, EPG&B, and Junior Clan, to name a few.

36. The dance workshop was organized by Yvonne Daniel, the U.S. academic and author of *Rumba* (1995).

37. Hoch's solo performance piece *Jails, Hospitals & Hip-Hop* was first published in text in 1998 and later translated into the 2000 film of the same title. The work's Cuban section involving Pablo grew out of Hoch's involvements with Havana's hip hop community, to which I will return, dating back to the mid-1990s.

38. Distributed by New York City–based Papaya Records, the disc featured Anónimo Consejo, Explosión Suprema, 100% Original, Instinto, Hermanos de Causa, Obsesión, Justicia, Junior Clan, Grandes Ligas, Reyes de las Calles, Bajo Mundo, Alto Y Bajo, and Cuarta Imagen.

39. Personal interview in English, September 24, 2012.

40. See chapter 1.

41. Pablo was initiated into Ifá around 2012 while living abroad in Edinburgh, Scot-

land, bestowing upon him religious status as a babaláwo, or religious leader/priest in Ocha-Lucumí.

42. The World Festival of Youth and Students, held periodically since 1947, was traditionally hosted in Soviet-aligned countries. The 1997 event, with the slogan "For Anti-Imperialist Solidarity, Peace and Friendship," was hosted in Villa Panamericana (Pan-American Village) in the municipality of Cojimar in Habana del Este. The facility and adjoining apartment complex was initially constructed to host the 1991 Pan-American Games.

Chapter 3. New Revolutionary Horizons

1. Although Magia and Alexey separated as a married couple in 2010, they continue to maintain an active partnership through their artistic work as Obsesión.

2. A Regla ferry, or *lanchita*, was hijacked in the summer of 1994, setting off the crisis of the huelgas discussed in chapter 2. A Regla ferry was again commandeered in 2003 by an armed group of Cubans attempting to flee to the United States. Following their apprehension by Cuban commandos, three hijackers were executed after a brisk tribunal hearing, triggering considerable international condemnation. The incident was the first of a series of hijackings in 2003—two involving domestic airplanes—that signaled an elevated point of social crisis amid Cuba's post-1989 hardships.

3. A 1974 Spanish-language translation of *The Autobiography of Malcolm X* published in Cuba has assumed collectible status within Afro-Cuban circles.

4. Personal interview in Spanish, August 1, 1999.

5. In ways reminiscent of other Caribbean settings (de Albuquerque 2000; Phillips 1999; Pruitt and Lafont 1995), Katrin Hansing (2001) suggests dreadlocks have also been taken up by some young black men involved in the informal tourist trade including forms of sex work. Within such economies of exchange, dreadlocks serve as an authenticating marker of black Caribbean masculinity, one often associated with a raced virility.

6. A recorded version of "Los Pelos" set to a funky bass line was released on Obsesión's 2007 album, *Supercrónica*.

7. Personal correspondence in Spanish, November 15, 2012.

8. DJ Roger Martínez left Obsesión and immigrated to the Los Angeles area in 2002. The duo of Obsesión was later joined by producer Yelandy Blaya roughly between 2003 and 2005, and DJ Isnay "El Jigue" Rodríguez between 2007 and 2012.

9. Though *mensaje* literally means "massage," Alexey explained that within this vernacular context it refers to Bandera's refusal to bow in the face of danger.

10. The line "no metan forros" translates literally as "don't mess with the cover/or lining," but in Cuban vernacular the expression is used to imply "do not tell lies or cheat." The expression thus doubles as a pun—i.e., "no metáforas" (no metaphors).

11. In Cuban vernacular, *rebambarambara* refers to a tremendous problem/fiasco/mess. In this context "¡Rebambarambara!" can thus be translated as "making hell!"

12. Following independence the former combatant leader Quintín Bandera was reportedly unable to find employment beyond that of a janitor. In 1906 he was assassinated by government troops after becoming involved in organizing resistance to the U.S.-aligned administration of Tomás Estrada Palma (Ferrer 1998b).

13. Personal interview in Spanish, August 11, 1999.

14. For a YouTube video of Alexey's "Esta es mi mama," see http://www.youtube.com/watch?v=Chd8THiZX1s, accessed February 13, 2014.

15. A hip hop/reggaetón CD compilation titled *Havana-Cultura* was later released under EGREM in 2009. *Obsesión* also represented the first hip hop album produced in Cuba. The album's producer, Afro-Cuban jazz pianist Roberto Fonseca, helped facilitate access to state recording facilities, and the album was distributed through state-run music stores for Cuban pesos rather than U.S. dollars, making it accessible to many young Cubans. Two earlier-recorded hip hop ventures by Primera Base and SBS (Sensational Boys of the Street) were produced overseas in Panama and Spain, respectively.

16. Barbito was a fellow member of the Diez y Diecinueve posse and director of then EPG who died of asthma complications around 1999. Barbito was known for his graffiti work, some of which adorns the patio adjoining Deno's home. The "B" in EPG&B was added after his death.

17. By late 2003, EPG&B began to unravel due to a series of precipitating events. One member of Grandes Ligas, Yaimir "Pitit" Jiménez, left Cuba for Switzerland on a fiancé visa earlier that year, while the remaining member, Yordis Villalon, was arrested for marijuana possession—an offense under Cuba's harsh drug laws that carries a minimum one-year prison sentence for even nominal traces.

18. Personal interview in Spanish, July 31, 2006.

19. Personal correspondence, November 11, 2009.

20. Parque Quinta de los Molinos was a former botanical garden and one-time residence of the Cuban independence leader General Máximo Gómez.

21. I will return to a more detailed discussion of Ariel Fernández Díaz's evolving position within AHS in chapter 5.

22. Ariel's high-tech DJ equipment was acquired through contacts in New York City.

23. A self-educated radical, prison organizer, and author of *Soledad Brother* ([1970] 1994) and *Blood in My Eye* ([1970] 1990), Jackson was gunned down by San Quentin prison guards for allegedly harboring a smuggled pistol, though many on the left suggest it was a staged political assassination.

24. Reyes de las Calles's "El mundo va a acabarse" is featured on the 2001 CD compilation *Cuban Hip-Hop All Stars, Vol. 1*, produced jointly by Pablo Herrera and Ariel Fernández Díaz.

25. U.S. artists involved in Black August's South African tour included Dead Prez, Talib Kweli, and Black Thought of the Roots—all of whom had previously performed or would soon perform in Cuba.

26. These same nationalist traditions drew upon their own concurrent streams of Third World internationalism from Frantz Fanon to Maoism (Bush 2009; Kelley 2003).

27. Pablo Milanés later composed "Canción para Angela Davis," a celebrated version of which he recorded with Silvio Rodríguez in 1975.

28. In 2013 Shakur's U.S. bounty was doubled to $2 million in addition to her rather dubious placement on the FBI's list of most wanted terrorists.

29. Personal interview, August 5, 2003.

30. Common's lyrics appear to draw broadly from narrative lines of Shakur's autobiography.

31. Personal interview in English, August 5, 2003.

32. Personal interview in Spanish, August 1, 1999.

33. See chapter 2.

34. Personal interview in English, July 26, 2012.

35. Personal interview in English, July 20, 2012.

36. The hotel-lined peninsula of Varadero is Cuba's preeminent beach location for foreign tourists, which has grown into something of a Cuban Cancún. For years it was designated as a dollar-only zone of commerce, and access to its white-powder, palm-treed beaches has long been restricted for most working-class Cubans.

37. Personal interview in Spanish, September 22, 2000.

38. Personal interview in English, January 10, 2002.

Chapter 4. Critical Self-Fashionings and Their Gendering

Epigraph: José Martí, La cuestión racial (Havana 1959), cited in Pérez (1999: 91).

1. Personal interview in English, August 5, 2003. All subsequent quotations of Nehanda Abiodun in this chapter are from this interview unless otherwise noted.

2. Personal interview in English, July 26, 2006. All subsequent quotations of Tomás Fernández Robaina in this chapter are from this interview.

3. This time frame reflected strategic considerations given the sensitivity of post-1959 Cuban scholarship on race.

4. Gómez was a white, Dominican-born general of the Cuban independence forces long celebrated as its supreme military leader, and hence a key hero of the Cuban republic.

5. Personal interview in Spanish, August 2, 2002.

6. Nicolas "Miko" Nocchi was the commercial force behind Orishas, a French-produced rap group of Havana expatriates who became an international sensation with the release of their premier album, A lo Cubano, in 1999.

7. Ire refers to a self-consciously "natural" vegetarian-centered lifestyle adopted by many Rasta practitioners.

8. Recorded versions of Hermanos de Causa's "Tengo" appear on Cuban Hip-Hop All

Stars, Vol. 1 (2001), and *La Causa Nostra* (Our cause), Hermanos de Causa's first self-released solo album (2003).

9. Original Spanish text, respectively: "Negro delincuente, concepto legendario / Visto como el adversario en cualquier horario" and "el armamento pesado calibre grueso, alta precisión / Impactando duro al blanco con mi vocación."

10. It is worth noting that this artist in question is one of the most highly visible and accomplished "white" members of Havana's rapero community.

11. Abakuá members have in recent years participated in a number of exchanges with Nigerian counterparts that, according to Kenneth Routon, have been used to lay claims to an African historical identity (and thus political legitimacy) autonomous of revolutionary jurisdiction and realms of state sovereignty (Routon 2005). The U.S.-based cultural historian Ivor Miller has been instrumental in helping facilitate a number of these encounters. As I have argued, similar appeals to Afro-alterity beyond the revolutionary national have comparable currents within Cuban hip hop.

12. Sanctions notwithstanding, gender and sexual fluidities do manifest to some degree within broader spheres of Afro-Cuban religiosity. While J. Lorand Matory's work on Brazilian Candomblé speaks eloquently per example to currents of female religious leadership within the broader circum-Yoruba Atlantic (Matory 2005), this has been less historically so in Cuba. Yet long-standing prohibitions on women's practice of Ifá divination in the Ocha-Lucumí tradition have for instance come under challenge by a rather controversial movement of *iyanifá*—female initiates to the sacred practice of Ifá divination historically the sole Cuban domain of male babaláwos.

13. The expression *asere* shares a broader Cuban history of urban address among black working-class men.

14. In addition to levels of cultural and liturgical opaqueness, histories of state harassment and efforts to regulate (if not eradicate) the Abakuá during revolutionary and prerevolutionary periods further discouraged initiates from public disclosure for risk of harassment (see Routon 2005).

15. Personal interview in Spanish, September 29, 2012.

16. An Afro-Cuban composer influential in the popular rise of Cuban rumba and son in the early to mid-twentieth century, Ignacio Piñeiro and his Septeto Nacional toured extensively in Europe and the United States and were featured in the influential "G.V. Series" (1933–58) of classic Cuban music impactive of many West and Central African popular music forms into the postcolonial period.

17. Another pioneering female artist was MC Monica, who performed alongside old-school MC Irak Saenz of the later duo Doble Filo.

18. For an innovative treatment of Las Krudas, see Celiany Rivera Valázquez's documentaries *T Con T: Lesbian Lives in Contemporary Cuba* (2008) and *Reina de mi Misma, Queen of Myself: Las Krudas d' Cuba* (2010).

19. Personal interview in Spanish, December 18, 2001. All subsequent quotations of Las Krudas in this chapter are from this interview.

20. While Pasa's and her sister Wanga's identification as black women might appear self-evident, Pelusa's very light-brown skin and reddish-tinged hair mark her nearer *jabá* or *trigeña* within Cuba's graduated racial classification system. Yet articulate with forms of black self-affirmation shared by other lighter-skinned MCs discussed earlier, Pelusa in my experience self-identifies politically as negra.

21. Kilay is an acronym of participating members' individual names.

22. Omega Kilay interview in Spanish, conducted with the assistance of Sue Harrod, September 9, 2006. All subsequent quotations of Omega Kilay members in this chapter are from this interview.

23. See the original Spanish text at http://www.hipzoma.com/proyectos/proyecto23/dossier_grupo.pdf, accessed September 12, 2011.

Chapter 5. Racial Challenges and the State

1. Personal interview in Spanish, December 22, 2001.

2. Roberto Zurbano assumed directorship of *Movimiento* following the 2005 departure to the United States of Ariel Fernández Díaz, who served as the magazine's first editorial director.

3. Personal interview in English, July 20, 2012.

4. See for instance Belafonte's rather intimate exploration of Afro-Cuban music traditions in his three-part hosted PBS series, "Roots of Rhythm" (1997).

5. Personal interview in English, August 5, 2003.

6. Personal correspondence in Spanish, November 15, 2012.

7. Personal interview in English, September 29, 2012.

8. Orishas' *A lo cubano* album was first released in Spain in 1999 under the Orishas moniker. The group has subsequently released an additional four alums.

9. Personal interview in Spanish, July 24, 2002.

10. The key organizers of the tour were the Miami Light Project under the directorship of Beth Boone, and the New York City–based International Hip Hop Exchange headed by Marinieves Alba.

11. U.S. journalist Eugene Robinson likened Ariel in this capacity to a Cuban "Minister of Hip Hop" (Robinson 2002).

12. Editorial consultants included Rubén Marín, Magia López and Alexey Rodríguez, Sekou Umoja, Yrak Saenz, Joaquín Borges-Triana, Roberto Zurbano, Tomás Fernández Robaina, Pablo Herrera, Victor Fowler, Ismael González Castañer, Tania Cañet, Yesenia Sélier, Tatiana Cordero, Gloria Rolando, Maikel García, and Grisell Hernández—virtually all of whom were Afro-Cuban.

13. Personal interview in English, January 10, 2002. All subsequent quotations of Ariel Fernández Díaz are from this interview.

14. There were in fact long tensions between Ariel and Pablo stemming in part from a mutual competiveness as two among the most resourceful, if not personally ambitious, members of Havana's hip hop community.

15. Such was also conferred to me in private conversations by Roberto Zurbano and Tomás Fernández Robaina.
16. See chapter 1.
17. Carlos Moore (1989) asserts significant numbers of those purged from the Partido Comunista de Cuba (PCC) were an older generation of black committee members, suggesting the move served in part to eliminate an established guard of influential black politicos.
18. The state-led effort was called "la campaña de rectificación."
19. Per diasporic comparison, consider Michael Hanchard's discussion of Brazil's movimiento negro in its efforts to forge an alternative "black" public sphere via Afro-Brazilian cultural strategies (Hanchard 1994).
20. Personal interview in Spanish, July 15, 2006.
21. Another noted expression of early state openings to racial discussion was a 1993-initiated study of Cuban racial attitudes by the Centro de Antropología de Cuba. The journal *Temas* also broke significant ground with a 1996 issue dedicated to scholarly debates on race and racial discrimination (cf. N. Fernandez 2001).
22. Personal interview in Spanish, August 16, 2002.
23. See the 1997 Decreto 217 Regulaciones Migratorias Internas para la Ciudad de La Habana y sus contravenciones (Decree 217 internal migration regulations for the City of Havana and its violations). See http://www.cuba-1.com/decreto-217-regulaciones -migratorias-internas-para-la-ciudad-de-la-habana-y-sus-contravenciones/, accessed May 2, 2015.
24. Yesenia Sélier, an accomplished dance performer, is currently working on a PhD in communications studies at New York University.
25. Diago is the grandson of the pioneering Afro-Cuban artist Roberto Diago (1920–57), from whom he takes his name. The elder Diago also widely exhibited work in Cuba and abroad.
26. Alejandro de la Fuente later helped curate an exhibition on the Santiago-based Grupo Antillano movement, whose artistic work spanning the late 1970s and early 1980s underscored the instrumentality of Africa and the Afro-Caribbean in the making of Cuban nationhood. See http://www.queloides-exhibit.com/Grupo-Antillano /tablet/index.html, accessed April 3, 2015.
27. A published novelist, Prieto was president of UNEAC from 1991 to 1997.

Chapter 6. Whither Hip Hop Cubano?

1. Personal interview in Spanish, July 31, 2006.
2. Original Spanish text: "Hacen revolución con sus textos, educan con su poesía" . . . "incomprendidos, censurados a pesar de portar la verdad en sus manos."
3. Among those participating in El Cartel were Explosión Suprema, Los Paisanos, and Hermanos de Causa. The Cuban hip hop documentary *East of Havana* (2006) gives center stage to a number of El Cartel members.

4. The documentary *La Fabrik: The Cuban Hip-Hop Factory* (2005) by the Cuban American filmmaker Lisandro Peréz-Rey narrates the experience of Obsesión and one member of Doble Filo on their 2003 performance tour to New York City.

5. Those profiled centrally in the film were Michel Hermida Martínez, aka Miki Flow, of Explosión Suprema; Magyori "La Llave" Martínez of EPG&B and Omega Kilay; and Soandres del Río of Hermanos de Causa.

6. Participating artists in the annual hip hop festival were customarily chosen by way of auditions before a panel assembled by AHS.

7. Personal interview in Spanish, July 31, 2006.

8. Although relatively scarce in comparison to other Caribbean settings, marijuana has long been available on the island in relatively small quantities. In conjunction with harsh mandatory penalties for possession (e.g., one-year minimum for possession of any recognizable trace of marijuana), the crackdown significantly impacted the availability and circulation of marijuana. While cocaine was said to have been available during my period of research in a significantly more limited degree, those who partook were significantly fewer in number and likely included foreign tourists given its prohibitive cost and scarcity.

9. Alternative Cuban brandings of reggaetón are *reguetón* or *cubatón*.

10. The now prolific genre, which fuses dancehall reggae rhythms with Spanish Caribbean hip-hop-inflected vocals, grew out of Afro-Panamanian pioneerings of *reggae en español*, coalescing among Puerto Rican artists and producers in the commercial formation and global popularization of today's reggaetón.

11. "Raggamuffin" or "ragga" is a style of Jamaican dancehall (reggae) music originating in the 1980s.

12. Personal interview in Spanish, July 10, 2001. All subsequent quotations from members of Crazy Man are from this interview.

13. For example, the former hip hop crew Gente de Zona shifted toward reggaetón early in their career, eventually garnering a spot as one of Cuba's premiere reggaetón groups.

14. Personal interview in Spanish, July 31, 2006.

15. Personal interview in English, July 26, 2012.

16. See the discussion of commodified blackness in chapter 1.

17. In addition to previously mentioned works, other foreign-produced documentaries on Cuban hip hop include *Young Rebels* (2005), directors Anna Boden and Ryan Fleck; *La Fabrik: The Cuban Hip-Hop Factory* (2005), director Lisandro Peréz-Rey; and *Cuban Hip Hop: Desde el Principio* (2006), directors Vanessa J. Diaz and Larissa Diaz.

18. See http://rootsofsalsa.com/details.php, accessed August 12, 2015.

19. With members from Haiti, Algeria, France, Argentina, Chile, Barbados, St. Vincent, and Grenada, the collective performs in French, English, Spanish, Haitian Creole, and Arabic.

20. As the nationalized, former family-run Bacardi rum company, the now-branded Havana Club International has operated since 1994 as a 50–50 joint venture with

the French distillery conglomerate Pernod Ricard, which has reportedly netted almost US$3 billion in international sales in the first quarter of 2012/13 (Pernod Ricard 2013).

21. See http://www.havana-cultura.com/en/int/now-showing-havana-cultura, accessed March 14, 2013.

22. For a comparative note, "Red Bull Street Kings" brass band competitions were hosted in 2010 and 2013 in New Orleans, awash with Red Bull logos, free cans of the drink, and an elaborately choreographed video production whose material is now part of a Red Bull promotional website.

23. In recent years Soandres has become active as a spoken-word poet.

24. Featuring invited MCs Papá Humbertico and El Discípulo, the original Spanish lyrics read: "Siempre a la ofensiva / En defensa de las vidas que anidan heridas / El rap es guerra / La lucha no está perdida / Liberen la verdad cautiva / No se detengan sigan / El rap es guerra / Quieren que llenemos nuestros demos de canciones movidas / Pero se olvidan que el rap es guerra."

25. Orginal Spanish lyrics read: "esclavo de tu nacionalidad, identidad y asuntos . . . esclavo de jodida y pausada agonía . . . esclavo de tus deberes, esclavo de tus derechos . . . esclavo de luchar sin cesar y no hallar felicidad."

26. Magia remains an active member of Obsesión with her artistic partner Alexey Rodríguez.

27. Personal interview in Spanish, October 5, 2009.

28. Personal interview in Spanish, October 30, 2011.

29. The example of Alan Gross, a recently freed USAID subcontractor jailed in Havana after being accused in 2009 of clandestinely distributing satellite phones and computer equipment to members of Cuba's Jewish community, stands as a high-profile illustration of this broader U.S. undertaking.

30. For additional conspiratorial details of USAID's Cuban hip hop scheme, see D. Butler et al. 2014a.

31. The title L3Y8 serves as a numerological reference to "Letras, Cultura y Hip Hop."

32. Personal interview in Spanish, September 29, 2012.

33. Personal interview in English, September 24, 2012.

34. See chapters 3 and 5.

35. Personal interview in English, July 26, 2012.

36. Personal interview in English, July 20, 2012. All subsequent quotations of Pablo Herrera in this chapter are from this interview.

37. See http://www.freedomcollection.org/regions/the_americas/cuba/ernesto_hernandez _busto/, accessed April 6, 2013.

38. Personal interview in English, July 26, 2012.

39. For related elaborations, see Morales 2013.

Postscript

1. During two New Orleans visits in which I was involved, Magia and Alexey combined visits to public schools and local cultural organizations, academic talks, and collaborative shows with local MCs and musicians. Institutional sponsorship of these tours was organized through the University of Michigan and the Washington-based lobby the Center for Democracy in the Americas.

2. Circum-Caribbean currents of cultural exchange have long tied New Orleans, Cuba, and Haiti, as have histories of political affinity as exemplified in General Antonio Maceo's 1884–85 exile in New Orleans while mobilizing Cuba's independence struggle with Spain.

References

Abu-Lughod, Lila. 1991. "Writing against Culture." In *Recapturing Anthropology: Working in the Present*, edited by Richard Fox, 137–62. Santa Fe: School of American Research Press.

Acevedo, Jesse. 2013. *Viva Cuba Libre: Rap Is War*. Documentary.

Acosta, Leonardo. 2003. *Cubano Be Cubano Bop: One Hundred Years of Jazz in Cuba*. Washington, DC: Smithsonian Books.

Alexander, Jacqui. 2006. *Pedagogies of Crossing: Meditations on Feminism, Sexual Politics, Memory, and the Sacred*. Durham, NC: Duke University Press.

Allen, Jafari. 2011. *Venceremos? The Erotics of Black Self-making in Cuba*. Durham, NC: Duke University Press.

Althusser, Louis. 1971. "Ideology and the State." In *Lenin and Philosophy and Other Essays*, 85–126. New York: Monthly Review Press.

Alvarez, Sonia, Evelina Dagnino, and Arturo Escobar, eds. 1998. *Cultures of Politics, Politics of Cultures: Re-visioning Latin American Social Movements*. Boulder, CO: Westview Press.

Anderson, Mark. 2009. *Black and Indigenous: Garifuna Activism and Consumer Culture in Honduras*. Minneapolis: University of Minnesota Press.

ARAC (Articulación Regional de Afrodescendientes de Latinoamérica y el Caribe). 2013. "Posición de la Articulación Regional de Afrodescendientes de Latinoamérica y el Caribe, en su Capítulo Cubano." *La Jiribilla*, April 5. Accessed May 15, 2013. http://www.lajiribilla.cu/articulo/4247/posicion-de-la-articulacion-regional-de-afrodescendientes-de-latinoamerica-y-el-caribe.

Arandia, Gisela. 2001. "¿Entendemos la marginalidad?" *Temas* 27 (October–December): 69–96.

————. 2013. "Construcción de consensos: ¿Podrá la sociedad cubana construir un consenso para romper con el racismo actual e histórico y, al mismo tiempo, aprovechar las oportunidades revolucionarias?" *La Jiribilla*, April 6–12. Accessed June 15, 2013. http://www.lajiribilla.cu/articulo/4403/construccion-de-consensos-podra-la-sociedad-cubana-construir-un-consenso-para-romper-c.

Arenas, Reinaldo. 1993. *Before Night Falls*. New York: Viking.

Armstead, Ronni. 2007. "Growing the Size of the Black Woman: Feminist Activism in Havana Hip Hop." *NWSA Journal* 19 (1): 106.

Arrizón, Alicia. 2002. "Race-ing Performativity through Transculturation, Taste and the Mulata Body." *Theatre Research International* 27 (2): 136–52.

Aschenbrenner, Joyce. 2002. *Katherine Dunham: Dancing a Life*. Champaign: University of Illinois Press.

Associated Press. 2001. "Cuba Attracts Million Tourists in First Half of 2001." Associated Press, July 4.

Austin, J. L. 1976. *How to Do Things with Words*. 2nd ed. New York: Oxford University Press.

Ayorinde, Christine. 2004. *Afro-Cuban Religiosity, Revolution, and National Identity*. Gainesville: University Press of Florida.

Babb, Florence E. 2004. "Recycled Sandalistas: From Revolution to Resorts in the New Nicaragua." *American Anthropologist* 106 (3): 541–55.

Baker, Geoffrey. 2011. *Buena Vista in the Club: Rap, Reggaeton, and Revolution in Havana*. Durham, NC: Duke University Press.

Baraka, Amiri (LeRoi Jones). 1966. "The Changing Same (R&B and the New Black Music)." In *Black Music*, 180–211. New York: William Morrow.

Behar, Ruth, ed. 1996. *Bridges to Cuba / Puentes a Cuba*. Ann Arbor: University of Michigan Press.

————. 1999. "Complex Relations: Contemporary Art in Cuba." Panel presentation, Austin Museum of Art, Austin, TX, September 25.

Bejel, Emilio. 2001. *Gay Cuban Nation*. Chicago: University of Chicago Press.

Belafonte, Harry, and Michael Shnayerson. 2011. *My Song: A Memoir*. New York: Knopf.

Benítez Rojo, Antonio. 1992. *The Repeating Island: The Caribbean and the Postmodern Perspective*. Durham, NC: Duke University Press.

Beoku-Betts, Josephine. 1994. "When Black Is Not Enough: Doing Field Research among Gullah Women." *NWSA Journal* 6 (3): 413–33.

Berg, Mette Louise. 2004. "Tourism and the Revolutionary New Man: The Specter of Jineterismo in Late 'Special Period' Cuba." *Focaal* 2004 (43): 46–56.

Blue, Sarah Andrea. 2004. "Socio-Economic Costs of Global Integration: Remittances, the Informal Economy, and Rising Inequality in Contemporary Cuba." PhD diss., University of California, Los Angeles.

Bolles, Lynn. 1996. *Sister Jamaica: A Study of Women, Work, and Households in Kingston*. Lanham, MD: University Press of America.

Borges-Triana, Joaquín. 2004. "La fabri_K: Obreros de la construcción y embajadores de la Creación." *Movimiento* 2: 5–10.

Bosch, Carles, and Joseph Maria. 2003. *Balseros*. Documentary, Spanish Television TV-3.

Bourdieu, Pierre, and Loïc Wacquant. 1999. "On the Cunning of Imperialist Reason." *Theory, Culture and Society* 16 (1): 41–58.

Brennan, Denise. 2004. *What's Love Got to Do with It? Transnational Desires and Sex Tourism in the Dominican Republic*. Durham, NC: Duke University Press.

Brock, Lisa, and Digna Castañeda Fuertes. 1998. *Between Race and Empire: African-Americans and Cubans before the Cuban Revolution*. Philadelphia: Temple University Press.

Bronfman, Alejandra. 2002. "'En Plena Libertad y Democracia': Negros Brujos and the Social Question, 1904–1919." *Hispanic American Historical Review* 82 (3): 549–87.

Brown, Elaine. 1993. *A Taste of Power: A Black Woman's Story*. New York: Anchor.

Brown, Wendy. 2003. *Edgework: Critical Essays on Knowledge and Politics*. Princeton, NJ: Princeton University Press.

Burnett, Victoria. 2011. "In a Shift, Cubans Savor Working for Themselves." *New York Times*, February 3.

Bush, Roderick. 2009. *The End of White World Supremacy: Black Internationalism and the Problem of the Color Line*. Philadelphia: Temple University Press.

Butler, Desmond, et al. 2014a. "Rajko Bozic, Rap Spy: How One Promoter Was Tasked by the U.S. to Sneak inside Cuba's Hip Hop Scene." December 12. Accessed December 14, 2014. http://news.nationalpost.com/2014/12/12/rajko-bozic-rap-spy-how-one-promoter-was-tasked-by-the-u-s-to-sneak-inside-cubas-hip-hop-scene/.

———. 2014b. "U.S. Secretly Infiltrated Cuba's Hip-Hop Scene to Spark Anti-Government Movement: Report." December 11. Accessed December 14, 2014. http://www.huffingtonpost.com/2014/12/11/secret-cuba-hip-hop-program_n_6306424.html.

Butler, Judith. 1990. *Gender Trouble: Feminism and the Subversion of Identity*. New York: Routledge.

Cabeza, Amalia. 2004. "Between Love and Money: Sex, Tourism, and Citizenship in Cuba and the Dominican Republic." *Signs: Journal of Women in Culture and Society* 29 (4): 987–1015.

———. 2009. *Economies of Desire: Sex and Tourism in Cuba and the Dominican Republic*. Philadelphia: Temple University Press.

Cabrera, Lydia. 1958. *La sociedad secreta Abakuá*. Habana: Ediciones C.R.

Carr, Barry. 1998. "Identity, Class, and Nation: Black Immigrant Workers, Cuban Communism, and the Sugar Insurgency, 1925–1934." *Hispanic American Historical Review* 78 (1): 83–116.

Castro, Fidel. 1961. "Palabras a los Intelectuales." Speech, Biblioteca Nacional José Martí, June 30. Accessed May 13, 2012. http://lanic.utexas.edu/project/castro/db/1961/19610630.html.

Castro, Raúl. 1974. *Trascendencia de la Revolución Cubana y denuncia del diversionismo ideológico imperialista*. Lima: Editorial Causachun.

César Jiménez, Julio, and Herson Tissert. 2004. "Sospechosos habituales: Algunos apuntes sobre el hip-hop en Santiago de Cuba." *Movimiento* 2: 40–45.

Chang, Jeff. 2005. *Can't Stop Won't Stop: A History of the Hip Hop Generation.* New York: St. Martin's.

Childs, Matt. 2006. *The 1812 Aponte Rebellion in Cuba and the Struggle against Atlantic Slavery.* Chapel Hill: University of North Carolina Press.

Clancy, Michael. 2002. "The Globalization of Sex Tourism and Cuba: A Commodity Chains Approach." *Studies in Comparative International Development* 36 (4): 63–88.

Clifford, James. 1986. "Introduction: Partial Truths." In *Writing Culture: The Poetics and Politics of Ethnography,* edited by James Clifford and George Marcus, 1–26. Berkeley: University of California Press.

Clytus, John, and Jane Rieker. 1970. *Black Man in Red Cuba.* Coral Gables: University of Miami Press.

Collins, Patricia Hill. 1990. *Black Feminist Thought: Knowledge, Consciousness, and the Politics of Empowerment.* Boston: Unwin Hyman.

Comaroff, John, and Jean Comaroff. 2009. *Ethnicity, Inc.* Chicago: University of Chicago Press.

Combahee River Collective. 1986. *The Combahee River Collective Statement: Black Feminist Organizing in the Seventies and Eighties.* New York: Kitchen Table Women of Color Press.

Companioni, Paula. 2013. "Articulación Regional de Afrodescendientes de Latino-américa y el Caribe: Una lucha contra toda discriminación." *La Jiribilla,* May 12. Accessed June 20, 2013. http://www.lajiribilla.cu/articulo/4839/una-lucha-contra-toda -discriminacion.

Cooper, Carolyn. 2004. *Sound Clash: Jamaican Dancehall Culture.* New York: Palgrave Macmillan.

Corrales, Javier. 2004. "The Gatekeeper State: Limited Economic Reforms and Regime Survival in Cuba, 1989–2002." *Latin American Research Review* 39 (2): 35–65.

Costa, Sérgio. 2002. "A Construção Sociológica da Raça no Brasil." *Estudos Afro-Asiáticos* 24 (1): 35–61.

Daniel, Yvonne. 1995. *Rumba: Dance and Social Change in Contemporary Cuba.* Bloomington: Indiana University Press.

Davies, Catherine. 2000. "Surviving (on) the Soup of Signs: Postmodernism, Politics, and Culture in Cuba." *Latin American Perspectives* 27 (4): 103–21.

Davis, Angela. 1999. *Blues Legacies and Black Feminism: Gertrude "Ma" Rainey, Bessie Smith, and Billie.* New York: Vintage.

Dawson, Michael. 1995. "A Black Counterpublic? Economic Earthquakes, Racial Agenda(s), and Black Politics." In *The Black Public Sphere,* edited by Houston Baker and Michael Dawson, 199–227. Chicago: University of Chicago Press.

de Albuquerque, Klaus. 2000. "In Search of the Big Bamboo: How Caribbean Beach Boys Sell Fun in the Sun." *The Utne Reader* (January–February): 82–86.

de la Fuente, Alejandro. 1999. "Myths of Racial Democracy: Cuba, 1900–1912." *Latin American Research Review* 34 (3): 39–69.

————. 2001. *A Nation for All: Race, Inequality, and Politics in Twentieth-Century Cuba.* Chapel Hill: University of North Carolina Press.

————. 2008. "The New Afro-Cuban Cultural Movement and the Debate on Race in Contemporary Cuba." *Journal of Latin American Studies* 40: 697–720.

————. 2010. *Queloides: Race and Racism in Cuban Contemporary Art/Raza y racismo en el arte cubano contemporáneo.* Pittsburgh: Mattress Factory.

de la Fuente, Alejandro, and Laurence Glasco. 1997. "Are Blacks 'Getting Out of Control'? Racial Attitudes, Revolution, and Political Transition in Cuba." In *Toward a New Cuba? Legacies of a Revolution,* edited by Miguel Angel Centeno and Mauricio Font, 53–71. Boulder, CO: Lynne Rienner.

de la Hoz, Pedro. 2012. "Ni la vulgaridad ni la mediocridad podrán mellar la riqueza de la música cubana." *Granma,* November 30. Accessed March 16, 2013. http://www .granma.cubaweb.cu/2012/11/30/cultura/artico2.html.

Delgado, Kevin. 2009. "Spiritual Capital: Foreign Patronage and the Trafficking of Santería." In *Cuba in the Special Period: Culture and Ideology in the 1990s,* edited by Ariana Hernández-Reguant, 51–66. New York: Palgrave Macmillan.

de Moya, Antonio. 2004. "Power Games and Totalitarian Masculinity in the Dominican Republic." In *Interrogating Caribbean Masculinities: Theoretical and Empirical Analyses,* edited by Rhoda E. Reddock, 68–102. Kingston, Jamaica: University of the West Indies Press.

de Santana Pinho, Patricia. 2010. *Mama Africa: Reinventing Blackness in Bahia.* Durham, NC: Duke University Press.

Desforges, Luke. 2000. "State Tourism Institutions and Neo-Liberal Development: A Case Study of Peru." *Tourism Geographies* 2 (2): 177–92.

Diawara, Manthia. 1998. *In Search of Africa.* Cambridge, MA: Harvard University Press.

Dilla Alfonso, Haroldo. 2002. "Cuba: The Changing Scenarios of Governability." *Boundary 2* 29 (3): 55–75.

Du Bois, W. E. B. [1903] 1989. *The Souls of Black Folk.* New York: Bantam.

Duggan, Lisa. 2004. *The Twilight of Equality?: Neoliberalism, Cultural Politics, and the Attack on Democracy.* New York: Beacon.

Duharte Jiménez, Rafael. 1993. "The 19th Century Black Fear." In *AfroCuba: An Anthology of Cuban Writing on Race, Politics and Culture,* edited by Pedro Pérez Sarduy and Jean Stubbs, 37–46. Melbourne: Ocean.

Dunham, Katherine. [1969] 1994. *Island Possessed.* Chicago: University of Chicago Press.

Duong, Paloma. 2013. "Bloggers Unplugged: Amateur Citizens, Cultural Discourse, and Public Sphere in Cuba." *Journal of Latin American Cultural Studies* 22 (4): 375–97.

Eckstein, Susan. 2010. "Remittances and Their Unintended Consequences in Cuba." *World Development* 38 (7): 1047–55.

"Edging Towards Capitalism." 2012. *The Economist* (March 24): 6.

Edwards, Brent Hayes. 2003. *The Practice of Diaspora: Literature, Translation, and the Rise of Black Internationalism.* Cambridge, MA: Harvard University Press.

Ellis, Keith. 1998. "Nicolas Guillén and Langston Hughes: Convergences and Divergences." In *Between Race and Empire: African-Americans and Cubans before the Cuban Rev-*

olution, edited by Lisa Brock and Digna Castañeda Fuertes, 129–67. Philadelphia: Temple University Press.

"Encuentro entre amigos." 2004. *Movimiento* 2: 18–23.

Espina, Rodrigo, and Pablo Rodríguez. 2006. "Raza y desigualdad en la Cuba actual." *Temas* 45: 44–54.

Essed, Philomena. 2002. "Everyday Racism: A New Approach to the Study of Racism." In *Race Critical Theories: Text and Context*, edited by Philomena Essed and David Theo Goldberg, 176–94. London: Blackwell.

Fanon, Frantz. [1952] 1967. "The Fact of Blackness." In *Black Skin, White Masks*. Translated by Charles Lam Markmann. New York: Grove Press.

Feld, Steven. 1984. "Communication, Music, and Speech about Music." *Yearbook for Traditional Music* 16: 1–18.

Fernandes, Sujatha. 2003. "Fear of a Black Nation: Local Rappers, Transnational Crossings, and State Power in Contemporary Cuba." *Anthropological Quarterly* 76 (4): 575–608.

———. 2006. *Cuba Represent! Cuban Arts, State Power, and the Making of New Revolutionary Cultures.* Durham, NC: Duke University Press.

———. 2007. "Proven Presence: The Emergence of a Feminist Politics in Cuban Hip-Hop." In *Home Girls, Make Some Noise: Hip Hop Feminism Anthology*, edited by Gwendolyn D. Pough et al., 5–18. Mira Loma, CA: Parker Publishing.

———. 2011. *Close to the Edge: In Search of the Global Hip Hop Generation.* New York: Verso.

Fernandes, Sujartha, and Jason Stanyek. 2007. "Hip Hop and Black Public Spheres in Venezujacqela, Cuba and Brazil." In *Beyond Slavery: The Multilayered Legacy of Africans in Latin America*, edited by Darien Davis, 199–222. Lanham, MD: Rowman and Littlefield.

Fernandez, Nadine. 1999. "Back to the Future? Women, Race and Tourism in Cuba." In *Sun, Sex, and Gold: Tourism and Sex Work in the Caribbean*, edited by Kamala Kempadoo, 81–92. Lanham, MD: Rowman and Littlefield.

———. 2001. "The Changing Discourse on Race in Contemporary Cuba." *Qualitative Studies in Education* 14 (2): 117–32.

———. 2010. *Revolutionizing Romance: Interracial Couples in Contemporary Cuba.* New Brunswick, NJ: Rutgers University Press.

Fernández, Raúl. 2006. *From Afro-Cuban Rhythms to Latin Jazz.* Berkeley: University of California Press.

Fernández Díaz, Ariel. 2000. "¿Poesía urbana? O la nueva trova de los noventa." *El Caimán Barbudo* 296: 4–14.

Fernández Robaina, Tomás. 1990. *El negro en Cuba, 1902–1958: Apuntes para la historia de la lucha contra la discriminación racial.* Havana: Editorial de Ciencias Sociales.

———. 1993. "The 20th Century Black Question." Excerpt from *El Negro in Cuba, 1902–1958.* In *AfroCuba: An Anthology of Cuban Writing on Race, Politics and Culture*, edited by Pedro Pérez Sarduy and Jean Stubbs, 92–105. Melbourne: Ocean.

———. 1996. "Cuban Sexual Values and African Religious Beliefs." In *Machos, Mar-*

icones, and Gays: Cuba and Homosexuality, edited by Ian Lumsden, 205–8. Philadelphia: Temple University Press.

———. 1998. "Marcus Garvey in Cuba: Urrutia, Cubans, and Black Nationalism." In Between Race and Empire: African-Americans and Cubans before the Cuban Revolution, edited by Lisa Brock and Digna Castañeda Fuertes, 120–28. Philadelphia: Temple University Press.

———. 2002. "El tratamiento del tema negro en el rap." La Jiribilla, August 1. Accessed June 21, 2012. http://www.lajiribilla.cu/2002/n67_agosto/1605_67.html.

———. 2005. "The Term Afro-Cuban: A Forgotten Contribution." In Cuban Counterpoints: The Legacy of Fernando Ortiz, edited by Mauricio Font and Alfonso Quiroz, 171–80. Lanham, MD: Lexington Books.

Fernández Tabío, Luis René. 1999. "La Dolarización y la Segunda Economía." Havana: University of Havana.

Ferrer, Ada. 1998a. "Rustic Men, Civilized Nation: Race, Culture, and Contention on the Eve of Cuban Independence." Hispanic American Historical Review 78 (4): 663–68.

———. 1998b. "The Silence of Patriots: Race and Nationalism in Martí's Cuba." In José Martí's "Our America": From National to Hemispheric Cultural Studies, edited by Jeffrey Grant Belnap and Raúl Fernández, 228–49. Durham, NC: Duke University Press.

———. 1999. Insurgent Cuba: Race, Nation, and Revolution, 1868–1898. Chapel Hill: University of North Carolina Press.

Fischer, Sibylle. 2004. Modernity Disavowed: Haiti and the Cultures of Slavery in the Age of Revolution. Durham, NC: Duke University Press.

Fontanar, Patricia. 2003. "Jóvenes cubanos piden legalización de la marihuana." El Nuevo Herald, February 19, 25A.

Foucault, Michel. [1969] 2002. The Archaeology of Knowledge. Translated by A. M. Sheridan Smith. New York: Routledge.

———. 1979. The History of Sexuality. Vol. 1, An Introduction. London: Allen Lane.

Fowler, Victor. 1998. La maldición: Una historia del placer como conquista. Havana: Editorial Letres Cubanas.

———. 2004a. "De Libros." Movimiento 2: 24.

———. 2004b. "De Libros." Movimiento 3: 20.

Fraser, Nancy. 1990. "Rethinking the Public Sphere: A Contribution to the Critique of Actually Existing Democracy." Social Text 25 (26): 56–80.

Frederick, Howard. 1986. Cuban-American Radio Wars: Ideology in International Telecommunications. Norwood, NJ: Ablex.

French, John. 2003. "Translation, Diasporic Dialogue, and the Errors of Pierre Bourdieu and Loïc Wacquant." Nepantla 4 (1): 375–89.

Fusco, Coco. 1998. "Hustling for Dollars: Jineterismo in Cuba." In Global Sex Workers: Rights, Resistance, and Redefinition, edited by Kamala Kempadoo and Jo Doezema, 151–66. New York: Routledge.

García, David. 2006. Arsenio Rodríguez and the Transnational Flows of Latin Popular Music. Philadelphia: Temple University Press.

García Canclini, Néstor. 1995. *Hybrid Cultures: Strategies for Entering and Leaving Modernity.* Minneapolis: University of Minnesota Press.

Gillespie, Dizzy. 1979. *To Be, Or Not . . . to Bop.* New York: Doubleday.

Gilliam, Angela, and Onik'a Gilliam. 1999. "Odyssey: Negotiating the Subjectivity of Mulata Identity in Brazil." *Latin American Perspectives* 26 (3): 60–84.

Gilroy, Paul. 1990. "'One Nation Under a Groove': The Cultural Politics of 'Race' and Racism in Britain." In *Anatomy of Racism*, edited by D. T. Goldberg, 263–82. Minneapolis: University of Minnesota Press.

———. 1991. "'Race,' Class and Agency." In *'There Ain't No Black in the Union Jack': The Cultural Politics of Race and Nation*, 15–42. Chicago: University of Chicago Press.

———. 1993. *The Black Atlantic: Modernity and Double Consciousness.* Cambridge, MA: Harvard University Press.

Godreau, Isar. 2006. "Forkloric 'Others': Blanqueamiento and the Celebration of Blackness as an Exception in Puerto Rico." In *Globalization and Race: Transformations in the Cultural Production of Blackness*, edited by Kamari Clarke and Deborah Thomas, 171–87. Durham, NC: Duke University Press.

Goldberg, David Theo. 1993. *Racist Culture: Philosophy and the Politics of Meaning.* Malden, MA: Blackwell.

———. 2009. *The Threat of Race: Reflections on Racial Neoliberalism.* London: Wiley-Blackwell.

Goldstein, Donna. 2003. *Laughter Out of Place: Race, Class, Violence, and Sexuality in a Rio Shantytown.* Berkeley: University of California Press.

González Bello, Neris, Liliana Casanella Cué, and Grizel Hernández Baguer. n.d. "El reguetón en Cuba: Un análisis de sus particularidades." Centro de Investigación y Desarrollo de la Música Cubana, Havana.

González Pagés, Julio César. 2004. "Feminismo y masculinidad: ¿Mujeres contra hombres?" *Revista Temas* 37–38: 4–14.

Gordon, Edmund T. 1998. *Disparate Diasporas: Identity and Politics in an African Nicaraguan Community.* Austin: University of Texas Press.

Gordy, Katherine. 2006. "'Sales + Economy + Efficiency = Revolution'? Dollarization, Consumer Capitalism, and Popular Responses in Special Period Cuba." *Public Culture* 18 (2): 383–412.

Gregory, Steven. 2006. *The Devil behind the Mirror: Globalization and Politics in the Dominican Republic.* Berkeley: University of California Press.

Guevara, Ernesto "Che." [1965] 2007. *El socialismo y el hombre en Cuba.* New York: Ocean.

Guillard Limonta, Norma. 2005. "Gender, Identity, Sexuality, and Social Communication in Hip-Hop." *Movimiento* 4: 46–50.

Guridy, Frank. 2010. *Forging Diaspora: Afro-Cubans and African-Americans in a World of Empire and Jim Crow.* Chapel Hill: University of North Carolina Press.

Guss, David. 2000. *The Festive State: Race, Ethnicity, and Nationalism as Cultural Performance.* Berkeley: University of California Press.

Habermas, Jürgen. 1989. *Structural Transformation of the Public Sphere: An Inquiry into a Category of Bourgeois Society.* Cambridge, MA: MIT Press.

Hagedorn, Katherine. 2001. *Divine Utterances: The Performance of Afro-Cuban Santeria.* Washington, DC: Smithsonian Institution Press.

Hale, Charles. 1997. "Cultural Politics of Identity in Latin America." *Annual Review of Anthropology* 26: 567–90.

———. 2002. "Does Multiculturalism Menace? Governance, Cultural Rights and the Politics of Identity in Guatemala." *Journal of Latin American Studies* 34: 485–524.

Hall, Stuart. 1980. "Race, Articulation and Societies Structured in Dominance." In *Sociological Theories: Race and Colonialism*, edited by UNESCO, 305–45. Paris: UNESCO.

———. 1992. "What Is This Black in Black Popular Culture?" In *Black Popular Culture*, edited by Gina Dent, 21–33. Seattle: Bay Press.

———. 1996. "Introduction: Who Needs 'Identity'?" In *Questions of Cultural Identity*, edited by Stuart Hall and Paul Du Gay, 3–17. London: Sage.

Hanchard, Michael. 1994. "Black Cinderella? Race and the Public Sphere in Brazil." *Public Culture* 7 (1): 165–85.

———. 1998. *Orpheus and Power.* Princeton, NJ: Princeton University Press.

———. 1999. "Afro-Modernity: Temporality, Politics, and the African Diaspora." *Public Culture* 11 (1): 245–68.

———. 2003. "Acts of Misrecognition: Transnational Black Politics, Anti-imperialism and the Ethnocentrisms of Pierre Bourdieu and Loïc Wacquant." *Theory, Culture and Society* 20 (4): 5–29.

Hanken, Ted. 2010. "Feeding Frenzy: Los Aldeanos y Silvito 'El Libre' Arrive in Miami." *El Yuma*, November 9. Accessed December 9, 2010. http://elyuma.blogspot.com /2010/11/feeding-frenzy-los-aldeanos-y-silvito.html#more.

Hansing, Katrin. 2001. "Rasta, Race and Revolution: Transnational Connections in Socialist Cuba." *Journal of Ethnic and Migration Studies* 27 (4): 733–47.

Haraway, Donna J. 1991. *Simians, Cyborgs, and Women: The Reinvention of Nature.* New York: Routledge.

Hardt, Michael, and Antonio Negri. 2004. *Multitude: War and Democracy in the Age of Empire.* New York: Penguin.

Harrison, Faye. 1995. "The Persistent Power of 'Race' in the Cultural and Political Economy of Racism." *Annual Review of Anthropology* 24: 47–74.

———. 1997. "The Gendered Politics and Violence of Structural Adjustment: A View from Jamaica." In *Situated Lives: Gender and Culture in Everyday Life*, edited by Louise Lamphere, Helena Ragoné, and Patricia Zavella, 451–68. New York: Routledge.

Hart Dávalos, Armando. 1990. *Cultura en revolución.* Mexico City: Editorial Nuestro Tiempo.

Harvey, David. 2007. "Neoliberalism as Creative Destruction." *The ANNALS of the American Academy of Political and Social Science* 610 (1): 22–44.

Hebdige, Dick. 1979. *Subculture: The Meaning of Style.* London: Routledge.

Helg, Aline. 1995. *Our Rightful Share: The Afro-Cuban Struggle for Equality, 1886–1912.* Chapel Hill: University of North Carolina Press.

———. 2000. *Lo que nos corresponde: La lucha de los negros y mulatos por la igualdad en Cuba,*

1886–1912. Havana: Casa Altos Estudios Fernando Ortiz. Originally published as *Our Rightful Share* (1995).

Hernandez, Tanya. 2002. "Buena Vista Social Club: The Racial Politics of Nostalgia." In *Latino/a Popular Culture*, edited by Michelle Habell-Pallan and Mary Romero, 61–72. New York: New York University Press.

Hernández Baguer, Grizel, Liliana Casanella Cué, and Neris González Bello. 2004. "El rap en Santiago de Cuba: Causas y azares." *Movimiento* 2: 46–51.

Hernández-Reguant, Ariana. 2004. "Copyrighting Che: Art and Authorship under Cuban Late Socialism." *Public Culture* 16 (1): 1–29.

———. 2005. "Havana's Timba: A Macho Sound for Black Sex." In *Globalization and Race*, edited by Kamari Clarke and Deborah Thomas, 249–78. Durham, NC: Duke University Press.

———. 2006. "Radio Taino and the Cuban Quest for Identi . . . qué?" In *Cultural Agency in the Americas*, edited by Doris Sommer, 178–202. Durham, NC: Duke University Press.

Herrera, Pablo, and Yesenia Sélier. 2003. "Rap cubano: Nuevas posibilidades estéticas para las canción cubana." *Boletín Música* 11–12: 96–101.

Hidalgo, Vilma, and Milagros Martínez. 2000. "Is the U.S. Economic Embargo on Cuba Morally Defensible?" *Logos* 3 (4): 100–120.

Hoch, Danny. 1998. *Jails, Hospitals and Hip-Hop/Some People*. New York: Villard.

———. 1999. "La Revolución Embraces Hip-Hop with Fidel's Blessing." *Village Voice*, October 5, 194.

hooks, bell. 2003. *We Real Cool: Black Men and Masculinity*. New York: Routledge.

Hurston, Zora Neale. [1935] 1990. *Mules and Men*. New York: Harper Perennial.

———. [1937] 1990. *Tell My Horse*. New York: Harper Perennial.

Jackson, George. [1970] 1994. *Soledad Brother: The Prison Letters of George Jackson*. New York: Lawrence Hill Books.

———. [1972] 1990. *Blood in My Eye*. Baltimore: Black Classic Press.

Jacques, Geoffrey. 1998. "CuBop! Afro-Cuban Music and Mid-Twentieth-Century American Culture." In *Between Race and Empire: African-Americans and Cubans before the Cuban Revolution*, edited by Lisa Brock and Digna Castañeda Fuertes, 249–65. Philadelphia: Temple University Press.

James, C. L. R. [1963] 1989. *The Black Jacobins: Toussaint L'Ouverture and the San Domingo Revolution*. New York: Vintage.

Jatar-Hausmann, Ana. 1999. *The Cuban Way: Capitalism, Communism, and Confrontation*. West Hartford, CT: Kumarian Press.

Jiménez, Félix. 2009. "(W)rapped in Foil: Glory at Twelve Words a Minute." In *Reggaeton*, edited by Raquel Rivera, Wayne Marshall, and Deborah Pacini Hernandez, 229–51. Durham, NC: Duke University Press.

Joseph, Peniel. 2002. "Where Blackness Is Bright? Cuba, Africa, and Black Liberation during the Age of Civil Rights." *New Formations* 45: 111–24.

Kapcia, Antoni. 2000. *Cuba: Island of Dreams*. New York: Berg.

Katel, Jacob. 2010. "Los Aldeanos and Silvito el Libre at Miami-Dade County Auditorium." *Miami New Times*, November 14. Accessed February 14, 2013. http://www.miami newtimes.com/2010–11–11/music/los-aldeanos-and-silvito-el-libre-at-miami-dade -county-auditorium-november-14/.

Kaup, Monika. 2000. "'Our America' That Is Not One: Transnational Black Atlantic Disclosures in Nicolas Guillén and Langston Hughes." *Discourse* 22 (3): 87–113.

Kelley, Robin D. G. 1997. "Looking to Get Paid: How Some Black Youth Put Culture to Work." In *Yo' Mama's Disfunktional! Fighting the Culture Wars in Urban America*, 43–77. New York: Beacon.

———. 2003. *Freedom Dreams: The Black Radical Imagination*. New York: Beacon.

———. 2012. *Africa Speaks, America Answers: Modern Jazz in Revolutionary Times*. Cambridge, MA: Harvard University Press.

Kempadoo, Kamala. 2004. *Sexing the Caribbean: Gender, Race, and Sexual Labor*. New York: Routledge.

Kingfisher, Catherine, and Jeff Maskovsky. 2008. "The Limits of Neoliberalism." *Critique of Anthropology* 28 (2): 115–26.

Klak, Thomas, and Garth Myers. 1998. "How States Sell Their Countries and Their People." In *Globalization and Neoliberalism: The Caribbean Context*, edited by Thomas Klak, 87–110. Lanham, MD: Rowman and Littlefield.

Knauer, Lisa Maya. 2008. "The Politics of Afrocuban Cultural Expression in New York City." *Journal of Ethnic and Migration Studies* 34 (8): 1257–81.

Kondo, Dorinne. 1990. *Crafting Selves: Power, Gender, and Discourses of Identity in a Japanese Workplace*. Chicago: University of Chicago Press.

Kun, Josh. 2005. *Audiotopia: Music, Race, and America*. Berkeley: University of California Press.

Kutzinski, Vera. 1993. *Sugar's Secrets: Race and the Erotics of Cuban Nationalism*. Charlottesville: University Press of Virginia.

Lane, Jill. 2005. *Blackface Cuba, 1840–1895*. Philadelphia: University of Pennsylvania Press.

Laurie, Nina, and Alastair Bonnett. 2002. "Adjusting to Equity: The Contradictions of Neoliberalism and the Search for Racial Equality in Peru." *Antipode* 34 (1): 28–53.

Levinson, Sandra. 2003. "An Exclusive Interview with Harry Belafonte on Cuba." *Cuba Now*, October 25. Accessed February 4, 2013. http://www.afrocubaweb.com/belafonte 03interview.htm.

Lilly Caldwell, Kia. 2007. *Negras in Brazil: Re-envisioning Black Women, Citizenship, and the Politics of Identity*. New Brunswick, NJ: Rutgers University Press.

Leogrande, William, and Julie Tomas. 2002. "Cuba's Quest for Economic Independence." *Journal of Latin American Studies* 34 (2): 325–63.

León, Argeliers. 1991. "Of the Axis and the Hinge: Nationalism, Afrocubanismo, and Music in Pre-Revolutionary Cuba." In *Essays on Cuban Music: North American and Cuban Perspectives*, edited by Peter Manuel, 267–82. Lanham, MD: University Press of America.

Lorde, Audre. 1984. "Uses of the Erotic: The Erotic as Power." In *Sister Outsider: Essays and Speeches*, 53–59. Freedom, CA: Crossing Press.

Lott, Eric. 1993. *Love and Theft: Blackface Minstrelsy and the American Working Class*. Oxford: Oxford University Press.

Lumsden, Ian. 1996. *Machos, Maricones, and Gays: Cuba and Homosexuality*. Philadelphia: Temple University Press.

Maguire, Emily. 2011. *Racial Experiments in Cuban Literature and Ethnography*. Gainesville: University Press of Florida.

Malcolm X. 1974. *Autobiografía Malcolm X*. Havana: Editorial de Ciencias Sociales, Instituto Cubano del Libro.

Mantienzo, María. 2004. "Así lo dicen sus textos." *La Jiribilla* 170. Accessed March 25, 2013. http://www.lajiribilla.cu/2004/n170_08/170_23.html.

Manuel, Peter. 1993. *Cassette Culture: Popular Music and Technology in North India*. Chicago: University of Chicago Press.

Martí, José. [1893] 1975. "Mi Raza." In *Obras completas*, vol. 2, 298–300. Havana: Editorial de Ciencias Sociales.

———. 1959. *La cuestión racial*. Havana: Editorial Lex.

Martínez-Echazábal, Lourde. 1998. "*Mestizaje* and the Discourse of National/Cultural Identity in Latin America, 1845–1959." *Latin American Perspectives* 25 (3): 22–42.

Martínez Furé, Rogelio. 1979. *Diálogos imaginarios*. Havana: Letras Cubanas.

———. 2000. "Homogenizing Monomania and the Plural Heritage." In *Afro-Cuban Voices: On Race and Identity in Contemporary Cuba*, edited by Pedro Pérez Sarduy and Jean Stubbs, 154–61. Gainesville: University Press of Florida.

Mateo, David. 2003. "No todos los negros tomamos café: Conversación con Roberto Diago." *La Gaceta de Cuba* (May–June): 22–26.

Matory, J. Lorand. 2005. *Black Atlantic Religion: Tradition, Transnationalism, and Matriarchy in the Afro-Brazilian Candomblé*. Princeton, NJ: Princeton University Press.

Mbembe, Achille. 2003. "Necropolitics." *Public Culture* 15 (1): 11–40.

McCarren, Felicia. 2013. *French Moves: The Cultural Politics of le hip hop*. London: Oxford University Press.

McClaurin, Irma. 1996. *Women of Belize*. New Brunswick, NJ: Rutgers University Press.

McClintock, Anne. 1995. *Imperial Leather: Race, Gender, and Sexuality in the Colonial Contest*. New York: Routledge.

Miller, Ivor. 2000. "A Secret Society Goes Public: The Relationship between Abakua and Cuban Popular Culture." *African Studies Review* 43 (1): 161–88.

———. 2005. "Cuban Abakuá Chants: Examining New Linguistic and Historical Evidence for the African Diaspora." *African Studies Review* 48 (1): 23–58.

Mintz, Sidney. 1986. *Sweetness and Power: The Place of Sugar in Modern History*. New York: Penguin.

Mitchell, Tony, et al., eds. 2002. "Global Noise: Rap and Hip Hop Outside the USA." Middletown, CT: Wesleyan University Press.

Mohanty, Chandra. 2003. *Feminism without Borders: Decolonizing Theory, Practicing Solidarity*. Durham, NC: Duke University Press.

Moore, Carlos. 1989. *Castro, the Blacks, and Africa*. Los Angeles: Center for Afro-American Studies, UCLA.

Moore, Robin. 1994. "Representations of Afrocuban Expressive Culture in the Writings of Fernando Ortiz." *Latin American Music Review* 15 (1): 32–54.

———. 1997. *Nationalizing Blackness: Afro-Cubanismo and Artistic Revolution in Havana, 1920–1940*. Pittsburgh: University of Pittsburgh Press.

———. 2006a. "Black Music in a Raceless Society: Afrocuban Folklore and Socialism." *Cuban Studies* 37: 1–32.

———. 2006b. *Music and Revolution: Cultural Change in Socialist Cuba*. Berkeley: University of California Press.

Moraga, Cherríe, and Gloria Anzaldúa, eds. 1981. *This Bridge Called My Back: Writings by Radical Women of Color*. Watertown, MA: Persephone.

Morales, Esteban. 2013. "Disidencia y contrarrevolución." *La Jiribilla*, June 10. Accessed July 12, 2013. http://www.lajiribilla.cu/articulo/4996/disidencia-y-contrarrevolucion.

Morejón, Nancy. 1979. "Mujer negra." In *Parajes de una época*. Habana: Editorial Letras Cubanas.

Moreno, Alfredo. 2009. "A Man Lives Here: Reggaeton's Hypermasculine Resident." In *Reggaeton*, edited by Raquel Rivera, Wayne Marshall, and Deborah Pacini Hernandez, 252–79. Durham, NC: Duke University Press.

Moreno, Jairo. 2004. "Bauzá–Gillespie–Latin/Jazz: Difference, Modernity, and the Black Caribbean." *South Atlantic Quarterly* 103 (1): 81–99.

Mullings, Leith. 2004. "Race and Globalization: Racialization from Below." *Souls* 6 (5): 1–9.

Muñoz, José Esteban. 1999. *Disidentifications: Queers of Color and the Performance of Politics*. Minneapolis: University of Minnesota Press.

Navarro, Desiderio. 2002. "In Medias Res Publicas: On Intellectuals and Social Criticism in the Cuban Public Sphere." *Boundary 2* 29 (3): 187–203.

Neal, Mark Anthony. 2005. *New Black Man*. New York: Routledge.

NewsMax.com. 2005. "Cuba and Venezuela Deepen Ties with Medical-Oil Swap." NewsMax.com Wires, July 13. Accessed April 13, 2012. http://www.newsmax.com/archives/articles/2005/7/13/101957.shtml.

Ng'weno, Battina. 2007. *Turf Wars: Territory and Citizenship in the Contemporary State*. Stanford, CA: Stanford University Press.

O'Connell Davidson, Julia. 1996. "Sex Tourism in Cuba." *Race and Class* 38 (1): 39–48.

Olavarria, Margot. 2002. "Rap and Revolution: Hip Hop Comes to Cuba." *NACLA Report on the Americas* 35 (6): 28–30.

Omi, Michael, and Howard Winant. 1994. *Racial Formation in the United States: From the 1960s to the 1990s*. 2nd ed. New York: Routledge.

Ong, Aihwa. 1999. *Flexible Citizenship: The Cultural Logics of Transnationality*. Durham, NC: Duke University Press.

————. 2006. *Neoliberalism as Exception: Mutations in Citizenship and Sovereignty.* Durham, NC: Duke University Press

Ortiz, Fernando. [1906] 1973. *Los negros brujos: Apuntes para un estudio de etnología criminal.* Miami: Ediciones Universal.

————. [1940] 1963. *Contrapunteo cubano del tabaco y el azúcar.* Havana: Dirección de publicaciones Universidad Central de las villas.

————. 1950. "La 'tragedia' de los ñáñigos." *Cuadernos Americanos* 9 (4): 79–101.

————. 1951. *Los bailes y el teatro de los negros en el folklore de Cuba.* Havana: Editorial Letras Cubanas.

Pacini Hernandez, Deborah, and Reebee Garofalo. 2000. "Hip Hop in Havana: Rap, Race, and National Identity in Contemporary Cuba." *Journal of Popular Music Studies* 11/12: 18–47.

————. 2004. "Between Rock and a Hard Place: Negotiating Rock in Revolutionary Cuba, 1960–1980." In *Rockin' Las Americas: The Global Politics of Rock in Latin/o America,* edited by Deborah Pacini Hernandez, Hector Fernandez L'Hoeste, and Eric Zolov, 43–67. Pittsburgh: University of Pittsburgh Press.

Palmié, Stephan. 2002. *Wizards and Scientists: Explorations in Afro-Cuban Modernity and Tradition.* Durham, NC: Duke University Press.

Paquette, Robert. 1988. *Sugar Is Made with Blood: The Conspiracy of La Escalera and the Conflict between Empires over Slavery in Cuba.* Middletown, CT: Wesleyan University Press.

Pardue, Derek. 2008. *Ideologies of Marginality in Brazilian Hip Hop.* New York: Palgrave Macmillan.

Pedrero, Mayckell. 2009. *Revolution.* Documentary.

Pérez, Louis. 1999. *On Becoming Cuban: Identity, Nationality, and Culture.* Chapel Hill: University of North Carolina Press.

Pérez Sarduy, Pedro, and Jean Stubbs, eds. 2000. *Afro-Cuban Voices: On Race and Identity in Contemporary Cuba.* Gainesville: University Press of Florida.

Perna, Vincenzo. 2005. *Timba: The Sound of the Cuban Crisis.* Burlington, VT: Ashgate.

Pernod Ricard. 2013. "Good Resilience of the Business." Press release, April 25. Accessed March 14, 2013. http://pernod-ricard.com/files/fichiers/Presse/Documents/Sales-Q3 -2012-2013-VA.pdf.

Perry, Keisha-Khan. 2012. "State Violence and the Ethnographic Encounter: Feminist Research and Racial Embodiment." *African and Black Diaspora Studies: An International Journal* 5 (1): 135–54.

Perry, Marc. 2004. "Los Raperos: Rap, Race, and Social Transformation in Contemporary Cuba." PhD diss., University of Texas.

————. 2008a. "Global Black Self-Fashionings: Hip Hop as Diasporic Space." *Identities: Global Studies in Power and Culture* 15 (6): 635–64.

————. 2008b. "Revolutionary Subjectivity in a 'Post-Fidel' Cuba?' *Transforming Anthropology* 16 (1): 74–76.

Phillips, Joan. 1999. "Tourist-Oriented Prostitution in Barbados: The Case of the Beach Boy and the White Female Tourist." In *Sun, Sex, and Gold: Tourism and Sex Work in* the *Caribbean*, edited by Kamala Kempadoo, 183–200. Lanham, MD: Rowman and Littlefield.

Pinho, Osmundo de Araújo, and Angela Figueiredo. 2002. "Idéias Fora do Lugar e o Lugar do Negro nas Ciências Sociais Brasileiras." *Estudos Afro-Asiáticos* 24 (1): 189–210.

Pollard, Velma. 2000. *Dread Talk: The Language of Rastafari*. Montreal: McGill-Queen's University Press.

Postero, Nancy. 2005. "Indigenous Responses to Neoliberalism: A Look at the Bolivian Uprising of 2003." *Political and Legal Anthropology Review* (POLAR) 28 (1): 73–92.

Pruitt, Deborah, and Suzanne LaFont. 1995. "For Love and Money: Romance Tourism in Jamaica." *Annals of Tourism Research* 22: 422–40.

Reed, Ishmael. 1998. "Black Pleasure—An Oxymoron?" In *Soul: Black Power, Politics, and Pleasure*, edited by Richard Green, 169–71. New York: New York University Press.

Reitan, Ruth. 1999. *The Rise and Decline of an Alliance: Cuban and African American Leaders in the 1960s*. East Lansing: Michigan State University Press.

Rivera, Raquel. 2003. *New York Ricans from the Hip Hop Zone*. New York: Palgrave Macmillan.

Rivera, Raquel, Wayne Marshall, and Deborah Pacini Hernandez, eds. 2009. *Reggaeton*. Durham, NC: Duke University Press.

Rivero, Yeidy. 2005. *Tuning Out Blackness: Race and Nation in the History of Puerto Rican Television*. Durham, NC: Duke University Press.

Robinson, Eugene. 2002. "The Rap Revolución." *Washington Post*, Sunday, April 14, G01.

Rodríguez, Yusimi. 2011. "Cuba Hip Hop Has Its Magic." *Havana Times*, December 22. Accessed December 14, 2012. http://www.havanatimes.org/?p=58058.

Roland, Kaifa. 2010. *Cuban Color in Tourism and La Lucha: An Ethnography of Racial Meaning*. New York: Oxford University Press.

Rosaldo, Renato. 1989. "Imperialist Nostalgia." In "Memory and Counter-Memory," edited by Natalie Zemon Davis and Randolph Starn, special issue, *Representations* 26 (spring): 107–22.

Routon, Kenneth. 2005. "Unimaginable Homelands? 'Africa' and the Abakuá Historical Imagination." *Journal of Latin American Anthropology* 10 (2): 370–400.

Safa, Helen. 1998. Introduction. In "Race and National Identity in the Americas," edited by Helen Safa. Special issue. *Latin American Perspectives* 25 (3): 3–20.

Sagás, Ernesto. 2000. *Race and Politics in the Dominican Republic*. Gainesville: University Press of Florida.

Said, Edward. 1979. *Orientalism*. New York: Vintage.

Saldaña-Portillo, María Josefina. 2003. *The Revolutionary Imagination in the Americas and the Age of Development*. Durham, NC: Duke University Press.

Sánchez, Yoani. 2009. "Computadora sin papeles." September 29. Accessed July 6, 2010. http://www.desdecuba.com/generaciony/?s=los+aldeanos&submit.x=17&submit .y=11&submit=Search.

Sánchez-Egozcue, Jorge Mario. 2007. "Economic Relations Cuba–US: Bilateralism or Geopolitics?" Paper presented at the Latin American Studies Association congress, Montreal, September.

Sánchez Taylor, Jacqueline. 2001. "Dollars Are a Girl's Best Friend? Female Tourists' Sexual Behavior in the Caribbean." *Sociology* 35 (3): 749–64.

Sanjek, Roger. 1990. *Fieldnotes: The Making of Anthropology.* Ithaca, NY: Cornell University Press.

Sansone, Livio. 2003. *Blackness without Ethnicity: Constructing Race in Brazil.* New York: Palgrave Macmillan.

Santos, Jocélio Teles dos. 2002. "De Armadilhas, Convicções e Dissensões: As Relações Raciais como Efeito Orloff." *Estudos Afro-Asiáticos* 24 (1): 167–87.

Saunders, Tanya. 2008. "The Cuban Remix: Rethinking Culture and Political Participation in Contemporary Cuba." PhD diss., University of Michigan.

———. 2009. "La Lucha Mujerista: Krudas CUBENSI and Black Feminist Sexual Politics in Cuba." *Caribbean Review of Gender Studies* 3: 1–20.

———. 2010. "Black Lesbians and Racial Identity in Contemporary Cuba." *Black Women, Gender and Families* 4 (1): 9–36.

Sawyer, Mark Q. 2005. *Racial Politics in Post-Revolutionary Cuba.* Cambridge: Cambridge University Press.

Scheper-Hughes, Nancy. 1992. *Death without Weeping: The Violence of Everyday Life in Brazil.* Berkeley: University of California Press.

Scher, Philip. 2011. "Heritage Tourism in the Caribbean: The Politics of Culture after Neoliberalism." *Bulletin of Latin American Research* 30 (1): 7–20.

Schwartz, Rosalie. 1998. "Cuba's Roaring Twenties: Race Consciousness and the Column 'Ideals de una Raza.'" In *Between Race and Empire: African-Americans and Cubans before the Cuban Revolution,* edited by Lisa Brock and Digna Castañeda Fuertes, 104–19. Philadelphia: Temple University Press.

———. 1999. *Pleasure Island: Tourism and Temptation in Cuba.* Lincoln: University of Nebraska Press.

Sélier, Yesenia. 2002. "Identidad racial de 'gente sin historia.'" *Caminos* 24/25: 84–90.

Sieder, Rachel 2002. "Introduction." In *Multiculturalism in Latin America: Indigenous Rights, Diversity, and Democracy,* edited by Rachel Sieder, 1–23. New York: Palgrave Macmillan.

Shakur, Assata. 2001. *Assata: An Autobiography.* Chicago: Chicago Review Press.

Sharma, Nitasha. 2010. *Hip Hop Desis: South Asian Americans, Blackness, and a Global Race Consciousness.* Durham, NC: Duke University Press.

Smith, Shawnee. 1998. "Cuban Hip-Hop Starts to Come into Its Own." *Billboard* 110 (38): 46.

Sokol, Brett. 2000. "Rap Takes Root Where Free Expression Is Risky." *New York Times,* September 3.

Stam, Robert, and Ella Shohat. 2012. *Race in Translation: Culture Wars around the Postcolonial Atlantic.* New York: New York University Press.

Stoler, Ann. 1995. *Race and the Education of Desire: Foucault's History of Sexuality and the Colonial Order of Things.* Durham, NC: Duke University Press.

Sublette, Ned. 2007. *Cuba and Its Music: From the First Drums to the Mambo.* Chicago: Chicago Review Press.

Tafoya, Sonya. 2004. *Shades of Belonging*. Pew Hispanic Center. Accessed March 12, 2014. 3/24/http://www.pewhispanic.org/files/reports/35.pdf.

Telles, Edward. 2003. "US Foundations and Racial Reasoning in Brazil." *Theory, Culture and Society* 20 (4): 31–48.

Thomas, Deborah. 2004. *Modern Blackness: Nationalism, Globalization, and the Politics of Culture in Jamaica*. Durham, NC: Duke University Press.

Trouillot, Michel-Rolph. 1995. *Silencing the Past*. New York: Beacon.

Trumbull, Charles. 2000. "Economic Reforms and Social Contradictions in Cuba." *Cuba in Transition* 10: 305–20.

Ulysse, Gina. 2008. *Downtown Ladies: Informal Commercial Importers, a Haitian Anthropologist, and Self-Making in Jamaica*. Chicago: University of Chicago Press.

Uma, Narayan. 2007. *Dislocating Cultures: Identities, Traditions, and Third-World Feminism*. New York: Routledge.

Vaughan, Umi. 2012. *Rebel Dance, Renegade Stance: Timba Music and Black Identity in Cuba*. Ann Arbor: University of Michigan Press.

Verán, Cristina. 1998. "¡Viva la rap revolución!" *The Source* 100 (January): 132–35.

Verdery, Katherine. 1996. *What Was Socialism, and What Comes Next?* Princeton, NJ: Princeton University Press.

Vrasti, Wanda. 2011. "'Caring' Capitalism and the Duplicity of Critique." *Theory and Event* 14 (4): 1–22.

Wacquant, Loïc. 2012. "Three Steps to a Historical Anthropology of Actually Existing Neoliberalism." *Social Anthropology/Anthropologie Sociale* 20 (1): 66–79.

Wade, Peter. 1995. *Blackness and Race Mixture: The Dynamics of Racial Identity in Colombia*. Baltimore: Johns Hopkins University Press.

———. 1999. "Working Culture: Making Cultural Identities in Cali, Colombia." *Current Anthropology* 40 (4): 449–71.

———. 2002. "Music and the Formation of Black Identity in Colombia." *NACLA: Report on the Americas* 35 (6): 21–27.

Wallace, Michele. 1979. *Black Macho and the Myth of the Superwoman*. London: Verso.

Warren, Jonathan. 2001. *Racial Revolutions: Antiracism and Indian Resurgence in Brazil*. Durham, NC: Duke University Press.

Watrous, Peter. 1997. "Eye of the Storm: The Artist and Cuba's Music Industry." *Descarga Newsletter*, April 1. Accessed May 3, 2012. http://www.descarga.com/cgibin/db/archives/Article3?Sw439qBb;;249.

West-Durán, Alan. 2004. "Rap's Diasporic Dialogues: Cuba's Redefinition of Blackness." *Journal of Popular Music Studies* 16 (1): 4–39.

Whitten, Norman, and Arlene Torres. 1998. "An Interpretive Essay on Racism, Domination, Resistance, and Liberation." In *Blackness in Latin America and the Caribbean*, edited by Norman Whitten and Arlene Torres, 3–34. Bloomington: Indiana University Press.

Williams, Eric. [1944] 1994. *Capitalism and Slavery*. Chapel Hill: University of North Carolina Press.

Williams, Raymond. 1977. *Marxism and Literature*. Oxford: Oxford University Press.

Yelvington, Kevin. 2001. "The Anthropology of Afro-Latin America and the Caribbean: Diasporic Dimensions." *Annual Review of Anthropology* 30: 227–60.

Yurchak, Alexei. 2003. "Russian Neoliberal: The Entrepreneurial Ethic and the Spirit of 'True Careerism.'" *Russian Review* 62 (1): 72–90.

Zurbano, Roberto. 2004a. "¡El Rap cubano! Discursos hambrientos de realidad (siete notas de viaje sobre el hip-hop cubano en los diez años del festival de rap de La Habana)." *Boletín de música cubana alternativa* I (November).

———. 2004b. "Se buscan: Textos urgentes para sonidos ambrientos." *Movimiento: Revista Cubana de Hip Hop* 3: 6–12.

———. 2006. "El triángulo invisible del siglo XX cubano: Raza, literatura y nación." *Temas* 46: 111–23.

———. 2009. "El Rap Cubano: Can't Stop Won't Stop the Movement." Translated by Kate Levitt. In *Cuba in the Special Period: Culture and Ideology in the 1990s*, edited by Ariana Hernández-Reguant, 143–58. New York: Macmillan.

———. 2013a. "For Blacks in Cuba, the Revolution Hasn't Begun." *New York Times*, March 23. Accessed April 16, 2013. http://www.nytimes.com/2013/03/24/opinion/sunday /for-blacks-in-cuba-the-revolution-hasnt-begun.html.

———. 2013b. "Mañana será tarde: Escucho, aprendo y sigo en la pelea." *Negracubana Tenía Que Ser*, April 15. Accessed May 6, 2013. http://negracubanateniaqueser.wordpress .com/2013/04/15/roberto-zurbano-reponde-manana-sera-tarde.

Index

Habana Aberita, 216

"Habana Joven, La" (Los Van Van), 113

Habana Vieja, 2, 16, 49, 51, 92, 160

Hall, Stuart, 10, 14–15, 78

Hanchard, Michael, 19–20, 65

Hancock, Herbie, 72

"Hands Off Assata" campaign, 118

Hart Dávalos, Armando, 242n16

Havana Cultura Tour, 219, 222

health care. *See* medicine, socialized

Heredia, Joel "Pando," 89, 244n33

Hermanazos, 228

Hermanos de Causa, 1, 3, 4, 53, 147–49,
180, 184, 196, 220, 244n38, 247n8,
250n3, 251n5

Hermanos Saíz. *See* Asociación Hermanos Saíz

Hermida Martínez, Michel "Miki Flow,"
217

Hernández Baguer, Grizel, 191

Herrera, Héctor, 121–22

Herrera, Pablo, 64–65, 67, 76–77, 85,
86–90, 106, 107f, 110, 113, 123, 125,
139, 167, 176, 178, 179, 180, 182, 185,
188, 195, 201, 215, 216, 226, 227–29,
231, 244n37, 244n41, 246n24, 249n12,
249n14

hip hop, Cuban: Africa as reference
point, 34, 70–71, 76, 83–85, 138, 143,
146, 163, 171, 226, 231; African diaspora, 6, 65, 71, 84, 87–90, 120–22, 139,
143, 236; birth of, 57–59; black assemblages, 86–90; black feminist queerings, 156–70; black identity, 14–19,
24–25, 52, 60–62, 78–85, 122, 136, 139,
146, 172–73, 225–27, 236–37; black
public sphere and, 188–97; community, 66–67, 75–78; diaspora, 214–19;
entrepreneurialism of, 200–201; as
gendered, 68, 93, 94–97, 103–4, 139,
149–70; as internal revolution, 131–33;
as movimiento, 3, 6, 15, 57, 213, 227;

nueva trova and, 199–200; performance
spaces, 75–78, 106–11, 200–201; rise
of, 52–55, 77–78; self-censorship
in, 105; state on, 5–6, 16, 72–75, 76,
104–5, 173–88, 200–205, 227–28;
textuality in, 83–84; vs. U.S., 121–22;
USAID and, 24, 224–25. *See also* annual
hip hop festivals; *raperos*

"Hip Hop Revolution" (Anónimo Consejo mantra), 131

Hoch, Danny, 86, 120

homosexuality. *See* queerness

huelgas (1994 riots), 73, 245n2

Hughes, Langston, 18, 32

Humbertico, Papá, 53–55, 220

Hurricane Charley, 201

Hurston, Zora Neale, 21

Ifá divination, 62, 88, 216, 243n7,
244n41, 248n12

Iglesia de Nuestra Señora de Regla, La,
92, 93

"Igual que tú" (Primera Base), 79–80

indio, 240n12

Instinto, 114, 156

Instituto Cubano de la Música, 110, 184,
185

Interactivo collective, 157, 218–19

Internet restrictions, 31

Inventos (E. Jacobs-Fantauzzi documentary), 119

Ivonnet, Pedro, 145–46

iyas de ocha, 92

iyawo, 61

jabao, 60–61, 240n12

Jackson, George, 111, 115, 246n23

Jacobs-Fantauzzi, Eli, 119

Jacobs-Fantauzzi, Kahlil, 119

Jacomino, Fernando León, 179

Jails, Hospitals & Hip-Hop (Hoch film), 86,
120, 244n37

Jamaica, 22, 70, 77, 161, 206, 207, 218, 251n11
jazz, 65, 69
Jesús María (barrio), 39, 51, 242n25
Jiménez, Adalberto, 73–74, 108
Jiménez, Yaimir "Pitit," 214
jineterismo practices, 46–48, 50, 86, 130, 158–60
Jóvenes Rebeldes, 106–7
Junior Clan, 106–8, 110, 122, 167, 171, 244n35, 244n38

Keloids. See *Quiloides/Keloids* (art show)
King, Martin Luther, Jr., 194
Kool Herc, 62, 70
Krudas, Las, 87, 160–67, 161f, 169–70, 216–17
Kweli, Talib, 118, 246n25

"Lágrimas negras" (Hermanos de Causa), 1, 3, 53, 147–49
Lay Apesteguía, Rafael, 204
Lee, Spike, 80
lesbianism. See queerness
Let's Get Free (Dead Prez), 120
Like Water for Chocolate (Common), 118
"Llaman puta, La" (Obsesión), 158–59, 166
"Lo Negro" (Acosta/Saladriga), 61, 142–43
López, Magia, 2, 91–105, 95f, 113, 139, 141, 142, 158–60, 167–68, 181, 183, 201, 218, 222–24, 226, 228. *See also* Obsesión
lucha, la, 7, 104, 146, 164, 218, 223, 252nn24–25
Lucumí. See Ocha-Lucumí

M1, 118, 120. *See also* Dead Prez
Maceo, Antonio, 8–9, 98, 100, 108, 141–42, 143, 145–46, 194–95, 253n2
Machado Leyva, Javier, 195

Madriguera, La, 110–11, 184
Maestra (Murphy film), 87
Malcolm X, 2, 30, 79–80, 93, 117, 133, 137, 194, 245n3. *See also* Malcolm X Grassroots Movement
Malcolm X (Lee film), 80
Malcolm X Grassroots Movement (MXGM), 89, 116
"Mambí" (Obsesión), 98–100, 103–4
Mandela, Nelson, 133
Manigua Brigade, 100
marginalization: gendered, 167; in official public spheres, 190, 193; racial, 1–2, 12, 17, 59, 68, 119–20, 149, 167, 237; socioeconomic, 13, 68; of youth, 23
marginalidad, 48, 152, 204
Mariel port, 36, 241n7; boatlift (1980), 73
Marín, Rubén, 80, 93
market capitalism. *See under* economies
maroon communities, 68–69, 135, 146
Martí, José, 9, 10, 110, 130, 135, 141, 149–50, 172, 194–95
Martíinez, Magyori "La Llave," 79f, 168–69, 217
Martínez, Roger, 98, 216, 245n8
Martínez Furé, Rogelio, 43, 146, 196, 242n17
masculinity: black, 27, 52, 68, 80, 93, 96, 104, 121, 139, 151–56, 167, 245n5, citizenship and, 94, 109, 139, 149–50, 162; Cuban heteromasculinity, 150–52, 162–63, 208; gendered hip hop, 149–56; machismo, 150–51, 162, 168
Matamoros, Miguel, 1, 148
medicine, socialized, 11–12, 30; marketization of, 37, 241n9
mestizaje, 17, 18, 81, 240n12
mestizo, 60, 67, 82–84, 143–44, 225, 240n12
Miki Flow. *See* Hermida Martínez, Michel
Milanés, Pablo, 119, 199, 247n27
"Mi nación" (Los Paisanos), 29, 53